ECONOMY AND SOCIETY IN THE EARLY GREEK WORLD

COLLECTED ESSAYS
BY

CARL ROEBUCK

ECONOMY AND SOCIETY IN THE EARLY GREEK WORLD

COLLECTED ESSAYS
BY

CARL ROEBUCK

With an Introduction and Bibliography
By
Carol G. Thomas

ARES PUBLISHERS INC.
CHICAGO   MCMLXXXIIII

ARES PUBLISHERS INC.
7020 NORTH WESTERN AVE.
CHICAGO, ILLINOIS 60645
Printed in the United States of America
International Standard Book Number:
0-89005-261-1

Introduction

In the preface to his *Ionian Trade and Colonization,* Carl A. Roebuck succinctly describes the principal themes which he has pursued throughout a long and scholarly career: "I found myself grappling with two problems of early Greek history which have been the subject of recent controversy, how to assess the economic factor and how to define the role of Ionia."[1] Few scholars have so thoroughly investigated the development of Ionia, especially its economic base, from the migrations in the early Dark Age to the period of the Persian Wars. Yet Professor Roebuck has always recognized that a society is far more than its economic system and that Ionia must be placed in the larger context of Greece as a whole. Hence his work has looked beyond Ionia and economics to the entire world of early Greece and has illuminated particularly the emergence of the distinctive product of the Dark and Archaic ages, the *polis.*

Roebuck's first published article, "A Note on Messenian Economy and Population," grew out of his dissertation and reflects his early interest in economic history. The study examines Messenia's agrarian base, discusses its productive capacity, and estimates its probable population. In 1945, when the article was published, Roebuck was justified in noting that little excavation had been done on Messenia's sites.[2] Since then the region has been extensively examined, notably by the University of Minnesota interdisciplinary team. Yet, in the words of Herman J. Van Wersch, one member of that team, Roebuck's article and published dissertation, *A History of Messenia From 369 to 146 B.C.,* remain the "only other population estimate for Messenia based on the production capacity of the region. . . ."[3]

The article reveals also its author's interest and solid grounding in archaeology, an interest that began in undergraduate study at the University of Toronto, was carried on in Master's work with Homer Thompson at the same University, and led to four years of work (1937-1940) at the American School of Classical Studies at Athens. In addition to dissertation research and writing, these four years were occupied with excavation with Oscar Broneer on the North Slope of the Acropolis and at Corinth. He has discussed the finds of this work in a number of articles and a monograph, *The Asklepieion and Lerna.* Archaeological evidence is a central feature in many of his historical studies as well. "The Economic Development of Ionia," for example, uses the evidence of pottery and coin hoards together with the archaeological reckoning of foundation dates, to assess the strength of Ionia's population, the size of its fleets, and its increasing need for large-scale trade. Similarly, in "The Grain Trade Between Greece and Egypt" he employs coin hoards to suggest the probable carriers among the Ionian states between Egypt and the Aegean. Using both archaeological data and literary evidence, Roebuck has examined "The Organization of Naukratis," in which he reassesses the role of Miletus in that settlement and examines the political structure of this early *emporion.* "Some Aspects of Urbanization in Corinth" provides

1. *Ionian Trade and Colonization* (Monographs on Archaeology and Fine Arts; Archaeological Institute of America and the College Art Association of America, IX; New York: Archaeological Institute of America, 1959).
2. "A Note on Messenian Economy and Population," *Classical Philology* 40 (1945) 149.
3. In Wm. A. McDonald and G.R. Rapp, Jr., eds., *The Minnesota Messenia Expedition* (Minneapolis: University of Minnesota Press, 1972) 186.

a masterly synthesis of the variety of evidence which exists for the emergence of Corinth as a city-state.

In the classroom no less than in his writing, Carl Roebuck has demonstrated the importance of archaeology. His lectures at Northwestern University provided excellent illustrations of the interaction of physical and literary evidence. To students who had not yet visited the site, his slides of the Acropolis and Agora clearly conveyed the importance of these areas in Athenian life. Nor were students allowed to forget the significance of numismatic or epigraphic evidence. The exercises he devised, although difficult and dreaded at the time, were of lasting value.

Yet, even in studies such as those cited above, which are most properly construed as archaeological in nature, other evidence is employed. Coin hoards, potsherds, and architectural remains are balanced by an examination of Greek tradition and the written records. Just as Roebuck's research draws on all varieties of evidence, so too does it embrace many concerns. His demonstration of the connections between economic developments and political structure reveals the influence of J.A.O. Larsen, his major professor at the University of Chicago where he received his Ph.D. degree in 1941. Larsen's name is associated inextricably with Greek leagues and federal associations and his legacy is clear in "The Early Ionian League," in which Roebuck, following the general outlines sketched by his mentor, concludes that, despite an initial compulsion toward political unity, a true federal union with regular institutions did not evolve before the League's dissolution in, probably, 493 B.C. In his later study, "Tribal Organization in Ionia," Roebuck begins with the structure of the primary settlements and traces change through the decadic organization resting on chiliastyes in the sixth century, a change that he describes as indicative of "adjustments made to include groups of Greek metics and of Anatolian natives in response to the pressures of urbanization as Ionia changed from an agrarian to a mixed economy."[4]

Comparable developments occurred on the mainland of Greece. In "Three Classes (?) in Early Attica," Roebuck discusses class structure and economic growth in the late Dark Age, questions similar to those raised in his Ionian studies. The developments in social structure and the rise of a complex division of labor by function are also primary considerations in "Some Aspects of Urbanization in Corinth," where the author documents increasing governmental direction with respect to domestic and foreign relations, the replacement of an older kinship structure by a territorial structure, specialization in industry, and regularization of trade.

Political unity on a grand scale is an issue in "The Settlements of Philip II with the Greek States in 338 B.C." Roebuck's early work with Messenia and the influence of Professor Larsen help to explain an interest in the separate settlements that shaped and defined the individual segments of Greece which Philip was preparing to incorporate into the League of Corinth. Roebuck's conclusion — that Philip hoped to organize Greece "as a quiet and co-operative ally," which would enable him to turn his attention to the projected war against Persia[5] — remains fundamental to the understanding of Philip's career and policy, as J.R. Ellis's recent study underscores.[6]

All these themes are brought together in the final paper of this collection. "Trade and Politics in the Ancient World" was the topic of the ancient history section of the Second International Conference on Economic History held at Aix-en-Provence in 1962. As one of the six participants, Carl Roebuck commented upon Édouard Will's analysis of Archaic Greece. Roebuck suggested that Greek expansion may have been

---

4. "Tribal Organization in Ionia," *Transactions and Proceedings of the American Philological Association* 92 (1961) 495.

5. "The Settlements of Philip II with the Greek States in 338 B.C.," *Classical Philology* 43 (1948) 90.

6. *Philip II and Macedonian Imperialism* (London: Thames and Hudson, 1976) esp. 144 f.

"the product of prosperity rather than poverty,"[7] since evidence indicates that a period of trade preceded colonial settlement. Such a thesis has been much debated; interestingly, the author of the most recent large-scale study of the Dark Age argues that "Much of this chapter will be devoted to the first western colonies; yet some thought must also be given to their commercial exchanges with the native peoples, which began well before the arrival of the first colonists."[8] Carl Roebuck's thesis reveals his continuing attention to the economy of early Greece. The focus of his comment, Ionian Asia Minor, is again indicative of his primary interests and is illustrative of his opinion that "the current impression of Ionian mediocrity in the 7th century needs revision."[9] The choice of Old Smyrna as a case study of changes in the early seventh century is appropriate to a historian drawing together the threads of a great variety of sources, archaeological as well as literary. In his discussion, Roebuck argues that the goods acquired in a pre-colonial trade — primarily metals and luxuries — were paid for by an agricultural surplus. With this point we have come full circle in the present collection of articles: Roebuck's study of Messenia provides the necessary framework for an understanding of how the productivity of Greece furnished that agricultural surplus.

* * * *

All this work ultimately focuses upon the emergence of the Greek *polis*, one of the most debated questions in the scholarship of ancient history. The debate is due not so much to the quarrelsome natures of the scholars concerned with the problem as to the composition of the *polis*. Although the city-state is an entity, it can be studied as an economic, political, religious, military, and / or social structure. In concentrating on one of those aspects, Carl Roebuck has done more than provide answers to specific questions of fact: he has revealed the interconnection between all the dimensions of the emerging state.

The value of Carl Roebuck's work has been recognized throughout his career: he was a Guggenheim Fellow in 1953-4, the President's Fellow of Northwestern University in 1962-3, and National Endowment for the Humanities Senior Fellow in 1968-9. The occasion of his retirement from Northwestern after twenty-seven years is an opportune time to demonstrate the importance of his scholarship by bringing his historical articles together under a single cover. We are in his debt.

* * * *

The editor would like to express gratitude to those people who made this collection possible. Covert correspondence with Mary Roebuck not only prepared the way for Carl's approval but also suggested the general form the volume should take; President Robert Strotz and Dean Clarence Ver Steeg of Northwestern University extended generous financial support "to honor one of our distinguished and loyal faculty members, Professor Carl Roebuck;" friends and colleagues have helped us avoid pitfalls and have supported the project with enthusiasm; Al. N. Oikonomides, Vice-President of Ares Publishers, Inc., has carried through the publication of the volume with spirit and efficiency. This degree of support serves to underscore the honor in which Carl Roebuck is held.

Seattle,   Carol G. Thomas
University of Washington

7. "Comment," *Deuxieme Conference Internationale d'Histoire Economique*, Aix-en-Provence, 1962, Vol. 1 (Paris: Mouton, 1965) 98.

8. J.N. Coldstream, *Geometric Greece* (London: Ernest Benn Ltd., 1977) 221.

9. "Comment," *op. cit.*, 98.

Bibliographica

Permission to reprint the articles included in this collection has been granted by the author and the original publishers. The editor thanks all publishers for prompt responses.

The University of Chicago for:

"A Note on Messenian Economy and Population," *Classical Philology* 40 (1945) 149-165.

"The Settlements of Philip II with the Greek States in 338 B.C.," *Classical Philology* 43 (1948) 73-92.

"The Grain Trade Between Greece and Egypt," *Classical Philology* 45 (1950) 236-247.

"The Organization of Naukratis," *Classical Philology* 46 (1951) 212-220.

"The Economic Development of Ionia," *Classical Philology* 48 (1953) 9-16.

"The Early Ionian League," *Classical Philology* 50 (1955) 26-40.

Dr. Marian H. McAllister for the publications committee of the American School of Classical Studies at Athens for:

"Some Aspects of Urbanization in Corinth," *Hesperia* 41 (1972) 96-127.

"Three Classes (?) in Early Attica," *Hesperia* 43 (1974) 485-493.

Prof. Douglas E. Gerber, Editor, *Transactions and Proceedings of the American Philological Association* for:

"Tribal Organizaton in Ionia," *Transactions and Proceedings of the American Philological Association* 92 (1961) 495-507.

Editions Mouton et Cie for:

"Comment" on the report of Édouard Will on Archaic Greek History, Deuxième *Conférence Internationale d'Histoire Économique,* Aix-en-Provence, 1962. Vol. 1, 97-106 (Paris: Mouton, 1965).

Additional Bibliography

A. Archaeological Articles

"The White Ground Plaques by the Cerberus Painter," *AJA* 43 (1939) 467-473.

"Pottery from the North Slope of the Acropolis 1937-38," *Hesperia* 9 (1940) 141-260.

"The Mavrozoumenos Bridge in Messenia," *Studies Presented to David Moore Robinson* (1951) 351-355.

"A Prize Aryballos" (with Mary Roebuck), *Hesperia* 24 (1955) 158-163.

B. Books and Monographs

A History of Messenia from 369 to 146 B.C. (University of Chicago Libraries, 1941)

The Asklepieion and Lerna, Corinth, Vol. XIV (American School at Athens, 1951)

Ionian Trade and Colonization (Monographs on Archaeology and Fine Arts; The Archaeological Institute of America and the College Art Association of America, IX; Archaeological Institute of America, New York, 1959)

The World of Ancient Times (Scribner's, New York, 1966)

The Muses at Work, editor (MIT Press, Cambridge, Mass., 1969)

Concordance

Since references in some of the articles refer to the page numbers of the original publications of earlier articles, the compilation of a concordance was necessary as a handy reference for the user of the volume.

CP 40 (1945),	149	1
	150	2
	151	3
	152	4
	153	5
	154	6
	155	7
	156	8
	157	9
	158	10
	159	11
	160	12
	161	13
	162	14
	163	15
	164	16
	165	17
CP 48 (1953),	9	21
	10	22
	11	23
	12	24
	13	25
	14	26
	15	27
	16	28
CP 45 (1950),	236	30
	237	31
	238	32
	239	33
	240	34
	241	35
	242	36
	243	37
	244	38
	245	39
	246	40
	247	41
CP 46 (1951),	212	44
	213	45
	214	46
	215	47
	216	48
	217	49
	218	50
	219	51
	220	52
CP 50 (1955),	26	54
	27	55
	28	56
	29	57
	30	58
	31	59
	32	60
	33	61
	34	62
	35	63
	36	64
	37	65
	38	66
	39	67
	40	68

TAPA (1961),	495	71
	496	72
	497	73
	498	74
	499	75
	500	76
	501	77
	502	78
	503	79
	504	80
	505	81
	506	82
	507	83
Hesp. 43 (1974),	485	85
	486	86
	487	87
	488	88
	489	89
	490	90
	491	91
	492	92
	493	93
Hesp. 41 (1972) pp. 97-127	same numbers	
CP 43 (1948)	73	131
	74	132
	75	133
	76	134
	77	135
	78	136
	79	137
	80	138
	81	139
	82	140
	83	141
	84	142
	85	143
	86	144
	87	145
	88	146
	89	147
	90	148
	91	149
	92	150
Comment (1962)	97	153
	98	154
	99	155
	100	156
	101	157
	102	158
	103	159
	104	160
	105	161
	106	162

ABBREVIATIONS:

CP = Classical Philology.
TAPA = Transactions and Proceedings of the American Philological Association
Hesp. = Hesperia.

List of Subscribers

Winthrop Lindsay Adams
Ernst Badian
Lawrence J. Bliquez
Eugene N. Borza
Stanley M. Burstein
William M. Calder III
Robert L. Carter
A.J. Christopherson
Louis Cohn-Haft
Frederick M. Combellack
Thomas H. Corcoran
C. Grier Davis, Jr.
Phillip H. DeLacy
Keith DeVries
Walter F. Donlan
Robert H. Drews
Harold D. Evjen
Terpsichore H. Tzavella-Evjen
Arther L. Ferrill
Richard I. Frank
Daniel H. Garrison
Jean Golden
A.J. Graham
William C. Grummel
Daniel P. Harmon
George Harris
Donald H. Hoffman
Chun-chieh Huang
Michael H. Jameson
Tom B. Jones
Solomon Katz
Thomas Kelly

James G. Keenan
Donald S. Lateiner
Valdis Leinieks
Malcolm McGregor
James D. Muhly
Douglass C. North
Mark D. Northrup
Louis A. Okin
Stewart I. Oost
James Packer
Lionel Pearson
John Peradotto
Anthony J. Podlecki
Anthony E. Raubitschek
Isabelle Raubitschek
James M. Redfield
Meyer Reinhold
A.L.H. Robkin
Christina Horst Roseman
Frederick A. Rusch
Linda W. Rutland
Raphael Sealey
William Shepherd
Stuart G.P. Small
Chester G. Starr
Grundy Steiner
Carol G. Thomas
Homer Thompson
Theodore J. Tracy
Howard F. Vos
Thomas N. Winter
John Wright

Contents

A NOTE ON MESSENIAN
ECONOMY AND POPULATION

MESSENIA is properly regarded as one of the regions in Greece unusually favored by nature in possessing a fertile soil, which, at an early date, excited the envy of the Spartans, who made it their conquest. This same fertility of soil enabled the Messenians, when their independence was established in 369 B.C., to be self-supporting so far as the staples of their food supply were concerned. Since Messenia played a minor part in Greek history and little excavation has been done on its sites, there is little evidence to fill in the details of this general picture. Most important is a group of inscriptions, including the well-known regulation of the mysteries celebrated in Andania,[1] dated about 100 B.C. Two other documents[2] refer to the collection for Roman purposes of an 8-obol tax (about 2 per cent), which was based on an estimate[3] of Messenian property at 1,256 talents. The tax inscriptions were published with a very useful commentary by Wilhelm[4] and have been noticed in some detail by both Rostovtzeff and Larsen in their recent studies of the economy of Greece in the Hellenistic and Roman periods.[5] The inscriptions seem to attest the prosperity[6] of the state and its timocratic social organization about 100 B.C. Their value, however, is impaired by the uncertainty whether they refer to all of Messenia or only to the city of Messene and its particular district. In addition, the population of the whole region and of the city and its district are unknown, which makes any estimate of the individual wealth, conjectured to be about one-fifth of a talent by Wilhelm,[7] too uncertain to be useful. Accordingly, it seems worth while to review the general considerations which must govern any estimate of Messenian economy, not so much in the expectation of finding definite answers to these problems as in the hope, at least, of defining them more precisely.

The total area of Messenia, including the islands off the coast, and in its greatest extent to the southeast, where the frontier with Laconia was delimited by the little Pamisus River (the modern Milia River), which flows into the sea by the village of Pephnos, has been estimated by Beloch as 2,901.5 sq. km.[8] About

[1] Ditt. *Syll.*[3], 736.

[2] *IG*, V, 1, 1432–33.

[3] There is some controversy whether the sum of 1,256 talents represents an estimate of the total value of all property or an assessment for the purposes of taxation, which may be only a certain (and unknown) proportion of that value (M. Rostovtzeff, *The Social and Economic History of the Hellenistic World* [Oxford, 1941], II, 751–52, 1147; III, 1606, n. 85). Rostovtzeff tentatively adopts the view that it is a total estimate and criticizes E. Cavaignac's attempt to break the figure into individual items, evaluate them, and show that it is a partial estimate (*Population et capitale dans le monde méditerranéen antique* [Strasbourg, 1923], pp. 128–32).

[4] A. Wilhelm, "Urkunden aus Messene," *Jahreshefte*, XVII (1914), 1–120. Another inscription (*IG*, V, 1, 1532), which was grouped with these by Wilhelm as a similar tax list, contains the name of a *polis* in a list of individuals. It is apparently a different type of document and has been restudied by M. N. Tod (*BSA*, XXVIII [1926–27], 151–57).

[5] Rostovtzeff, *op. cit.*, II, 750–54, 1147–48; J. A. O. Larsen, "Roman Greece," *An Economic Survey of the Roman World* (Baltimore, 1938), IV, 419–20, 430.

[6] F. M. Heichelheim, while not objecting explicitly to the acceptance of 1,256 talents as the taxable capital of the state, has argued that the sum represented a low standard of wealth and is an indication of poverty rather than of prosperity in Messenia (*Wirtschaftsgeschichte des Altertums* [Leiden, 1938], II, 1093).

[7] *Op. cit.*, p. 113.

[8] K. J. Beloch, *Die Bevölkerung der griechischrömischen Welt* (Leipzig, 1886), p. 114. Beloch gives the southeast boundary of Messenia as Thalamae, which lay several miles south of the Milia River but

65.8 per cent of the region, however, is mountainous,[9] so that there are only about 992 sq. km. of comparatively level land.[10] The proportion of level to mountainous terrain is one of the highest in Greece;[11] but, of course, all the level area is not equally fertile and suited to the production of cereals. The soil of the Akritas peninsula on the southwest is chalky, and its yield of grain is poor. On the other hand, the alluvial soil of the plains drained by the system of the Mavrozoumenos and Pamisus rivers—the Soulima plain in northwestern Messenia, the upper and lower plains in central Messenia—and of the small coastal plains on the west coast is well suited for the production of grain and, even in summer, is well watered by the rivers and numerous springs.[12] The total area of the alluvial soil in the most important district—the upper and lower plains—is estimated at about 407 sq. km.[13] and of the flat land alone in the upper and lower plains, at about 217 sq. km.[14] Thus the area on which the traditional reputation of Messenia for fertility rested is quite small when considered in relation to its total surface. In addition, it is probable that, as at present, small parts of the lower plain near the modern town

of Hagios Floros[15] and along the Pamisus River were too marshy to be cultivated, although it is scarcely possible to estimate their size.

Although some Messenian towns are mentioned in the *Iliad* and the *Odyssey*,[16] the reputation for fertility which the whole region enjoyed came into being in the early stages of the Spartan conquest. At that time, Tyrtaeus expressed the feeling of the Spartans that Messenia was a "good land to till, a good land to plant."[17] The tradition was further developed in Athens during the latter period of the Spartan occupation of Messenia, when the Athenians were backing the cause of the helots and possibly feeling some envy at the thought that Sparta had a fertile region at its absolute disposal, while Athens' own food supply was threatened by invasion or by the cutting of the routes from the Black Sea. Thus, Euripides wrote of Messenia, contrasting it to Laconia, as "rich in produce, watered with

presumably controlled the territory extending up to its bank. This stream was made the boundary between Messenia and Laconia by the adjudication of 338 B.C. (Roebuck, *A History of Messenia from 369 to 146 B.C.* [Chicago, 1941], pp. 56–57).

[9] A. Jardé, *Les Céréales dans l'antiquité grecque* (Paris, 1925), p. 65, n. 1.

[10] This is not to be confused with the estimate given by Wilhelm (*op. cit.*, pp. 112–13) of *ca.* 990 sq. km. for the territory of Messene and its own district.

[11] See the table printed by Jardé (*op. cit.*, p. 65, n. 1).

[12] *Ibid.*, pp. 64, 75; A. Philippson, *Der Peloponnes* (Berlin, 1892), pp. 373, 496–97.

[13] Philippson, *op. cit.*, pp. 381, 576. Philippson's estimate of 407 sq. km. for the upper and lower plains includes both the flat land of the plains and the low tables and hills (*Neogenhügel*) around their edge, on which many of the villages are set. Thus it does not include the Soulima Valley or the small coastal plains of the west coast.

[14] Wilhelm, *op. cit.*, p. 114.

[15] The sources of the Pamisus River are situated in this region. M. N. Valmin has remarked on the measures apparently taken to lay the foundations of the temple of the river-god, Pamisus, in the marshy soil (*The Swedish Messenia Expedition* [Lund, 1938], p. 422).

[16] When Achilles was offered some Messenian towns by Agamemnon to cease his sulking and return to the battle, certain epithets are used of them. Hira is called grassy; Antheia had deep pastures; Pedasus was covered with vines; the country folk were rich in sheep and oxen (*Il.* ix. 150–54). When Telemachus journeyed from Pylos to Sparta, he passed through the wheat-bearing plain, apparently the lower plain (*Od.* iii. 495). While these epithets are in part conventional or designed to impress Achilles with the desirability of the towns, they give a picture of production which held true for Messenia in later periods. For the Homeric towns, which are to be located in the southern part of Messenia, see Valmin, *Etudes topographiques sur la Messénie ancienne* (Lund, 1930), pp. 206–13; for the route of Telemachus' journey see Macdonald, "Where Did Nestor Live?" *AJA*, XLVI (1942), 541–43.

[17] Tyrtaeus Frag. 4. 3 [Diehl]; Schol. Plato *Laws* i. 629 a [Becker]. Pausanias also remarks on Messenian fertility in the legendary section of his account (iv. 4. 3; 15. 6), and Strabo observes that the lower plain was called *Makaria* (viii. 4. 6). It is possible that the name was bestowed on the region because of its fertility (Valmin, *Etudes topographiques*, pp. 39–40).

countless streams, furnished with good pasture for both cattle and sheep, not cold in the blasts of winter, nor again too hot in summer; whose fertility is greater than words can express";[18] and Plato, or some student of Plato, as if it were a commonplace, referred[19] to the number of horses and other animals bred in Messenia.

The Spartans, however, seem to have used only the upper plain, the lower plain west of the Pamisus River,[20] and probably the Soulima plain[21] for their *kleroi*,

while the coastal region was occupied by perioecic towns, except for the district of Pylos in the central part of the west coast. We know from Thucydides that the region of Pylos was at least partly wooded and undeveloped,[22] since the Athenians were able to get a foothold there without opposition. The general picture, then, of Messenia under the Spartan occupation was probably one of cereal production on the Spartan *kleroi*[23] in the plains and of stock-raising in the hills surrounding them. The perioecic towns would have cultivated the small plains and hillsides in their own neighborhood, while on the west coast was the undeveloped area around Pylos. Thus, in the Greece of the late fifth and early fourth centuries, Messenia presented the spectacle of a region with part of its best land exploited by another state and part of it undeveloped, so that it was capable of supporting a larger population than it had. These impressions might well outweigh the con-

[18] The passage is quoted by Strabo (viii. 5. 6) from an unidentified play (*Tragicorum Graecorum fragmenta*, ed. A. Nauck [2d ed.; Leipzig, 1889], 1083).

[19] Plato *Alcibiades I* 122 d.

[20] Roebuck, *op. cit.*, pp. 28–31.

[21] Valmin has suggested in his publication of a small structure near Vasiliko, at the entrance to the Soulima plain from the upper plain, that the former was Arcadian territory until the beginning of the fifth century B.C., when it was captured by the Spartans in the third Messenian War ("Ein messenisches Kastell und die arkadische Grenzfrage," *Skrifter utgivna av Svenska Institutet i Rom*, V, Part I, 59–76). In the building, which was plausibly identified as a small fort housing a garrison, an inscribed sherd was found with a name, Παυκᾶ Εὐτρεσίο[υ], which Valmin considered to be that of a man from Eutresis in Arcadia. Since it is unlikely that an Arcadian would be serving in a Spartan garrison in the fifth century, he has argued that the district west of the fort—all northwest Messenia—was Arcadian. The general thread of the argument runs that northwest Messenia is geographically linked more closely to Phigaleia and Triphylia than to Messenia and that Arcadia, through its control of these districts, sought to control northwest Messenia. As historical confirmation of this the following arguments are used: the presence of an Arcadian soldier; the reassertion of the Arcadian claim to Triphylia after 369 B.C.; evidence that the Soulima plain was Arcadian after 180 B.C. To answer these in detail: From a purely geographical point of view the Soulima plain is as closely linked to the Messenian upper plain as it is to Phigaleia, and Phigaleia is more closely linked to Messenia than it is to the Arcadian center of gravity around Megalopolis and Mantinea (Meyer, "Phigaleia," P.-W., XIX, 2067–68); granting that Pankas was an Arcadian, he might have been present as an ally of the Messenians to fight the Spartans; while it is true that Arcadia pressed its claim to Triphylia after 369 B.C., there is no reason to suppose that northwestern Messenia was regarded as part of Triphylia or Lepreon, for Scylax (*Periplus* 45) specifically noticed Cyparissia as Messenian; the argument that the Soulima plain became a part of Arcadia after 180 B.C. is unintelligible as presented by Valmin, who seems to have confused his own previous views (Roebuck, *op. cit.*, p. 103, n. 167). Thus it is scarcely proved that the Soulima plain district was Arcadian *ca.* 500 B.C. It may still have been Messenian, but in any case

it became Spartan well before the Peloponnesian War. The status of the Soulima plain under Spartan control, however, is not clear, although it is probable that Cyparissia and Aulon to the west were perioecic towns (*ibid.*, p. 30).

[22] Thuc. iv. 3. 2–3, 8. 6; ii. 25. 1 (referring to Mothone).

[23] Attempts have been made to estimate the production of the *kleroi* in Laconia and Messenia from Plutarch's notice of the amount paid to his landlord by the helot (Plut. *Lycurg.* 8). Kahrstedt's view ("Die spartanische Agrarwirtschaft," *Hermes*, LIV [1919], 279–94) is criticized as basically unsound by Jardé (*op. cit.*, pp. 109–12); but Jardé's own discussion is invalidated because he assumes that the whole of Messenia was Spartiate territory and does not make allowance for the land of the perioecic towns. Messenia was probably never entirely Spartiate territory, for it was conquered piecemeal; and by the time the whole region had come into Spartan hands, the perioecic towns had been established along the coasts. Thus Jardé's figure of 140,000 hectares of cultivable ground, of which possibly 10 per cent was in vineyards and orchards, for the *kleroi* is too high (it is almost one-half of the total area of the whole region). If the helot population is calculated by using his suggested figures (a *kleros* of the maximum size of 36 hectares for grain; 3,500 *kleroi* in Messenia; 40 helots to the *kleros*), the result is about 140,000 persons, which seems too high when compared to my later calculations (see below, p. 162).

sideration that the fertile area was, in itself, quite small.

Agriculture necessarily became the basis of Messenian economy after the establishment of the state as an independent power in 369 B.C. There was no tradition of skill in the arts and crafts, no metal resources; nor was the position of Messenia, remote from the Aegean and Italian trading routes, such as would enable it to become a trading state of any importance. Further, Messenia possessed no special product like the silphium of Cyrene on which it might have capitalized. The population, in which the helot element must have predominated, was trained only in agriculture and was in possession of a country capable of further settlement. New towns were founded,[24] as well as the capital city on the slopes of Mount Ithome; but none, it is to be noticed, on the flat land of the upper and lower plains or on that of the Soulima plain. Andania,[25] near modern Polichne, on the upper plain gained further importance, but as a religious sanctuary rather than as a *polis*. Accordingly, the areas of production must have remained much the same as in the period of Spartan occupation. The fertile plains would have been used largely for the production of grain,[26] the hills about them for grazing animals, and the small towns on the coast would utilize the little

plains and hills near their walls and would fish in the waters offshore.

Such is the impression given by the scanty literary notices. In 221 B.C., when Dorimachus, the Aetolian, was stationed at Phigaleia to organize forays on Messenian territory, the first raids were made in the hilly border district with animals as their especial booty.[27] One particularly venturesome raid, made while Dorimachus was in the city of Messene accounting for his actions, was directed against the farm of a certain Chyron near the city.[28] The farm was evidently an establishment of some size, which would combine grain- and stock-raising and is the first example of the large estates which are known to have existed in the Roman period as Italian landowners settled in the country.[29] In modern times the upper and lower plains have been extensively used for growing fruit, particularly figs and oranges rather than vines and olives. There is a reference to vines in Messenia in Homeric times,[30] but none for any period to olives or figs, although the low fertile land was suitable for them. It is probable that some were grown, but the paramount necessity of grain production makes it likely that the proportion was low.[31]

It is probable that Messenia was self-

---

[24] The new towns seem to have been Corone, possibly Kolonides, and Haliartus (Roebuck. *op. cit.*, p. 39). No doubt there was also a development of the Pylos area, if not a new settlement there (*ibid.*, p. 29, n. 9). Villages (not *poleis*) would have been built on the low hills at the edge of the plain rather than on the flat, as, for example, the sites near Pidima, Kortzaousi, Kalogeraki, and Karteroli in the lower plain (Valmin, *Etudes topographiques*, pp. 52–64) and Desylla, Aetos, and Stylari in the upper plain and the Soulima plain (*ibid.*, pp. 89–90, 102 ff.).

[25] Valmin has identified Andania with the remains near Polichne on the western edge of the upper plain (*Etudes topographiques*, pp. 89–98).

[26] Grain production on the plains is not mentioned specifically in the sources, but it is apparent from the accounts of the various invasions of Messenia that the plains were so used (see below, n. 46).

[27] Pol. iv. 3. 9–10.

[28] *Ibid.*, iv. 4. 1.

[29] *IG*, V, 1, 1433. 24–26; 1434. It seems probable that the names with feminine terminations in *IG*, V, 1, 1532, should also be regarded as estates. That list, then, would record the payments by individuals, estates, and a community, the *polis* of the Pylanians. The document is being further studied by Sterling Dow.

[30] *Il.* ix. 152. Pedasus is identified by Pausanias (iv. 35. 1) with Mothone, which apparently retained the tradition of a wine-producing center; for, according to one legend, the city of Mothone was named after Methone, the daughter of Oineus. The name Oenussae was borne by the islands lying off Mothone (Valmin, *Etudes topographiques*, pp. 211–12).

[31] Jardé has suggested that 10 per cent of the cultivated land was in orchards and vineyards during the period of the Spartan occupation (*op. cit.*, p. 112).

supporting in its food supply, although that is largely a deduction drawn from the fertile nature of the country and the absence of any evidence to the contrary. Some indication of it may be seen in an inscription dated vaguely in the second or first century B.C., regulating the grain supply of the town of Thouria.[32] The inscription gives no hint of a shortage of grain but is concerned with disposing of the surplus with as much profit to the city as possible, presumably to citizens of its own district. It is to be noted that Thouria, at least for the period of this inscription, had full control over its own grain supply and was not subject to the authority of Messene. One statement which might seem to indicate that Messene itself was not self-supporting is to be found in Polybius' account of the revolt of Messene against the Achaean League in 183–182 B.C. At that time, the League asked the Roman senate to place an embargo on the export of arms and grain to Messene by Italian merchants.[33] The request was made, however, during the winter of 183–182 B.C., and the Achaean plan of campaign was evidently to destroy the harvest of 182 B.C., which would ripen in June, thus enabling them to starve out the city.[34] The episode indicates rather that the city's supply was arranged on a harvest-to-harvest basis and that any surplus, as in Thouria, was disposed of by sale rather than stored to form a reserve.[35]

While agriculture formed the basis of the Messenian economy, there would, of course, be craftsmen and artisans who produced most of the articles for local use and were employed in the trades necessary for the life of the community. Not enough material is available from Messenian sites of the period of its independence to discuss the types or the quality of locally manufactured articles. Certain general statements, however, may be made. The stone used in Messenian buildings and fortifications is local, and their construction would have afforded some employment at various periods. A supply of leather and wool was probably obtained from the animals raised. There are clay beds, which would have been used for the manufacture of pottery and tiles. Valmin has discovered an establishment for refining salt on Venetiko Island.[36] Metal would have had to be imported, for the most part in the form of manufactured articles, as was noticed in the case of the arms in 183–182 B.C. Presumably the silver plate and the fine textiles mentioned in the inscription from Andania[37] were imported from the Hellenistic centers of manufacture, although there is a hint in the sources that flax may have been grown in Messenia.[38]

The only products available for foreign trade would have been of an agricultural nature—live animals, possibly a small amount of grain, and other produce. The trade may have had rather more importance than one is at first sight inclined to assign to it. It is noteworthy that, except for Messene and Thouria, the larger

[32] *IG*, V, 1, 1379. I have followed the interpretation of L. Robert, "Notes d'épigraphie hellénistique," *BCH*, LII (1928), 426–32. The Delian accounts of the early second century B.C. also seem to indicate how the grain supply might be a source of profit to the community (Larsen, *op. cit.*, pp. 344–48).

[33] Pol. xxiii. 9. 12.

[34] For the chronology and events of the revolt see Roebuck, *op. cit.*, pp. 95 ff.

[35] One objection, of course, to basing any conclusion on this episode is that the harvest of 183 B.C. may have been poor. That, however, seems unlikely, as the Messenians would not have chosen to revolt at the particular time they did. The revolt seems to have

started in the autumn of 183 B.C. when the harvest and summer produce would have been gathered. The Achaean request, made to the senate in the winter after an initial failure to crush the revolt, was designed to cut off all possibility of external supply.

[36] *Études topographiques*, p. 160.

[37] Ditt. *Syll.*[3], 736.

[38] Thuc. iv. 26. 8.

towns were all on the coast and the Achaean League made it a point of policy in its gradual absorption of Messenia to cut them off from the capital city. Pylos was detached sometime before 220 B.C.,[39] and the process was completed in 182 B.C., when Abia, Pharae, and Thouria became independent members of the League.[40] There is no indication that any one of these coastal towns served as an especial port for the capital. So far as communications go, Corone and Cyparissia were best situated to serve such a purpose. It is possible that some ships for Messene sailed up the Pamisus River, which was said by Pausanias to have been navigable for about 10 stades from its mouth.[41] If so, one would expect to find some sort of harbor facilities on its bank, although none have been found or are mentioned in the sources. A certain amount of trade moved through Cyparissia, for an inscription[42] of the late fourth century B.C. contains provisions for collecting a tax on imports and exports by sea from that port. Unfortunately, no figures are given from which their volume might have been calculated. Also, a sufficient number of ships was found along the coast to transport the levy ordered from Messenia by Philip V for his attack on Cephallenia in 218 B.C.[43]

The only specific notice of export trade is found in the story told by Polybius of the Messenian merchant, Nikagoras, who helped to arrange the death of King Cleomenes of Sparta when the latter was in exile at Alexandria.[44] Nikagoras was evidently a person of more than local importance, for he entertained Archidamus

of Sparta about 238 B.C., when the latter fled from Cleomenes. At a later date, when Nikagoras took a cargo of horses to Alexandria, he was induced to co-operate with Sosibius, the first minister and virtual ruler of Egypt, in engineering a plot against Cleomenes. Polybius mentions the horses only incidentally; but it is probable, when we recall Plato's remark about the breeding of horses there at an earlier date, that they were bred in Messenia. Further, the trade carried on by Nikagoras was evidently of some importance if he was known to Sosibius. All this evidence of trade indicates that it was by sea rather than by land; and such was probably the case, as the routes into Messenia are through difficult mountain country[45] leading only from Elis, Arcadia, and Sparta, of which the economy was of the same agricultural type as that of Messenia and thus would offer markets only in times of temporary shortage.

The following statements, then, about the economy of Messenia seem justified: It was based on agriculture, of which the chief products were cereals and stock. The cereal production was probably concentrated largely on the plains, while cattle, sheep, and goats were pastured on the surrounding hills. The larger estates, on which horses could best be bred, would have used some of their area for pasture and some for the production of barley used in feeding the horses. The production of foodstuffs was apparently sufficient for the population and left a small margin for export. The exports were agricultural products and horses, while the imports would have been fine articles, such as silver plate and textiles, and such necessities as metal, which were not found in Messenia. For the period of the

---

[39] Roebuck, *op. cit.*, p. 69, n. 12.

[40] Pol. xxiii. 17. 2.

[41] Paus. iv. 34. 1.   [42] *IG*, V, 1, 1421.

[43] Pol. v. 3. 3, 4. 4. They could not, however, cope with the Illyrian pirates, who were making raids on the coast *ca.* 230 B.C. (*ibid.* ii. 5. 1–2).

[44] *Ibid.*, v. 37.

[45] Roebuck, *op. cit.*, pp. 1–28. Communications inside Messenia were not difficult and were the object of some care, as the elaborate triple bridge over the Mavrozoumenos River near Meligala indicates.

Thourian grain inscription the various towns seem to have regulated their own supplies, presumably the product of their dependent districts. Our view of the production as a whole should be controlled by the fact that the most fertile and the largest level area was only about 217 sq. km. in size.

From these observations an important question arises. Is it possible to limit with some degree of accuracy the districts dependent on the various cities and, above all, on Messene itself? If it is possible, in the case of the latter a rough estimate might be made of its grain production and, from that, a maximum figure set for the population. It would be particularly desirable to work out these limits for the period of about 100 B.C., so that more use could be made of the tax inscription; but information for the period after the Roman settlement of Greece in 146 B.C. is very scanty. Yet there is some reason to believe that, about 100 B.C., Messene was in possession of the same district which it controlled before the city's entrance into the Achaean League in 182 B.C., and it is possible to fix the limits of the city's district for the period before 182 B.C. with some probability. Further, the information obtained for that period is not meaningless for the tax inscription, since Messenia did not suffer so severely during the troubled years between 230 and 146 B.C. as did many other regions of the Peloponnesus.[46]

In estimating the production of grain

and the population of the district of Messene, the assumption is made that both it and the other towns used, as a normal practice, only the grain grown in their own districts for their food supply. The grain regulation from Thouria seems to indicate that that was true at one period; but it is not clear whether the document is to be dated before or after 182 B.C., when Messene lost political control of Thouria, which became an independent member of the Achaean League.[47] An indication that it may well have been true of the preceding period is that various Messenian towns were detached from the Messenian political organization in 191 B.C., as territorial entities capable of taking their place as independent members of the League.[48] Between 191 and 183 B.C., Messene's grievances against the Achaean League centered around the question of the return of exiles,[49] which

[46] It will be apparent from the following summary of invasions and raids that no very serious or lasting damage was done. Messenia was not laid waste during the Cleomenean War (Pol. iv. 5. 5). It was raided by Dorimachus in 221 B.C. from Phigaleia, and it was invaded twice during the Social War, but neither the raids nor the invasions were on a large scale (Roebuck, op. cit., pp. 72, 79–80). In 215–214 B.C. a civil outbreak occurred in which over two hundred people were killed, but there seems to have been no property damage and order was soon restored (ibid., p. 82). Shortly afterward Philip V, when his agent, Demetrius of Pharos, had failed to take Messene, laid the country waste. That would involve the loss of the harvest, destruction of orchards, vineyards, and farm buildings (ibid., p. 83). In 202–201 B.C. Nabis made a partially successful raid, in which some movable property was carried off from Messene, but later it may have been recovered in part (ibid., pp. 88–89). In 191 B.C. forces of the Achaean League devastated the fields, but Flamininus settled the affair before much harm was done (ibid., pp. 92–93). In 182 B.C. the forces of the Achaean League again destroyed the harvest; some territory was detached from the city and a number of prominent citizens sent into exile, but the latter were allowed to return in 179 B.C. (ibid., pp. 101–5). In 146 B.C. the Messenian levy raised for the revolt of the Achaean League against Rome did not leave Messenia and, in the ensuing settlements, land taken from the city in 182 B.C. was apparently restored (ibid., pp. 105–7). This list of the recorded disasters between 230 and 146 B.C. shows only two serious crises: the events of 215–214 B.C. and the results of the revolt against the Achaean League. Neither of these, however, seems to have been particularly destructive of property, which it would tax the resources of the state to replace. Messenia was primarily an agricultural state, so that occasional loss of the harvest would result in acute temporary distress; but it would not have been subject in the same degree as the more industrialized states to the long-term economic factors which gradually impoverished Greece in the Hellenistic period, or, before 146 B.C. at least, to crippling Roman confiscations and levies.

[47] Pol. xxiii. 17. 2.

[48] Roebuck, op. cit., pp. 93–94.

[49] Ibid., pp. 94–95.

was a political, rather than an economic, problem. Their return would affect the ownership of properties and give rise to a host of legal problems, but not necessarily lessen the capacity of the land to produce food. Thus the city of Messene was able to support itself between those years; but after 182 B.C., when the upper plain was given to Megalopolis, a three-year period of relief from taxation by the Achaean League was necessary for economic readjustment.[50] Accordingly, the attempt seems justifiable to define the limits of the territory of Messene's own district and to base an estimate of production and population on it.

The city of Messene was situated on the west slope of Mount Ithome and surrounded by a fortification wall of which the circuit was about 9 km. and extended up the slope to include the summit of the mountain. The site was well chosen to control the upper and lower plains, the Soulima plain to the northwest, and the rolling hills to the southwest. During its period of independence, Messene assured its control by a number of towers and forts placed at strategic points.[51] In the upper plain the only site of importance was Andania, a sanctuary. In the lower plain there were no town sites of importance in the area west of the Pamisus River; but east of the river, at the edge of the plain, was Thouria, which would presumably control an area of the plain as its own dependent district. The natural limits for the Thourian district are: on the south, the hills which cut off the little plain of Pharae; on the west, the Pamisus River; on the north, the line of hills running westward to the Pamisus by Skala.[52] When this area is taken from Messene's

own district, the latter would have included the lower plain west of the Pamisus River and the whole of the upper plain. It is also likely from the absence of town sites that the hills west of the Pamisus were included as far as the Bias River,[53] which would form the boundary with Corone. It is also likely that the Soulima plain on the northwest, as far as the hills by Kopanaki, formed a part of Messene's district; for in a boundary delimitation, apparently to be dated shortly after 182 B.C., Messene was allowed to hold the area of Doris (the Soulima plain) but lost the upper plain to Megalopolis.[54] In addition to this whole contiguous territory, Messene possessed the *Ager Denthaliatis* of unknown extent, but possibly only a small tract near the sanctuary of Artemis Limnatis east of Pharae in Taygetus.[55] Thus, to trace the district's boundary line: on the west, the coastal range and its northern prolongation in the hills by Kopanaki; on the north, along the gorge of the Neda River to Mount Tetrazi; on the east, along the range of Taygetus to the hills by Skala and thence along the Pamisus River to the sea; on the south, the shoreline of the Gulf of Messenia as far as the Bias River, which flowed from the west coastal range.[56]

The hilly regions of the district, as was previously suggested, would have been used primarily for grazing and the fertile plains for cereal production. The district

[50] Pol. xxiv. 2. 3; for the loss of the upper plain see below, n. 54.

[51] Roebuck, *op. cit.*, pp. 39–40.

[52] Valmin, *Etudes topographiques*, pp. 61, 65–66, 122–25; Roebuck, *op. cit.*, p. 103, n. 168.

[53] Valmin, *Etudes topographiques*, p. 179.

[54] Roebuck, *op. cit.*, p. 102, n. 167.

[55] *Ibid.*, pp. 118–21.

[56] Wilhelm has made an estimate (*ca.* 990 sq. km.) of the area of the district of Messene and traced its boundaries (*op. cit.*, pp. 112–13). His delimitation of the boundaries is based only on geographical considerations, as, in part, is my own. There are a few unimportant differences: the line of hills by Kopanaki seemed a preferable boundary to the Kyparisseis River because the fort of Stylari, which would control the route through them, lies near by. The Bias River on the southwest would form a better boundary than the Karias River, since it is a more important stream. The area of the territory remains approximately the same.

east of the Pamisus River, which presumably belonged to Thouria, is roughly
equivalent to the Soulima plain in area.
Therefore, if we take 200 sq. km. as the
area of the fertile plain land available to
the citizens of Messene, we should not be
far wrong. The total area of the district
was about 1,000 sq. km.,[57] so that about
800 sq. km. consisted of hilly and mountainous terrain. Possibly one-quarter[58] of
the latter would have been cultivated and
the whole of the plains, which together
make about 400 sq. km. of cultivated
land.[59] About 10 per cent of that may
have been in orchard and vineyard,[60]
which would leave 360 sq. km. available
for cereal production. Half of that would
lie fallow every year, according to the
usual practice of Greek agriculture, so
that 180 sq. km., or 18,000 hectares,
would have been available each year
for production.

The problem of estimating the production of cereals on that acreage and then
determining the mean annual ration per
person, which would enable a maximum
limit to be set for the population, is, of
course, beset with numerous difficulties.

At best, it is possible to work out only an
approximation, but even the factors by
which such results must be calculated are
by no means certain. In the first place,
was barley or wheat the principal crop?
Since the yield of barley is greater than
that of wheat, but the nutritive value of
wheat greater than that of barley,[61] it
makes considerable difference which grain
was used as the staple food. If both were
used, what was the ratio between them?
Then, as we have pointed out, pro-
portionately more animals, particularly
horses, seem to have been bred in Messenia
than, for example, in Attica, so that an
allowance should be made for the amount
of grain which they consumed. In setting
the amounts of the production and the
food ration in modern metrical standards,
it is necessary to choose between the system of Hultsch,[62] with a *medimnos* of
52.53 liters, and that of Viedebantt,[63]
with a substantially smaller *medimnos* of
40.9334 liters. While it is scarcely possible
to answer these questions in a very decisive manner, yet, with the help of Jardé's
valuable study on the production of
cereals and with the peculiar conditions of
Messenia in mind, some results can be
obtained which tally reasonably well with
the scanty evidence bearing directly on
the question of Messenian population.

To consider, first, the problem of production: The alluvial soil of the Messenian
plains is very fertile and would yield good
returns of either wheat or barley; but under such favorable conditions the cost
of producing wheat, when its higher nu-

[57] Wilhelm, *op. cit.*, p. 112; see the preceding note
also. The following table, which is based on Philippson's measurements (*op. cit.*, pp. 381, 576), lists the
areas of the various types of land: (1) the area of the
lower and upper plains (flat alluvial land) was *ca.* 217
sq. km.; (2) the area of the alluvial hilly land ringing
the plains was *ca.* 190 sq. km.; (3) the area of mountainous and nonalluvial land was *ca.* 600 sq. km. In
No. 1 the area of the district of Thouria was subtracted and that of the Soulima plain added, which left
ca. 200 sq. km. I have referred to the hilly alluvial
land and the mountainous terrain together as making
up the remaining 800 sq. km.

[58] Jardé, *op. cit.*, p. 110, n. 2. The estimate is made
of the hill country in Laconia.

[59] This estimate makes the proportion of cultivated
land in the district about 40 per cent of its total area.
That is a higher percentage than that suggested by
Jardé for the estate of Phainippos in Attica (24.7 per
cent) and that of Dionysos in Heraclea (33 per cent)
and for the whole Peloponnesus in modern times (25
per cent) (*ibid.*, pp. 78—79). In the case of the Messenian district, however, we are dealing with a small
area which had an unusually high percentage of fertile
land and the estimate seems reasonable.

[60] *Ibid.*, p. 112.

[61] N. Jasny, "Competition among Grains in Classical
Antiquity," *American Historical Review*, XLVII
(1942), 752–53. According to Jasny, wheat of average
quality has a nutritive value of 10 per cent more than
barley in terms of weight and 35 per cent more in terms
of volume.

[62] F. Hultsch, *Griechische und römische Metrologie*
(2d ed.; Berlin, 1882), pp. 99–111, 703.

[63] O. Viedebantt, "Medimnos," P.-W., XV, 86–87;
"Die athenischen Hohlmasse," *Festschrift für August
Oxé* (Darmstadt, 1938), pp. 135–46.

tritive value is considered, is about equal to the cost of production of the more prolific barley.[64] Then, although barley was originally the principal cereal consumed in Greece,[65] there was a preference for wheat as food;[66] and, in the Hellenistic period, wheat seems to have become the main item of diet when it could be obtained. Thus it seems probable that in the Messenian plains in the third and second centuries B.C. wheat would have been the main crop both because of the natural preference for it and because its cost of production would not have been appreciably more than that of barley. Some barley would have been grown, no doubt, both as food for animals,[67] particularly horses and mules, and on the poorer soil of the mountain fields. It seems justifiable, however, to make a general estimate of the production and food ration in terms of wheat and to subtract from that an allowance for the consumption of barley by animals.

The average yearly yield of wheat in Greece in antiquity has been estimated by Jardé at 8–12 hectoliters per hectare and of barley at 16–20 hectoliters per hectare.[68] Although there should have been a maximum yield from the Messenian plains, it would be wiser to use the mean figures of 10 for wheat and 18 for barley by way of compensating for the poor seasons. In estimating the amount of barley pro-

duced for the animals, the result has to be entirely conjectural, for neither the amount of the ration nor the number of grain-eating animals is known. Sheep, goats, pigs, and cattle could have lived by grazing and such fodder as the Greeks provided for their animals—straw and leaves. Horses and mules, however, would need barley as part of their diet, and the donkeys, although needing it to work efficiently, probably received the short end of available supplies. It is known that on one occasion 250 Messenian cavalry were levied and on another, 200.[69] Jardé, in estimating the number of horses bred in Attica, fixed on 3,000 in proportion to a cavalry force of 1,200.[70] If the same ratio is used, the number of horses in Messenia may be estimated as 625; but, since horses were exported, relatively more would have been bred, possibly 1,000. Again using the same ratio between horses, mules, and donkeys as for Attica,[71] there would have been about 2,100 mules and 1,500 donkeys. Thus the total yearly consumption of barley by that number of animals would amount to about 56,780 hectoliters, for the production of which about 3,154 hectares of land would have been necessary.[72] When this is subtracted from the 18,000 hectares of land available

---

[64] Jasny, op. cit., pp. 753–54.

[65] L. Gernet, "L'Approvisionnement d'Athènes en blé au Vᵉ et au IVᵉ siècle," Mélanges d'histoire ancienne, XXV (1909), 293–94; Jardé, op. cit., pp. 123–24.

[66] Jardé, op. cit., p. 130.

[67] Ibid., p. 125, n. 1. It is possible that during the period of the Spartan occupation of Messenia the amount of barley grown was greater, for contributions to the syssitia were made in barley flour (Plut. Lycurg. 12), which would come in part from the kleroi in Messenia. Yet, for the reasons suggested above, it seems likely that the percentage of barley became substantially smaller during the period of Messenian independence.

[68] Op. cit., p. 60.

[69] Pol. iv. 15. 6; v. 20. 1. These levies were made during the Social War and, at that time, were presumably drawn from the whole territory of Messenia with the exception of Pylos, which had already become a member of the Achaean League (Roebuck, op. cit., p. 69, n. 12). Strictly speaking, the above estimates, starting from these figures, should be applied to the whole of Messenia and not to the city district of Messene alone. Yet, since the well-watered region of the city district would have been the site of the horse-breeding estates, it seems better to apply the estimate only to that area.

[70] Op. cit., p. 127.

[71] Ibid., pp. 126–27. I have estimated the number of mules and donkeys in relation to the number of 625 horses to preserve the ratio as used for Attica.

[72] It is calculated that, in modern times, mules and horses (weighing ca. 260 kg.) eat about one-thirtieth of their weight per day, of which two-thirds are in fodder and one-third in grain (ibid., pp. 125–26), while donkeys (weighing ca. 120 kg.), Jardé estimates, would

yearly for the production of cereals, there remain 14,846 hectares, on which, as we have suggested, wheat for human consumption would have been grown. Assuming that the average yield per hectare was 10 hectoliters, then 148,460 hectoliters would have been produced annually. One-sixth of that would have been necessary for seed,[73] which leaves 123,717 hectoliters for consumption by the population.

It remains to decide upon the mean annual consumption of wheat per person. Jardé cites considerable evidence to show that the traditional Greek ration, with some variations, was one Attic *choenix* (*ca.* 1 liter) per day for an adult male[74] and, using that as a basis, estimates that a woman would have eaten three-quarters of a *choenix* and a child one-half a *choenix*, thus obtaining a mean ration per person of about 2.60 hectoliters per year.[75] Jardé, however, has interpreted this as a minimum ration and established a maximum ration of 4.11 hectoliters per year, based on the daily allowance of 1½ *choenikes* of wheat recorded as paid to two stonemasons of Delos in 282 B.C.[76] This in-

stance of the higher ration is isolated and should scarcely be taken as a typical example of a food ration. Thus, Glotz[77] and Larsen[78] have explained it as part salary—that is, the amount contained an excess, which is to be regarded as part of the workmen's pay. If this interpretation is correct, the maximum ration disappears, and the minimum ration of Jardé's calculations is established as the normal ration. The latter would seem to be better justified on the general grounds that it is unlikely that Delos, which imported its grain, would have a substantially higher ration than Athens.

The problem is complicated, however, in that Jarde's interpretation finds some support in the fact that the Delian masons were allowed indifferently either 1½ *choenikes* of wheat or 3 *choenikes* of barley flour. This seems to establish a ratio of 1:2 between wheat and barley flour, and there is some evidence cited as pointing to that as the normal ratio elsewhere in Greece. In practice, this means that a person would eat twice the volume of barley flour as of wheat. Aside from the physical distaste or even disability (3 liters, almost an American gallon, of barley flour per day for a Delian) involved in such a diet, the ratio does not represent the nutritive value of the grains, which would have been roughly established in antiquity by practice, if not by scientific methods; for wheat is said to have a nutritive value of 35 per cent more than barley in terms of volume. The ratio of

---

have received no more than half that proportionate amount in grain. Thus 1,000 horses would eat 2,889 kg. per day; 2,100 mules would eat 6,067 kg. per day; 1,500 donkeys would eat 1,000 kg. per day—in all, 9,956 kg. per day, or 3,633,940 kg. per year, which would be equivalent to 56,780 hectoliters (64 kg. is the average weight of barley per hectoliter [*ibid.*, p. 109, n. 4]). Since the average yield of barley in Greece was *ca.* 18 hectoliters per hectare, *ca.* 3,154 hectares of land would have been necessary to produce that amount of barley.

[73] Estimates of the amount used for seed vary about the proportion of 15 per cent.

[74] Jardé, *op. cit.*, pp. 129–30. It is also to be noted in this connection that the ration of the Roman legionary soldier (Pol. vi. 39. 13) was about two-thirds of an Attic *medimnos* of wheat per month, which amounts to about 1 *choenix* per day.

[75] *Op. cit.*, pp. 132–35.

[76] *IG*, XI, 158, 37 ff.; Jardé, *op. cit.*, pp. 129, 135. Gernet (*op. cit.*, p. 294, n. 7) also noticed this higher Delian ration but did not attempt to establish it as a maximum ration, although he regarded the ration of 1 *choenix* per day as a minimum.

[77] G. Glotz, "Les Salaires à Délos," *Journal des savants*, XI (1913), 211–12.

[78] *Op. cit.*, pp. 410, 413. The system of giving both grain and money suggests that the origin was a system of rations plus cash, but later at times probably more than the normal ration was given as extra pay. Thus this payment in grain to the workmen may be a survival of a traditional practice retained by Greek conservatism in such matters and would not be a typical instance of granting food rations.

1:2 has already been questioned[79] on these grounds and, as an examination of the evidence will show, rightly so, for it rests largely on this Delian inscription. Glotz has explained the ratio as one of price relationship, since the price of wheat was normally double that of barley flour.[80] This explanation, however, is only satisfactory from the point of view of the employer who paid the salary. It would cost him an equal amount of money to buy 1½ *choenikes* of wheat or 3 of barley flour. Perhaps that is sufficient explanation; yet the employee would have profited by being paid in barley, for he would not need to eat twice as much of it as of wheat to live and could have sold the excess for more than the excess wheat.[81] This is an uneconomic practice, but, in the case of Delos, we may find the explanation for the variation in grains in the temporary availability of either wheat or barley.[82] These speculations at least show that it is unwise to consider that a ratio of 1:2 is established between wheat and barley flour as a food ration by the inscription.[83] The other evidence which Jardé cited for the ratio is equally unsatisfactory. The terms granted by the Athenians to the Spartans besieged on Sphacteria allowed them 2 Attic *choenikes* of barley flour per day.[84] This was interpreted by Jardé as the normal Athenian ration and thus double the ration of wheat, which was 1 *choenix* per day. Yet it is possible that the terms were rather the expression of a desire to humiliate or to weaken the Spartans, for the amount of wine allowed the prisoners in the terms was less than the normal amount brought by the Spartans to their *syssitia*.[85] Similarly, 2 *choenikes* of barley flour was less than the usual Spartan consumption.[86] An inscription from Mykonos[87] records the payment to a cook, after a sacrifice, of 2 *choenikes* of barley flour; but that is not unmistakably a food ration. It might be part salary, and, in any case, it does not agree with the supposedly higher Delian ration of 3 *choenikes* per day, as one might expect. Thus it does not seem that the ratio of wheat to barley flour as 1:2 is sufficiently well established for it to be used as a norm in calculating consumption. It is clear, however, that for a very long time barley was a staple food in the Greek diet. Since the traditional ration of 1 *choenix* per day seems to have been established at an early period, when barley would have been used as much as, if not

[79] Jasny, *op. cit.*, p. 752, n. 11. He has accepted the explanation of the ratio as one of price relationship but has not discussed the other evidence cited in support of it.

[80] G. Glotz, "Le Prix des denrées à Délos," *Journal des savants*, XI (1913), 20; see also Larsen (*op. cit.*, pp. 383–86), who has observed that "this should not be made into a hard and fast rule."

[81] This is evident if a price of 100 is assumed per *choenix* of wheat and of 50 for barley flour. The workman would receive 1½ *choenikes* of wheat and eat one, selling the remaining half at 50. If he received 3 *choenikes* of barley flour and ate 1.35, he could sell 1.65 *choenikes* at 82.50.

[82] Jardé, *op. cit.*, p. 170.

[83] Jardé (*ibid.*, p. 131, n. 3) has rejected the explanation of the ratio as one of price, on the grounds that there would be a variation in the ration when the price of wheat varied in relation to that of barley or when the price of wheat varied in itself. Yet there does not seem to be any other evidence in which information about the prices of wheat and barley and an allowance of the grains in a ratio of 1:2 coincide.

[84] Thuc. iv. 16. 1.

[85] Jardé, *op. cit.*, p. 130, n. 4.

[86] Plut. *Lycurg.* 12. Each person was to furnish monthly 1 *medimnos* (Aeginetan) of barley flour. If the same amount was consumed in meals at home, the total consumption would be 2 *medimnoi* per month or ca. 4½ Attic *choenikes* per day (Jardé, *op. cit.*, p. 129, n. 4). Although the Spartan manner of life demanded a heavy diet, this amount seems very large. The quantity used for meals at home, however, is conjectural; but, even if it is disregarded, the amount contributed to the *syssitia* is still slightly higher than the allowance granted to the men on Sphacteria. It is unlikely that a Spartan would himself eat his whole contribution to the *syssitia* (Busolt-Swoboda, *Griechische Staatskunde* [Munich, 1920–26], II, 699–700). It is possible, of course, that the amount allowed in the truce was determined by the available supply which could be brought to Pylos. In that case it should not be used as evidence of a food ration.

[87] Ditt. *Syll.*³, 1024.

more than, wheat, and to have become a moral precept among the Pythagoreans, it is possible that originally either 1 *choenix* of wheat or of barley was meant.[88] It is thus important to decide whether a ration should be established in terms of wheat or of barley; for, if the 1:2 ratio did not exist between them, the greater productivity of barley would enable a country with a constant supply of the latter to support a larger population than it could on the same acreage of wheat. In the case of Messenia it has been argued that wheat was its natural crop and that calculation may be made in terms of wheat consumption.

The normal ration for an adult male, then, may be taken as 1 *choenix* per day, and the mean annual ration per person as 2.60 hectoliters. In obtaining this latter figure, Jardé has made use of the standard fixed by Hultsch, in which the *medimnos* is made equivalent to 52.53 liters. That of Viedebantt was equivalent to 40.9334 liters, so that, if it is accepted, there would be considerable difference in the ration when expressed in modern standards. Both systems agree in the fractional divisions of the *medimnos* (into 48 *choenikes*, etc.) and in making the *kotyle* the connecting link between the Athenian system of liquid and dry measures. Both, too, since they are worked out by mathematical calculations exercised on the literary evidence, attain an accuracy in decimal points to which ancient measures in actual use would not have uniformly conformed. On the whole, such archeological

evidence as we have tends to support the system of Hultsch.[89] Thus Jardé's figures may be used without change.

[88] The earliest notice of the ration is found in Herodotus (vii. 187. 2), who calculates the amount of food necessary for the army of Xerxes on the basis of 1 *choenix* of wheat per man per day. The Pythagorean precept, μηδ' ἐπὶ χοίνικα καθίσαι (Plut. *Moralia* 704 a; Athenaeus x. 452 e; Diog. Laert. viii. 18), is interpreted as providing one's daily food; and Alexarchus (Athenaeus iii. 98 e) calls a *choenix*, "daily-feeder." In neither case is it stipulated whether a *choenix* of wheat or barley is concerned, but the precept loses some of its force if it is applied to wheat only.

[89] The literary evidence, on which both systems depend, is later than the period (before contact with the Romans may have influenced the Athenian measures) for which it is desirable to fix the "Solonian" measures. The so-called *Tabula Vetustissima* and the metrical notices, which are mostly for small units, in the medical writers included in the corpus of Galen offer most information. They do not inspire much confidence, however, for, besides being late, they necessitate some textual emendation to bring them into line with one or the other of the systems. On the whole, that of Hultsch requires fewer changes in the texts than that of Viedebantt; but the basis of his system—that the Athenian *medimnos* was equal to 6 Roman *modii*—has been used by Viedebantt as the basis for a measure which is called "der sizilische u. spätattische *Medimnos*," which, it is suggested, was established in the second century A.D. (P.-W., XV, 89–90.)

Two official measures, however, recently found in Athens, which were in use in the fifth century B.C., seem to fit into the system of Hultsch. One of these was found in a well on the North Slope of the Acropolis (Broneer, "Excavations on the North Slope of the Acropolis, 1937," *Hesperia*, VII [1938], 222–24, 251). It seems to have been thrown into the well between *ca.* 461 and 425 B.C. Its stamp proves it a public measure, and its volume was *ca.* 3.200 liters—that is, about three times the volume of the *choenix* as established by Hultsch (1.094 × 3 = 3.282 liters) and equivalent to his estimate of the *chous* (3.283 liters). Broneer considered it a dry measure of 3 *choenikes'* volume rather than a *chous*. The other measure is the *klepsydra* from the Agora (Young, "An Athenian Clepsydra," *Hesperia*, VIII [1939], 274 ff.), which is marked XX (2 *choes*) and holds the contents of the measure from the North Slope twice, thus also fitting into the system of Hultsch. Mrs. Young dates the filling of the well in which the *klepsydra* was found as *ca.* 400 B.C., but it is a question of some importance whether the *klepsydra*'s use is to be placed before or after 403 B.C., when the Athenian measures are said to have been restored on the Solonian standards (Andocides i. 83). Mrs. Young favored a date immediately before 403 B.C. for the use of the vessel, in which case it would presumably be on a non-Solonian standard. This would mean that the measure from the North Slope would also be non-Solonian, which is rather surprising, as its period of use was apparently in the mid-fifth century. Unfortunately, the dates suggested for the filling of the Agora well and the use of the *klepsydra* cannot be pressed, so that we might definitely place the use of the *klepsydra* either before or after the decree reported by Andocides. If it is to be placed before, Athens was presumably on a different standard in the fourth century B.C., and that view receives some support from the fact that the volume of a fourth-century measure in the National Museum in Athens does not fit as a unit into the standard of the two fifth-century measures. It does, however, accord with the system of Viedebantt.

Viedebantt, in his latest discussion of the Athenian dry measure (*Festschrift für August Oxé*, pp. 135–46) based his system primarily on the information given

The amount of wheat available for consumption in the district of Messene was estimated to be 123,717 hectoliters. When the normal ration of 2.60 hectoliters is divided into that, a maximum figure of 47,583 is obtained for the population. This figure, of course, includes men, women, and children of all classes. The proportion of free to slave and of poor to well-to-do cannot be calculated, although it is probable that there were a relatively large slave population and well-to-do group in Messene.[90]

In making an estimate of the production and population of the rest of Messenia (an area of about 1,900 sq. km.) it is scarcely possible to take all the necessary factors of its varied character—the soil quality, the relatively deserted condition of the islands, and the greater proportion of

mountainous terrain—into account. Probably an estimate of 25 per cent of the total area as cultivated land would be a maximum. Thus 427.5 sq. km. would have been available for grain production, which, using the same methods of calculation as for the district of Messene, indicates a yearly production of 178,125 hectoliters of wheat for consumption. That would support a population of about 68,510. This figure would be reduced somewhat by the amount of grain needed for animals; possibly about 65,000 would be a reasonable estimate. The estimated population for all Messenia, then, would be about 112,500, of which about 42 per cent lived in the city of Messene and its district.[91] This proportion would enable the city to exercise the control over the whole district of Messenia which its political history shows to have been a fact.

There is little help to be obtained from the usual sources for estimating population to check this maximum figure. No numbers of the population are given in the literary sources for any period, although there are a few general remarks to be taken into account. Plutarch observed[92] that the *plethos* of Messenia was not less than that of Laconia before 369 B.C. *Plethos* may, however, mean resources or extent in general rather than population specifically, and the statement is evidently a part of the Spartan propaganda[93] circulated to support their claim to Messenia after its loss. Beloch, on the assumption that the populations of Messenia and Laconia were equal in density, has suggested a figure of 80,000 for about 400 B.C., which seems reasonable.[94]

about the size of the *choenix* in the inscription concerning Attic measures dated *ca.* 100 B.C. (*IG*, II², 1013. 24–26; "Der athenische Volksbeschluss über Mass und Gewicht," *Hermes*, LI [1916], 120 ff.); on the measure in the National Museum, which is identified as a *choenix* and has a measured volume of 0.865 liter; and on metrical information in the late literary evidence. Mrs. Young has already pointed out (*op. cit.*, p. 280, n. 37) that this inscription is usually interpreted as representing a change in the Athenian system of measures to conform to the increasing internationalism of trade. It might also be observed that only the depth of the *choenix* is given in the inscription (5 *daktyloi* = 10.25 cm., if Viedebantt uses a correct estimate of the Attic foot); and, to get an estimate of the volume, it has to be assumed that the diameter of the vessel was equal to its depth and that it had straight sides (the measure from the North Slope had incurving sides). Granting that the measure from the National Museum was a public measure, it is not certainly identified as a *choenix*, and it does not seem to have been examined and measured recently (Viedebantt cites an unpublished measurement for its volume of 0.865 liter, made by Pernice). Thus, although its volume conforms to that of the theoretical *choenix* of the inscription, it should not be accepted as an official fourth-century *choenix* without further examination. Viedebantt, in using the literary evidence, has made considerable textual emendation rather than to fit his standard than on any paleographical grounds. That can be valid only if the standard is correct. Thus, neither system is to be accepted without some misgivings, but that of Hultsch would seem to be established for the fifth century B.C. at least and preferable in the present state of our knowledge.

[90] Rostovtzeff, *op. cit.*, II, 753–54.

[91] The total cultivated area of Messenia would have been, according to these estimates (400 + 475), 875 sq. km., or about 30 per cent of the total area.

[92] *Agesilaus* 34. 1.

[93] Roebuck, *op. cit.*, pp. 43–45.

[94] *Op. cit.*, pp. 147 ff.

It seems probable that there was some increase in population in the years immediately following 369 and 338 B.C., Messenia's two "foundation" dates, for the returning exiles and new settlers from elsewhere in Greece may well have outnumbered the Spartan landlords, garrison troops, and pro-Spartan perioeci who were killed or left the region.[95] This level would be maintained or increased in the third century, which was relatively peaceful; but probably Messenia, although not to such an extent as the rest of the Peloponnesus, shared in the general decline noticed by Polybius[96] in the first half of the second century. The latter part of the second century would bring about another increase, followed, in turn, by a decline in the disturbed conditions of the first century B.C., as Strabo comments on the deserted condition of the land in his own time.[97]

The only specific figures which we have for Messenia are those of two military levies during the period of the Social War, one of 2,500 infantry and 250 cavalry, the other of 2,000 infantry and 200 cavalry.[98] The levies were presumably made from all Messenia, with the exception of Pylos,[99] at that period; but they are not complete, and their proportion is unknown. The second is specifically mentioned as a corps d'élite by Polybius. It is impossible for the third century B.C., when levies were made from the well-to-do class rather than from the whole male population and when they are incomplete, to make any actuarial estimate from the figures.[100] Yet the proportion seems not

incompatible with the suggested maximum of about 112,500 for the population of all Messenia; for in Athens in the crisis of 323 B.C. only between 3 and 4 per cent of the total population was used for military service.[101]

There are two complete ephebe lists from Thouria dated to the late second century B.C., one containing 19 names,[102] the other, which is presumably for two years, 38 names.[103] Another ephebe list of A.D. 246, found at Corone but considered to have come originally from Messene, is incomplete and contains 80 names.[104] The difficulty, of course, with such lists for the Hellenistic and Roman periods is that the ephebeia was not compulsory and the ephebes came only from the well-to-do class. Beloch has suggested that the lists for Thouria indicate an adult citizen population of over 1,000 and for Messene

---

Les Assemblées de la Confédération achaienne [Bordeaux, 1938], p. 87, n. 5). Beloch and Wilhelm make no attempt to use these figures, but Lipsius suggests that they indicate 7,000 citizens ("Die attische Steuerverfassung und das attische Volksvermögen," Rh. Mus., LXXI [1916], 184).

[101] A. W. Gomme, The Population of Athens in the Fifth and Fourth Centuries B.C. (Oxford, 1933), pp. 8, 17–18, 26, Table 1.

[102] IG, V, 1, 1384.

[103] Ibid., 1385. This document is usually considered to be an ephebe list, although it lacks a heading similar to that of IG, V, 1, 1384. It has, however, some puzzling features: the apparent mention of brothers (lls. 8–9, 11–12, in Col. 1), and of the same (?) individuals who are found in IG, V, 1, 1384. Another list (IG, V, 1, 1386) of the same period contains 13 names of tritirenes, possibly those in the third year of their status as eirenes, arranged by tribes. The number for the tribe Daiphontis is complete with eight names, for Aristomachis, incomplete with five names. There were five tribes in Messene and Thouria; but, while they may have been equal in numbers at first, the passage of time brought natural changes, as the estimates for the separate tribes in the tax inscription for Messene show (IG, V, 1, 1433). Thus it is probably incorrect to assume that the total number of the tritirenes was about forty. For the Messenian tribes see Roebuck, op. cit., p. 113, n. 25.

[104] IG, V, 1, 1398. The large number of names on the list seems incompatible with a site of the small size and relative unimportance of Corone (Beloch, op. cit., p. 149).

---

[95] Roebuck, op. cit., p. 34.

[96] Pol. xxxvi. 17.

[97] Strabo viii. 4. 11.

[98] Pol. iv. 15. 6; v. 20. 1.

[99] Roebuck, op. cit., p. 69. n. 12.

[100] These levies were called out under the direction of the Achaean League, but the proportion of the levy for the League itself is also unknown (Aymard,

of over 5,000 citizens.[105] Wilhelm, using the latter figure, suggested[106] 6,000 households as a probable number for Messene and its district about 100 B.C. These lists, however, like the military levies, are of little use in arriving at any estimate of the total population of either Thouria or Messene; but, in spite of the discrepancy in date between the documents from the two places, they may well indicate the relative proportion between them, that is, Messene was over four times as large as Thouria.

Estimates of the population of Messene and its district have been made by Wilhelm and Cavaignac. Wilhelm utilized Beloch's estimate of the density of population in Epirus in 168 B.C. (38 per square kilometer) and his own estimate of 6,000 households for Messene about 100 B.C. to suggest a total of 39,600.[107] This agrees reasonably well with our figure of 47,583 as a maximum, when it is considered that there was probably some surplus of grain for export trade. Cavaignac estimated the population as 30,000, basing his calculations on the productive capacity of the region; but his delimitation of the boundaries of the district is inexact.[108]

While it is impossible to arrive at any figure for the population of either Messene and its district or for the whole of Messenia on the available evidence, yet Wilhelm's conjecture of 39,600 as the population of the city of Messene and its district accorded very well with our estimate based on the productive capacity of the region and is not contradicted by the indications of the ephebe lists or of the military levies. Accordingly, it seems reasonable to adopt the conjecture that the population of Messene and its district was about 40,000 when the state was in a comparatively prosperous condition and that the population of the whole of Messenia, including the above figure, was about 90,000.

The boundaries of the district were estimated, however, for the period before Messene lost a portion of it to Megalopolis in 182 B.C. It is likely, although certainly

[105] *Op. cit.*, p. 149. Beloch's estimate seems very high on any actuarial basis, although he is including the citizens of the poorer classes. If we use the same calculations as Roussel has done for the Delian ephebe list of 119 B.C., we obtain a well-to-do class in Thouria of 2,128 men, women, and children and in Messene of 8,960 (*BCH*, LV [1931], 441–42).

[106] *Op. cit.*, p. 113.

[107] *Ibid.*, pp. 113–14. Wilhelm also cited some figures from the census of 1907 for the eparchy of Messenia, which is smaller in extent than the ancient district of the city, noting that, at present and probably in antiquity, the density is much greater for the lowland than for the mountains, although in antiquity it would not have been so great as at present. Comparisons with modern Greece are useless for our purposes because of the different type of economy and the rapid increase in population in modern times. The figures for the *nome* of Messenia (area 3,341 sq. km., including the region on the north up to the Alpheius River) are interesting. In the census of 1889 the population was 183,232, with a density of 55 per square kilometer which represented an increase in density from 20 in 1838 (*La grande encyclopédie*, art. "Grèce"). In 1920 (area then 3,369 sq. km.), before the influx of refugees from Asia Minor, the population was 217,285, with a density of 64 (*Enciclopedia universal illustrada*, art. "Grecia"). In 1928, although very few refugees settled in the southwestern Peloponnesus, the population had increased to 247,907 with a density of 74 (*Der grosse Brockhaus*, art. "Griechenland"). The district is one of the most thickly populated regions of modern Greece.

[108] *Op. cit.*, pp. 128–32. He also estimated the population of Messene alone as 10,000–15,000 by the similarity of its size with that of Mantinea and Megalopolis. We do not know, however, how large an area of the total inclosure the house blocks covered. The line of fortification is evidently dictated by strategic considerations, as is usual in cities of the fourth century and the Hellenistic period. Cavaignac has made two conjectures, one designed to fit the figure of 1,256 talents as the total wealth of Messene, in which the city's district is considered to have included only the upper and lower plains; the other, based on a district which includes Cyparissia and gives no specific boundaries, estimated at 1,000–1,500 sq. km. The latter would have possessed a capital of nearer 3,000 than 1,250 talents. Thus Cavaignac argues that the figure of 1,256 talents was only a partial estimate of Messenian capital. His argument is considerably weakened by a misinterpretation of Wilhelm's view, for Wilhelm's estimate of the district of Messene is approximately that of Cavaignac's second conjecture, and Wilhelm's discussion of the capital is based on it, not on the whole territory of Messenia, as Cavaignac assumed. For a criticism of Cavaignac's assumptions about the value of the capital items see Rostovtzeff, *op. cit.*, III, 1606, n. 85.

not proved, that Messene recovered control of its district but not of the whole of Messenia after 146 B.C. Possession of the *Ager Denthaliatis* was confirmed about 140 B.C.,[109] and Messene was evidently in control of Andania and, with it, the upper plain at the time of the inscription which regulated the celebration of the mysteries (*ca.* 100 B.C.).[110] Yet an indication that Pharae was independent of Messene before about 80 B.C.[111] and the activity of Thouria in conducting its own affairs[112]

[109] By the Milesian arbitration (Ditt. *Syll.*³, 683).

[110] Roebuck, *op. cit.*, p. 106.

[111] *Ibid.*, pp. 107–8.

[112] The inscription by which the Thourian grain supply was regulated (see above, n. 32) gave no hint of control of the town by Messene; similarly, another inscription—a decree of the Thourian *synedroi*, commemorating a boundary dispute with Megalopolis (Valmin, "Inscriptions de la Messénie," *Bull. Lund*, 1928–29, pp. 108–23, No. 1; Roebuck, *op. cit.*, p. 103, n. 168), reveals Thouria taking independent action in its foreign policy. These documents are dated, as are the ephebe lists (nn. 102 and 103) in the second or first centuries B.C. on epigraphic grounds. It is unlikely that any of them are to be placed before 182 B.C., when Thouria became an independent member of the Achaean League. Therefore, they are to be set either between 182 and 146 B.C., when the town was a member of the League, or after 146 B.C., when it was either independent or under the control of Messene. Larsen has already suggested that some of the inde-

hint that political control over the whole region of Messenia had not been restored. Thus it seems probable that the tax decree should be understood as applying to Messene and its district, not to the whole of Messenia, and that Wilhelm's estimate of the economic information contained in it and his conjecture of the wealth of each household at one-fifth of a talent have some validity. All the evidence which we have cited pointed to Messene's having been a small, relatively wealthy, agricultural state. Its political history of circumspect alliances and neutrality and its almost complete lack of artistic achievement are such as one might expect from a community of that type.

DALHOUSIE UNIVERSITY
HALIFAX, CANADA

pendent coinage of the Messenian towns might be dated after 146 B.C. (*op. cit.*, p. 334), and I have indicated that the usual date of the Thourian coinage—240–182 B.C.—is incompatible with what we know of conditions in Messenia at that time (Roebuck, *op. cit.*, p. 114). Accordingly, both some of the coinage and some of the inscriptions mentioned above may well be dated after 146 B.C. and be taken as an indication that Thouria remained independent of Messene by the settlement of 146 B.C.

THE ECONOMIC DEVELOPMENT
OF IONIA

WHILE the history of Greece before 550 B.C. has always been an obscure period which scholars endeavored to illuminate *per obscuriora*, one tenet seemed to be securely fixed in our textbooks and histories: that the Ionian Greeks of the eastern Aegean played a leading role in the development of archaic Greece. Yet, in the last generation specialized archeological work has removed Panionism, Ionia as the source and inspiration, from the study of early Greek art and the implications are now spreading to other fields. In the last five years two articles, in particular, have been published from which I should like to summarize some conclusions as a starting point for my own remarks on economic development. They are Mr. George Hanfmann's article, "Archaeology in Homeric Asia Minor"[2] and Mr. R. M. Cook's "Ionia and Greece in the Eighth and Seventh Centuries B.C."[3] Hanfmann concluded that Greek settlement of the eastern Ionian area began *ca.* 800 B.C. in Samos and Chios and that only in the course of the succeeding century did Greek settlers win the Ionian sites on the adjacent coast.[4] If this is so, Ionian development was not parallel in form to that of Old Greece, which rose from the matrix of the migrations and settlements following the collapse of the Mycenean civilization. Instead, it was a colonial development which might resemble that of the western Greeks in Sicily and South Italy, for it was almost contemporary with them.[5]

Cook's article has extended the problem from origins to a general assessment of the place of Ionia in Greek development. As he observes, there are no direct estimates of the early importance of Ionia in the Greek sources;[6] but these are hardly to be expected in Herodotus and Thucydides, I think, for the intellectual climate of fifth century Athens was not sympathetic towards the Ionian Greeks, who had not only lost a war with Persia, but were charged with dragging Athens into one. Despite Herodotus' obvious approval of these views and minimization of Ionia[7] his account carries the material for its refutation. A study of details leaves the impression that Ionia was very important, indeed, in the latter part of the archaic period. Cook concludes that the colonial activity of Ionia was on a smaller scale than that of Old Greece and began later. He distinguishes, however, between the character of colonization from each region: that of the Ionians was complementary to the parent-city while the western colonies of Old Greece were intended to be economically independent, to rid the motherland of surplus inhabitants and to create a new state.[8] This seems an important distinction with interesting implications for the degree of economic development to which the founding cities of mainland Greece and Ionia had respectively attained. With regard to trade, Cook concludes that Old Greece was generally earlier in trading than East Greece, but points out that the evidence is not yet conclusive.[9] He also observes that discussions of trade are almost necessarily based on the distribution of pottery. Yet, in the East Greek area, at least, pottery was not an important article of trade. It merely indicates a "hidden" trade carried on by the East Greeks in trading posts, a trade which may have started before they established the post and which did not exchange pottery for the objects sought.[10]

These are the main points. We might begin with the problem of the strength of the Ionian states and that of Old Greece. Lack of evidence, of course, precludes the possibility of arriving at any definite figure for the population of a Greek state in the archaic period, but, in Herodotus, there are some indications of naval strength for the period from 550 B.C. to the Persian Wars, from which we may also conjecture backwards. They reveal that individually and collectively the fleets of Ionian cities were as large, if not larger, than those of Old Greece and of the New Greece in the west until Athens and Syracuse built navies *ca.* 480 B.C. which upset the maritime balance of the Aegean and Tyrrhenian seas; probably, too, the trireme was first used extensively by Ionian Greeks. The number of sailors required to man the ships indicates a population far above the productive capacity of the states to feed. Grain had to be imported on a large scale. Timber for ship building would also have been an important and necessary import.

Herodotus, in his description of the battle of Lade, fought between those Ionians still in the war and the Persians in 494 B.C., gives us a fleet list.[11] He represents the contingents of the Ionian alliance as made up by almost a scraping of the bottom of the barrel. Their total is 353 triremes. Of that number, Chios furnished 100, Miletus, threatened by land attack as well, 80, Lesbos 70, and Samos 60. The other units were very small, ranging from Phocaea's 3 to

the Tean 17. These were warships, of course, but the Ionians also had merchant ships in service during the revolt, engaged in bringing supplies from the Black Sea.[12] Possibly their crews were transferred to the warships for this last great sea battle. The total number is to be compared to the collective strength of the Greeks at Artemisium, 325 at the highest estimate,[13] and at Salamis, 310 according to Aeschylus.[14] Beloch pertinently notes that neither Athens, nor Syracuse, at the height of their naval power, mustered such a fleet as that at Lade on any one occasion.[15] Three questions arise: Is the total compatible with what we know of Ionian fleets on other occasions? Are the figures for the individual contingents approximately correct? Were the ships at Lade really triremes? All can, I think, be answered affirmatively.

Scholars have generally accepted the total at Lade as approximately correct or little exaggerated; so, too, with the totals for Artemisium and Salamis. In the case of the Ionian fleet at Lade, the obvious comparison is with the contingents supplied to the Persians in 480 B.C. Tarn's detailed study of that problem contains the incidental verdict that at Lade the Greeks would have had 300 ships at least;[16] Beloch, while criticising Tarn's reconstruction for the Persian War, accepts the figure for Lade as little exaggerated.[17] The number is also compatible with the number of 200 ships reported by Herodotus for Artaphrenes' expedition against Naxos in 499 B.C.[18] This was a levy, of course, not a total mobilization; it was the nucleus of the fleet which the Ionians used in the revolt.

The figures for the individual contingents can be checked to some degree for Chios and Samos. Herodotus places Polycrates' fleet at 100 pentekonters near the outset of his career, ca. 540 B.C.;[19] later it is observed that he sent a detachment of 40 triremes to support Cambyses in Egypt.[20] A century later, in 440 B.C., in its revolt against Athens, Samos mustered 50 triremes and 20 transports, according to Thucydides.[21] Thus, the figure for Samos of 60 in 494 B.C. seems to agree with what is known of Samian naval strength 50 years before and after that date. When Chios was a member in good standing of the Athenian Empire, it contributed, together with Lesbos, fleets of 50 and 55 triremes to the service of Athens and the League.[22] These were levies only and we get a picture of total Chian strength in the period of the Sicilian expedition and the ensuing revolts against Athens. The Athenians levied about 25 Chian ships which were lost in Sicily.[23] Yet, in 412 B.C. Chios satisfied the Spartans that it could contribute 60 triremes to a revolt against Athens.[24] Here again, the figure of 100 triremes from Chios in 494 B.C. seems compatible with what is known of its later strength. Apparently, then, Herodotus' figures for both states are accurate and he gives us a valid picture of relative sea power among the Ionian states: Chios, Miletus, Lesbos, Samos in that order. Herodotus tells us that the Samians had the best reputation[25] — a result presumably of Polycrates' efforts to found a maritime empire.

It is instructive to compare these fleets with what we know or conjecture of the fleets of Old Greece and of the west at the same period: Aegina, perhaps 80; Athens, 70, 20 of which were rented from Corinth; Corinth, probably higher than either, but it sent only 40 ships as its contribution to the fleets at Artemisium and Salamis;[26] Corcyra could afford to make a brave showing with 60 after the battle of Salamis had

been fought and won.[27] For Sicily and South Italy Dunbabin has suggested 60 ships at the most for the fleets of Hippokrates and Anaxilas ca. 490 B.C.[28] Athens and Syracuse could and did build great fleets shortly after this, but on the Herodotean evidence, the Ionian states were predominant in sea power before 490 B.C. It is significant that the strongest state in Old Greece, Sparta, was a land power whose strength rested on its hoplites. This actual predominance of sea power in Ionia was apparently obtained in part by readiness to make innovations, to adopt the trireme. Herodotus describes the Ionian fleet at Lade as made up of triremes[29] and recent discussion of the development of the Greek ship has demonstrated that he makes a careful distinction between pentekonters and triremes, thus using the terms deliberately and presumably correctly. It is suggested that the Ionian Greeks passed out of the pentekonter stage between the coming of the Persians, ca. 540 B.C., and the battle of Lade. Polycrates has the credit for building the first fleet of triremes.[30] This Ionian innovation would have been a response to the threat of Persian encroachment, just as the building of large new fleets in Athens and Syracuse was a response to the threats of Persian and Carthaginian attack. Objection might be raised that the Ionians began to build large fleets only when threatened by Persia. Yet Herodotus stresses the sea power of the islanders at the time of Croesus' conquests ca. 560 B.C.[31] Perhaps the extensive use which Phocaea made of pentekonters for its long voyages to the west in the seventh century marks the beginning of large Ionian navies.[32] The tradition of strong sea power would, then, go back into the seventh century.

If triremes were used at Lade we are enabled to make some estimates of the number of men in naval service during the Ionian Revolt. It is likely that slaves would have been used sparingly in such a critical situation so that our estimate would be of free citizens under arms. Herodotus' normal figure for the complement of a trireme is 200.[33] Possibly there were fewer on board the early triremes, but Herodotus tells us that in the case of Chios, at least, 40 marines were also put on board.[34] Using the figure of 200 for each trireme, the following totals are obtained: Chios, 20,000; Miletus, 16,000; Lesbos, 14,000; Samos, 12,000. Probably for the island states these represent almost full mobilization, but for the mainland cities, such as Miletus, substantial forces would have been left on guard. If the usual ratio of about 1 to 4 for adult males of military age to total population is applied, we obtain figures for the free population as follows: Chios, ca. 80,000; Miletus, ca. 64,000; Lesbos, ca. 56,000; Samos, ca. 48,000. To these should be added an unknown number of slaves. Possibly it was already very large in Chios, for Thucydides, in the late fifth century, states that the island possessed more slaves than any other Greek state except Sparta with its helots.[35]

These figures indicate that in each of the states mentioned the population was in considerable excess of the productive capacity of the cultivable land in the state. Chios, for example, had to import grain for well over a third of its population.[36] Some of this surplus population was no doubt going into mercenary service; Herodotus observes that 30,000 Ionians and Carians were in the army of Apries of Egypt ca. 570 B.C.[37] If this figure is correct, we are confronted with a phenomenon like that of fourth century Greece when thousands of men were entering the armies of Persia. Some were also filtering into Thrace, the Black Sea area and to the far west, but not in any organized colonial movement on a large scale. All the Phocaeans and Teans would have stayed at home, if possible. Generally speaking, the larger Ionian states must have been trying to feed their people by the importation of grain, paying for it and providing employment by the development of special products, of industries and of such services as a carrying trade, and, withal, finding the surplus to erect such structures as the great temples on Samos and at Ephesus. These last are at least evidence of considerable technical ability, skill in craftsmanship, and wealth, if not of the best taste. In the period of the mid- and later sixth century, certainly, Ionia seems to have been predominant in sea power and to have created a well developed and advanced import trade — a trade in bulk goods like grain which is significantly different from the importation of luxury goods on a small scale for a part of the population.

From the point of view of economic history this solution, by the development of sea trade in bulk goods and mass volume, is more important than a small trickle of luxury goods and exotics such as may be found even in very primitive cultures. Volume trade will involve radical changes in the economic, social and political structure of the state, the other need not. What is important in a comparison of the colonizing and trading activity is not so much the date at which it begins, but the date at which it assumes this significant character.[38] We might now try to answer the important question: When did the size of the population bring about the need for such a trade?

According to the reduced foundation dates, based on archeological evidence, for Naukratis and the Black Sea colonies, it was probably the last quarter of the seventh century. At that time there is a significant cluster of foundations: Naukratis, 615/610 B.C.; Istrus, Olbia, and Apollonia Pontica, 610/600 B.C.[39] The significance lies not so much in the fact that the Black Sea region and Egypt were opened up to trade and settlement at a much later date than the Italian west, but that colonies in these places were primarily trading factories in food-producing regions. Presumably the capacity of the Black Sea region as a producer of grain and fish would have become known in the course of the several generations of inhabitation in the Propontis colonies,[40] but there was hardly an incentive to settlement in such an uncongenial region until there was a need for its products. Egypt, as a source of luxury articles and bric-à-brac, was probably known much earlier to occasional traders, but Naukratis, as I have argued elsewhere, was established to provide the facilities for a bulk trade in grain.[41] Herodotus characterizes both it and the Black Sea cities as emporia,[42] essentially trading places, and recent Russian work describes the early settlements as trading factories until well down into the sixth century, when they began to take on a more permanent and independent character.[43]

This solution to the problem of overpopulation enabled the Ionian states to support a surplus population of some size and to develop a strength and complexity of economic organization out of proportion to their relatively small land area. Was Old Greece able to do the same? Corinth and Aegina made use of Naukratis and Egyptian grain from the foundation of the emporion,[44] but if they were importers of grain before that date, it would have been from and through the Sicilian and South Italian colonies. There is trade, of course, from the early eighth century,[45] but it seems significant that large scale production and export of Corinthian pottery does not begin until the development of Early Corinthian black-figure ware ca. 625 B.C.[46] Export of silver to the west starts only after 600 B.C.[47] Athens is hardly a factor until the middle of the sixth century.[48] It looks very much as if both Old and Ionian Greece were experiencing the same rhythm of economic development. That is, the economically significant point in the development of trade in the Aegean comes in the last quarter of the seventh century. Qualitatively and temporally it is parallel in Old Greece and Ionia.

There seems also to be little significant difference of period in the earliest trading activity when trade sought luxury products or metals. In the west Cyme is the earliest Greek colony, probably founded ca. 750 B.C. and, to judge from the bypassing of Sicilian and South Italian sites, designed as a trading post, perhaps to get metals.[49] In the east the earliest East Greek establishment was probably at Al Mina near the mouth of the Orontes in northern Syria; the settlers were evidently East Greeks to judge from their pottery, but perhaps from the Cycladic and Rhodian area rather than the Ionian. From the third quarter of the eighth century, however, Al Mina presumably provided an outlet for the luxury goods of the east.[50] This trade raises a difficult question. How were the goods paid for? If by their own pottery the East Greeks were very good traders, indeed, to judge from the poor quality and sparse quantity of pottery found on sites up the Orontes valley. Possibly silver and gold were exchanged as in Egypt, if we judge from a silver coin hoard of the late archaic period found farther to the south at Ras Shamra.[51] In this connection it is interesting to speculate whether the East Greeks, the Ionians in particular, were obtaining precious metals from Thasos in the late eighth century; the deposits are said by Herodotus to have been known to the Phoenicians.[52]

In both Old Greece and in Ionia colonization followed upon these early trading ventures. Emigration was apparently earlier and on a larger scale from Old Greece to the west, but that may merely indicate that there was more elbow room in the region close at hand to Ionia. For example, the Chian colony at Maroneia in Thrace was early enough to be mentioned by Homer and Archilochus as a source of good wine.[53] Chios and Samos were able to establish enclaves on the adjacent Anatolian coast, to the dissatisfaction of their neighbors, Erythrae and Priene.[54] There was room for small settlements in Aeolis and inland from the coast, as at Larisa.[55] Perhaps a filling out of the region adjacent to Ionia and Aeolis corresponded to the first wave which took Old Greece to the west; then, early in the seventh century, movement began into the Propontis and into eastern Thrace.[56] This early colonization may have been akin to that of the west, primarily agricultural; but soon East Greece seems to have been ready to take advantage of the facilities for trade and to lay the foundations for the significant trading colonies of the late seventh century.

We have thus worked our way backwards to the early archaic period which Hanfmann has suggested as the time when movement into Ionia was completed. It seems, however, that movement out had already started. This early movement may not have been caused by excess population. Motives of trade should receive more emphasis in early colonization. But could the Ionian cities have reached the peak of population attested for the sixth century if they were founded only in the eighth century? Further, there scarcely seems time for a fixing of organization such as evidently went on in the Ionian cities before the early colonial movement. For example, tribal names of seemingly local origin are common to both Miletus and to its early colony, Cyzicus; to Samos and to its colony, Perinthus. These are not the old Ionian tribal names, but developments from a mixing of Greek emigrants and natives, the results of struggles and adjustments.[57] This, however, is leading to a discussion of the social and political organization. In the economic development, I suggest that the significant factor is development by sea power and sea communications, the significant time is the last quarter of the seventh century, and that there is a similar rhythm between Old Greece and Ionia, the expression of which naturally took slightly different forms in the somewhat different areas. This similar rhythm, moreover, may suggest a similar origin in the conditions of post-Mycenean Greece.

NORTHWESTERN UNIVERSITY

NOTES

1. This paper was presented in a symposium on the subject, "The Role of Ionia in the Development of Classical Greek Culture," at the meeting of the American Philological Association in Princeton on December 27, 1951. I have made a few slight changes in the text and added notes.

2. *AJA*, LII (1948), 135–55.
3. *JHS*, LXVI (1946), 67–98.
4. Hanfmann, *op. cit.*, p. 155.
5. Thucydides (1. 12. 4) perhaps couples the Ionian migration with the colonization of Italy and Sicily; *perhaps*, for his reference to it is placed before the latter in

the order of his text and in this paragraph he is spanning a period of five centuries in a few sentences.

6. Cook, *op. cit.*, pp. 67 ff.

7. This disparagement is Herodotus' usual attitude to the Ionians and probably represents views current in the fifth century after the Persian Wars (1. 143. 2; 4. 142; 5. 69. 1; 6. 12–13. 1; Gomme, *Commentary on Thucydides*, I [Oxford, 1945], 127). He makes an exception, of course, of Athens whose bitterness towards the Ionians during the Wars appears in Themistocles' message on the rocks of Euboea (8. 22. 1–2). There are, however, traces of a different evaluation of the Asiatic Ionians (see 5. 28), as well as the detail which is developed in the course of this paper. Thucydides, too, reflects the disparagement, particularly in hortatory speeches by Dorian commanders who do not make any reservation in favor of Athens (1. 124. 1; 5. 9. 1; 7. 5. 4; 8. 25. 3). Thucydides' most damaging evidence, of course, is his scant mention of Ionian sea power in his sketch of early Greek development. In it, Corinth is singled out (1. 13. 2) as a leader and the Ionian fleet mentioned only for the time of Cyrus and Cambyses (1. 13. 6), while the Ionian fleets of the Revolt are passed over in favor of those of Corcyra and Sicily. These emphases are perhaps to be explained by the nature of Thucydides' analysis. It is primarily in terms of naval power in war, although he represents Corinth's maritime growth as commercial in the first instance; further, his views are formed from his estimate of the efficiency and uses of Athenian naval power in the fifth century. From this point of view, Ionian naval power was effective for the islanders in the time of Cyrus and Cambyses; it did not attain its proper end during the Revolt, while before Cyrus there was no occasion for its use in large scale warfare.

8. Cook, *op. cit.*, pp. 78–79.

9. *Ibid.*, p. 87.

10. *Ibid.*, p. 80. This seems to be true of trade with Egypt and Syria, but it may not be the case in Thrace and the Black Sea area. Egypt and Syria had a developed industry of their own and no need of such Greek products in volume, but Thrace and the Black Sea region probably absorbed Ionian industrial products on a large scale. Thus, in Egypt the finds of Greek pottery outside Naukratis are scanty (Cook, *JHS*, LVII [1937], 236–37; Roebuck, *CP*, XLV [1950], 236) and in North Syria the chief quantity of pottery is from Al Mina rather than the sites farther inland on the route to the interior (see note 50 below). Thrace, of course, awaits excavation and the material from the Black Sea a re-examination in the light of revised chronology and estimates of trading activity.

11. Her. 6. 8.

12. Her. 6. 5. 2–3, 26. 1.

13. Beloch, *GG²*, II, 2, 62–67.

14. Aeschylus *Persians*, 339–40.

15. Beloch, *op. cit.*, II, 1, 15, n. 1; see note 30 below.

16. Tarn, *JHS*, XXVIII (1908), 228.

17. Beloch, *loc. cit.*; so, too, How and Wells, *Commentary on Herodotus*, II (Oxford, 1928), 68; Köster, "Studien zur Geschichte des antiken Seewesens," *Klio*, *Beiheft*, XXXII (1934), 98.

18. Her. 5. 31. 4.

19. Her. 3. 39. 3.

20. Her. 3. 44. 2. This detachment probably represented less than half of his fleet since the ships were manned by malcontents and Polycrates would feel it necessary to keep a substantial margin of safety.

21. Thuc. 1. 116. 1.

22. In 440 B.C. at the time of the Samian revolt 55 triremes were levied from both islands (Thuc. 1. 116–17); in 430 B.C., 50 triremes were levied (Thuc. 2. 56. 2).

23. The exact number of Chian ships levied for the first expedition in 415 B.C. is unknown. Thucydides, however, names only Chios specifically among the allies furnishing 34 ships in all, which indicates that the Chians

furnished the largest separate unit (Thuc. 6. 43); later a levy of 5 was made (Thuc. 7. 20. 2).

24. Thuc. 8. 6. 4. Presumably the 7 collected by Athens as a pledge of good faith before the revolt (Thuc. 8. 9–10) were numbered among the 60.

25. Her. 5. 112. 1; 6. 8. 2.

26. Beloch, *GG²*, II, 2, 63–67; Athens had rented 20 from Corinth to increase its small fleet of 50 for the war against Aegina (Her. 6. 89, 92, 132). The figure for Aegina is conjectural.

27. Her. 7. 168. 2.

28. Dunbabin, *The Western Greeks* (Oxford, 1948), pp. 199, 404–5.

29. Her. 6. 8. 2; Herodotus also describes the vessels picked up from Lesbos as triremes (6. 5. 2–3).

30. J. A. Davison, *CQ*, XLI (1947), 18–24; G. S. Kirk, *BSA*, XLIV (1949), 142.

31. Her. 1. 26–27, 143; cf. also Thucydides' statement about the strength of the Ionian fleets at the time of Cyrus' conquests (note 7 above).

32. Her. 1. 163.

33. Her. 7. 184. 1; 8. 17.

34. Her. 6. 15. 1.

35. Thuc. 8. 40. 2; Roebuck, *CP*, XLV (1950), 245, n. 41.

36. The total area of Chios is given by Beloch as 826.7 km.² (*Die Bevölkerung der griechisch-römischen Welt* [Leipzig, 1886], p. 224). Of that about 20% would be suitable for cereal production, while the remainder would be mountainous or usable for grazing only. Since we know that Chios produced olives and vines in the sixth century (Roebuck, *CP*, XLV [1950], 240 and 245, notes 38 and 40) a further deduction of 10% of the area for cereals should be made (Roebuck, *CP*, XL [1945], 157, n. 60). Thus, *ca.* 150 km.² remains. Of that area one-half would lie fallow each year according to the usual practice of Greek agriculture: *ca.* 75 km.² would be available for the annual crop. The crop would presumably be in both barley and wheat, but we do not know the relative proportions. For the purpose of these calculations, to allow as much production as possible, we will assume it was entirely in barley with a yield of 18 hectolitres per hectare (Roebuck, *op. cit.*, p. 158). The average annual yield of barley would have been 135,000 hectolitres. The mean annual ration of barley per person may be calculated as 2.60 hectolitres (Roebuck, *op. cit.*, pp. 159–61). Chian production, then, would feed a population of about 52,000. Actually it would provide for less since some barley would have been needed for animals and probably some wheat was produced, the yield of which was about half that of barley. Our estimate of the population was a minimum of 80,000 so that grain would have had to be imported for more than 30,000 persons per year. Similar calculations might be made for the other islands, the area of which is known (for fifth century Lesbos see D. P. Mantzouranis, *The Annual Agricultural Revenue of Lesbos in Antiquity* [Mytilene, 1950]). We can scarcely make them, however, for Miletus since the amount of land which it controlled in the fertile Maeander plain is unknown.

The above calculation is primarily designed to show that there was need of imported grain in substantial volume in the East Greek states. It is illuminated by hints in the literary sources that such was the case: Teos — the well-known inscription (Tod, *GHI*, No. 23. 6–12) which curses those who prevent the importation of grain into Teos and (probably) re-export it after it has been brought in; this seems better taken as showing a normal condition of scarcity than a temporary one due to disorganization after the Persian Wars (so Hunt, *JHS*, LXVII [1947], p. 70, n. 15); Miletus — Herodotus represents Miletus as importing grain during the siege of Alyattes (1. 16–22), but that may have been only an abnormal war-time condition resulting from the destruction of Milesian harvests; Lesbos — Histiaeus did not find enough grain for his forces on Lesbos (Her. 6. 28. 2) so that he crossed to the mainland to reap the harvest (see also Thuc. 3. 2. 2, where the Lesbians are described as accumulating a stock of grain from the Black Sea before they venture to revolt). In addition to these specific indications we know that Ionian ships were engaged in bringing supplies from the Black Sea during the Revolt (above, note 12). Mainland Greeks also imported grain at the time of the Persian Wars (Her. 7. 147).

37. Her. 2. 163. 1; for mercenaries in the archaic period see Parke, *Greek Mercenary Soldiers* (Oxford, 1933), pp. 3–13.

38. Cf. the remarks of Heichelheim, *Wirtschaftsgeschichte des Altertums*, I (Leiden, 1938), 244 ff.

39. Cook, *JHS*, LVI (1946), 76–78.

40. Colonial settlement in this region seems to have begun on some scale in the early part of the seventh century; Cook, *loc. cit.* and Rhys Carpenter, *AJA*, LII (1948), 1–10.

41. Roebuck, *CP*, XLV (1950), 236–37.

42. Roebuck, *CP*, XLVI (1951), 215 and 219, n. 22.

43. S. A. Zebelev, *Vestnik Drevnei Istorii*, 1938, 2, pp. 154 ff.; A. A. Essena, *Vestnik*, 1946, 3, p. 222; K. M. Kolobotha, *Vestnik*, 1949, 2, pp. 130 ff.

44. Roebuck, *CP*, XLV (1950), 237–38.

45. Dunbabin, *The Western Greeks*, pp. 3, 214; Dunbabin ascribes great importance to the grain trade in the seventh century.

46. Dunbabin, *ibid.*, pp. 225 ff.; the most important period of the Potters' Quarter in Corinth begins with Early Corinthian (A. N. Stillwell, *Corinth*, XV, 1 [Princeton, 1948], 15–20).

47. C. H. V. Sutherland, *AJP*, LXIV (1943), 137 ff.; Dunbabin, *The Western Greeks*, pp. 246 ff. The very important article of E. S. G. Robinson on the dating of the coins in the Ephesus base (*JHS*, LXI [1951], 156–67) places the beginning of coinage in Ionia in the last half of the seventh century; this involves scaling down the dates of the mainland Greek coinages since they are apparently derivative.

48. While the change in Athenian economy no doubt started in the Solonian period its significant point in the sense described above is rather in the time of Peisistratus. Athenian pottery fully replaces Corinthian in the west about the middle of the sixth century (Dunbabin, *The Western Greeks*, p. 226), but Athenian coins do not appear until the end of the century (*ibid.*, p. 249). In Egypt, there is some Athenian pottery almost from the foundation of Naukratis, but the bulk of it falls after the middle of the century (Roebuck, *CP*, XLV [1950], 244, n. 19); while there are a few coins before 550 B.C., their number begins to increase steadily only in the latter part of the century (*ibid.*, p. 237 and p. 244, n. 16). In Syria at Al Mina the earliest Attic material is of the last quarter of the sixth century although the nearby Sabouni has some early Attic black-figure ware and a few pieces are reported from other Syrian sites (*JHS*, LVIII [1938], 21 and LIX [1939], 1–44). At Al Mina, however, there is a gap in the material between the end of the seventh and

the last quarter of the sixth century which is difficult to account for; Robertson (*JHS*, LXVI [1946], 125) suggests that a gradual change was made from East Greek to Athenian orientation in the course of the century. The earliest Athenian coins found there are tetradrachms of the latter part of the fifth century (Robinson, *Num. Chron.*, XVII [1937], 182–96). The earliest Athenian pottery from the Black Sea sites is a fragment from a pot by the painter of Acropolis 606 in the second quarter of the sixth century (Beazley, *The Development of Attic Black-Figure* [Berkeley, 1951], p. 40).

49. Dunbabin, *The Western Greeks*, pp. 5–8, 458, 461.

50. Robertson (*JHS*, LX [1940], 2–21) and Cook (*JHS* LXVI [1946], 78–79) find nothing that need go back into the first half of the eighth century although Smith considers the settlement dated from *ca.* 800 B.C. (*Antiquaries' Journal*, XXII [1942], 87–112). I am indebted to Mr. G. Swift of the Oriental Institute for allowing me to inspect the material from the Institute's investigations in the Amk plain.

51. Schaeffer, *Mélanges Dussaud*, XXX (1939), 1, 461–87. The majority of the coins are Thraco-Macedonian (33 out of 38), the others from Salamis in Cyprus. Another hoard is reported from the mountains between Antioch and Latakia (Noe, *Bibliography of Greek Coin Hoards*, No. 55). It, too, consisted of Thraco-Macedonian coins. The presence of the Cypriote coins suggests that Cypriotes brought this silver to the Syrian ports, but presumably Ionian traders from the northern Aegean would have brought it to Cyprus as they apparently did to Egypt (Roebuck, *CP*, XLV [1950], 238–40); W. Schwabacher notes the importance of Thraco-Macedonian silver for the trade with Syria (*Skrifter Utg. av Svenska Inst. i Rom*, XV [1950], 142–43).

52. Her. 6. 47.

53. *Iliad* 9. 71–72; *Odyssey* 9. 196–98; Archilochus, Frag. 2 (Diehl). For the date of colonization in this region see Cook, *JHS*, LXVI (1946), 71. Unfortunately for the chronology, Homer, whose references to Thrace indicate some knowledge and trading connections, and Archilochus, important for the colonization of Thasos, Maroneia and Stryme, afford our literary evidence.

54. *RE*, VI (Stuttgart, 1909), 585; IA² (Stuttgart, 1920), 2213.

55. Greek occupation of Larisa is apparently to be dated *ca.* 700 B.C. (Hanfmann, *AJA*, LII [1948], 146). Larisa's location, inland from the coast, indicates that it would hardly be a *primary* Greek settlement in Asia Minor, but would rather mark an expansion inland, just as Greek influence began to affect Sardis *ca.* 700 B.C. (Hanfmann, *op. cit.*, pp. 152–54). There may be some reflections of this movement in the literary sources; e.g., the traditions of Ionian settlement of Phocaea from Teos and Erythrae, of Clazomenae from Colophon (Wilamowitz, *SB Berlin*, [1906], 55–57; Caspari, JHS, XXXV [1915], 177–78); of the capture of Aeolian Smyrna by the Colophonians (Her. 1. 149–50).

56. See notes 40 and 53 above.

57. Nilsson, *Cults, Myths, Oracles, and Politics in Ancient Greece* (Lund, 1951), pp. 143–49.

THE GRAIN TRADE BETWEEN
GREECE AND EGYPT

IN RECENT years our increasing knowledge of archaic Greek pottery, a large amount of which was found in Naukratis, and the study of the early coin hoards found, for the most part, in the Delta have aided substantially in the clarification of the problem of the trade relationship between the Greek states and Egypt in the archaic period. The use of this evidence, however, involves many difficulties so that any complete interpretation, in conjunction with the literary evidence, is still premature. Hasebroek and Milne[2] have emphasized the consideration that the pottery from Naukratis, and presumably that found in small quantities elsewhere in Egypt,[3] was imported (or, in the case of some groups, made locally) for the use of the Greeks, largely for dedications in their own sanctuaries. It was hardly imported for sale in quantity to Egyptians. Possibly some of those Greek states to which pottery fabrics found at Naukratis have been ascribed were concerned rather with profiting from the sale of their vases and such products as wine and oil to the Greek community than with buying Egyptian commodities. Some states may not have been the carriers of their own pottery, while others, such as Aegina and Teos, which did not have a pottery fabric for export, are credited by Herodotus[4] with an interest in the Egyptian trade. Thus, aside from the technical questions of sorting out the various fabrics, assigning them to centers of manufacture and working out their chronology —still far from settled in the case of the East Greek wares—we are faced with the problem of how reliable an index the pottery is for trade connections with Egypt

since, in itself, it was not an article of exchange in quantity. It seems necessary to consider the case of each of the major states involved in the light of other evidence and of their own needs rather than to make a simple equation of pottery fabric, its known or conjectured producer, and an interest in purchasing Egyptian commodities.

The numismatic evidence, however, is probably a more reliable guide to the general nature of the trade. The uniform pattern of composition in the archaic hoards[5] and their discovery at scattered points in the Delta seem to indicate that certain Greek states were responsible for bringing the coins to Egypt to buy commodities in quantity from the Egyptians. This evidence, first brought into prominence by Dressel and Regling, and recently discussed by Milne and Sutherland,[6] shows that in the archaic period, as later, Egyptian grain was the chief article of trade in quantity and that it was paid for in large part by silver from the Thraco-Macedonian silver producing region. While the origin of much of this silver is certain, it is highly improbable that its producers carried it to Egypt or consumed Egyptian grain in any quantity. Thus, the question of which Greek states were the chief carriers and consumers arises. In the present article I shall attempt to find a solution by reviewing the evidence of the hoards and attempting to relate it in some degree with the activity of various states at Naukratis as indicated by the archaeological and literary material. Naukratis itself must have been the most important center, if not the only one, of this trade.[7] A solution will be of value, not only for the particular problem of trade, but for the light thrown on the early economic development of certain Greek communities in their perennial attempt to ensure their food supply.

The Egyptian hoards, both of the archaic and classical periods,[8] frequently contain not only minted coins, but also bars and lumps of silver and clippings from coins; some hoards, in fact, are made up entirely of unminted silver and clippings.[9] This silver was evidently used in Egypt as a bullion currency, since Egypt had no minted money of its own, and represents, so to speak, a small surviving portion of Egypt's favorable trade balance. Much of it must have been melted down. Presumably Greek buyers went out into the Delta to make their purchases of grain although we may assume that most deliveries and shipments were made from Naukratis. This infiltration of individual Greeks is apparently reflected in the sporadic finds of Greek pottery, mentioned above; it was true also of the period of Herodotus, since he mentions Greek residents in various cities.[10] The coins, with the important exception of those of Miletus,[11] are of large denominations so they must have been brought into the country for large scale purchases of goods and do not represent the specie spent by travellers and sailors. Many of them, as well as the bars of silver, are marred by cuts, made to determine whether the metal was solid or plated. The coins, of course, are of various standards, according to their mints, and the bars show no relation in weight to each other or to any standard.

The most striking feature of the composition of the archaic hoards is the uniform representation and the great preponderance of coins from the Thraco-Macedonian area—about 30% of the total. Presumably a large part of the unworked silver might safely be assigned to the same region, an article of export pre-

ceding and accompanying the minted coins. The coins are not only from the Pangaeus region proper: from the cities of Thasos, Neapolis, Lete, and the native tribes of the mining area, but from the adjacent regions of the Chalkidike and western Thrace. The Chalkidic cities represented are: Acanthus, Dicaea, Scione, Mende, Terone, Sermyle, and Potidaea;[12] from western Thrace: Abdera and Dicaea, but not Maroneia. It is unlikely that any of these places were carrying the silver of this region to Egypt or importing Egyptian grain in large quantity.[13] The coins from the cities on the periphery of the mining region would indicate that the carriers are to be sought among the states having trading relations with them and a known activity in Egypt. It is improbable that the silver would pass through another intermediary handler.

The states from the area of mainland Greece best represented in the hoards are Athens, Aegina, and Corinth. Athens has forty-seven coins, Aegina thirty-two, and Corinth twenty, but some qualifications are necessary on the score of date. The Aeginetan coins are almost entirely of the type with older incuse, dated in the late seventh and earlier part of the sixth century.[14] Many of the Corinthian coins are of similarly early date and none are found in the fifth century hoards.[15] On the other hand there are only two Athenian coins of the *Wappenmünzen* type, dated by Seltman 594–62 B.C.; possibly three others are earlier than the middle of the century, but there is a steady and marked increase only after that period.[16] Evidently Aegina and Corinth were the states most interested in the Egyptian trade in the early part of the sixth century and were gradually replaced by Athens in the latter part of the century.

Aegina has usually been considered the most active of these states in the trade with Egypt, even to the extent of establishing a virtual monopoly over the distribution of Egyptian grain in the central and western Aegean regions.[17] There would seem to be a reflection of this, of course, in Herodotus' list of the states with sanctuaries at Naukratis, for Aegina is the only state from the western Aegean so represented.[18] Since Aegina had no exportable pottery fabric in this period, it is scarcely possible to use the fairly substantial amount of Corinthian and Attic pottery of the first part of the sixth century found at Naukratis[19] in a comparison. It has, in fact, been suggested that Aeginetans were the carriers of the pottery.[20] While these considerations may well reflect the fact that Aegina carried the bulk of the grain imported by the western and central Aegean states, the view that it exercised a monopoly seems open to some question. In the first place it is necessary to assume for the establishment of this monopoly a rather long period of Aeginetan trade in Egypt before the last quarter of the seventh century when Greek pottery appears, *i.e.*, when Greek settlement was made.[21] This is possible, but it would also seem necessary to assume close commercial connections between Corinth and Aegina after that date. There is a relatively large number of Corinthian coins as compared to Aeginetan in the hoards. Moreover, a substantial number of Egyptian objects were found at the Corinthian sanctuary of Perachora.[22] Did Corinth buy both grain and such objects from Aeginetan merchants? She might have done so before the last quarter of the seventh century, but seems to have been breaking away from the Aeginetan monetary area during that period and attaching herself to the Euboean.[23] On the whole it seems unlikely, since we know that Corinth had ships and was already interested in trading eastwards across the Aegean, as the Corinthian pottery found in Rhodes indicates. Certainly, Corinth's main sphere of

trade and source of grain was in the west, but she was apparently interested also in the Egyptian supply and probably paying for it with silver from the Thraco-Macedonian region. In the Zagazig hoard was a Corinthian coin made by overstriking a Thraco-Macedonian piece.[24] While the sources of Corinthian silver are not definitely known,[25] the foundation of and continued efforts to hold Potidaea, and the Corinthian monetary affiliation with Euboea and through Euboea with the colonies of the Chalkidike, seem to point to the Pangaeus region as one of the areas on which the city relied. On the other hand Aegina probably drew her silver from the island of Siphnos.[26] Athens, however, after the middle of the sixth century, as a result of Peisistratus' personal interests in the mining region, brought some of this Thraco-Macedonian silver to Egypt, probably in the form of its own minted coin.[27] The greater part of it was probably carried by the East Greeks, whose connections with both Thrace and Egypt were closer than those of the western Aegean states.

It has already been suggested by Milne and Sutherland[28] that the Ionian states were the chief carriers of the silver, obtaining it by an exchange of textiles and other manufactured goods with the natives. The coins from the East Greek area considerably outnumber those from the western Aegean and show representation from a variety of states. While this variety of coinage might represent a general consumption of Egyptian grain and a close interweaving of trade connections, there are certain states whose coinage predominates and which appear to have been very prominent at Naukratis. If their connection with the Thraco-Macedonian district can be established it seems reasonable to see in them the main carriers and, perhaps, consumers of the grain.

For convenience of discussion we might

divide the East Greek states into a northern area including the islands and mainland cities from Caria north and a southern group centering around Rhodes—the Dodecanese islands, Lycia, Cilicia, and Cyprus. Although the trade of this last group with Egypt was presumably of as much importance as that of the northern group of cities, to judge from the relative quantity of their coins, it seems hardly necessary to consider it for our purposes since there does not appear to be any evidence of a strong Rhodian or Cypriote connection with the Thraco-Macedonian region. Cyrene, too, as might be expected, has a substantial representation in the hoards, but again there is no reason to suppose that Cyrenean traders went to the northern Aegean.

Of the northern group of states Miletus has twenty-five coins in the hoards, Chios seventeen, Samos seven, Phocaea five, and Teos three. The Tean representation is misleadingly small since some of its inhabitants fled from the prospect of Persian rule to recolonize Abdera ca. 545 B.C. Abdera's coinage is dated to the period after this transplantation[29] and some of its coins were found in the hoards. Phocaea, too, suffered a partial removal to the west ca. 540 B.C. after failing to come to an agreement with Chios for the purchase of the Oenussae Islands.[30] The absence of Lesbian coins is somewhat surprising in view of the other evidence of the presence of its citizens in Naukratis[31] but perhaps is to be explained by the fact that its colonial ventures and political interests were in Aeolia and the Thracian Chersonese rather than in the Thraco-Macedonian region. Of this group we might eliminate Samos as an important carrier. It has a relatively small representation compared to that of Miletus and Chios and what evidence we have for the source of its silver would seem to indicate Siphnos rather than the north.[32] Possibly, too,

its connections with Egypt, well attested for the tyranny of Polycrates, were rather later in origin than those of the other states mentioned.[33] Phocaea might also be eliminated, on the considerations that its trading interest was in the far west, and the source of its silver probably Tartessus.[34] It would seem that Miletus, Chios, and, to a lesser degree, Teos are left as probable carriers.

The claims of Miletus would seem to be less justified than those of Chios. It does have more coins in the hoards than any other East Greek state, but they are all of small denominations and are found in only two hoards.[35] This would suggest that, while Miletus may have been a carrier, it was not a purchaser of grain on its own account. It is, indeed, rather difficult to understand why it should have purchased Egyptian grain considering the agricultural development of its own local territory[36] and its connections with the Euxine. These latter would have been in the process of development during the early sixth century, if the revised foundation dates suggested for the Black Sea colonies are correct.[37] Further, Miletus does not appear to have had direct connections with the Thraco-Macedonian district, for its colonial activity was directed to the Hellespont and to the Black Sea. As we shall demonstrate below the view of its reputedly important position at Naukratis is open to some modification. On the whole, then, Miletus' participation in the grain trade with Egypt was probably limited to carriage for the smaller islands and cities in its vicinity.

Chios has, of course, long been recognized as one of the wealthy and economically advanced Ionian states of the archaic period. There is some evidence to suggest that its agriculture was early transformed towards specialized viticulture and olive production, which would, of course, have the effect of making it dependent on imports of grain. While the literary references to its famous wine begin only in the fifth century,[38] the amphora appears as a symbol on the coins soon after the middle of the sixth century;[39] if the story of Thales' corner of olive presses is to be believed, the island was growing olives in the early sixth century.[40] The record of Chios as the earliest "slave-state" of Greece,[41] making use of purchased barbarian slaves, might indicate an extensive use of slaves in agriculture and possibly in industry, while its citizens engaged in trade.[42]

Chios was, then, a wealthy state presumably in need of imported grain. It is significant that relief was not sought in colonization on any scale and equally significant that the only colonial foundation of importance was made very early in western Thrace at Maroneia.[43] This colony was not in the silver producing region, but could have served as a depot for trade with the inland tribes[44] and a calling point en route to Thasos. Some reflection of rivalry with Paros and Thasos in this region survives in the literary tradition,[45] but, if Archilochus' taste for Ismarian wine has any significance beyond a Homeric reminiscence, there was trade also.[46] It seems a not unreasonable assumption that Chian wine, olive oil, and manufactured goods may have been sent to the Greek coastal cities and the inland tribes in exchange for silver and slaves before the period of extensive agricultural development in Thrace.[47] We have little archaeological evidence of Chian trade with this region except some pottery found at Thasos and Neapolis (Kavalla),[48] but there has been little excavation and publication. In view of certain characteristics of the Chian coinage of the archaic period, it seems probable that such a connection existed.

Chios stood somewhat apart from the other Ionian states in that the principal fabric of its coins was silver,[49] not elec-trum, which indicates that it had access to supplies of silver. The source could scarcely have been Siphnos,[50] and it is unlikely that it was Asia Minor, or Chios would have struck more electrum. It apparently made little effort to acquire electrum, for its commercial relations with the coastal cities of Asia Minor do not appear to have been extensive.[51] The island found itself or placed itself in a trading situation in which silver was needed, that is for the trade with Egypt, where electrum coins are conspicuous by their scarcity. Chios evidently had sufficient silver and sufficient trade to create a standard of its own, which fitted easily into either the Milesian or Euboic standards.[52] The symbols on its earliest coins, found, significantly enough, in Egypt, are similar to those of the early Thraco-Macedonian group.[53] Further, when Abdera began to coin after its recolonization by Teos, it did so on a standard related to the Chian, which would indicate one area of Chian influence in this region.[54] Chios, then, would appear to be chief carrier of the Thraco-Macedonian silver to Egypt and a large importer of Egyptian grain. It might also, of course, have distributed silver to the Rhodian area. Probably, too, Chios imported grain from the Black Sea when the export trade of its cities had developed; if the size of the Chian war fleet is any gauge of that of its merchant fleet, the latter was larger than that of any other Ionian city, since Chios had one hundred vessels in the combined fleet of 353 which fought against the Persians at Lade,[55] while Miletus provided eighty, Lesbos seventy, and Samos sixty.

It is probable that Teos, too, shared in this trade in grain with Egypt. The recolonization of Abdera is an indication of its interest in the Thraco-Macedonian region; further, its colonial activity in the Milesian preserve of the Cimmerian Bosporus shows that it was on good terms with Miletus and Chios in the early sixth century.[56] In Naukratis, too, Teos was of more prominence than the bare reference of Herodotus implies. Teos' need for imported grain is attested in the early fifth century by the well known inscription invoking curses on those who prevented its import and engaged in its re-export.[57]

When the evidence of Naukratis is considered the position of Miletus seems to be paramount at first sight. According to the tradition reported by Strabo[58] Miletus was the founder of Naukratis. There is no doubt that the sanctuary of Apollo, from which such a large amount of dedicated pottery has been obtained, was that of the Milesian Apollo.[59] Miletus was formerly considered to have made and carried to Naukratis a large part of the "Rhodo-Milesian" ware found on the site.[60] The dedicatory inscriptions to Apollo, written in Ionic and without designation of the worshipper's nationality were confidently assigned to Milesians on the assumption that they must have been the dedicators in their own shrine.[61]

When the material is examined, however, this picture of Milesian predominance is seen to be in need of revision, particularly in favor of Chios. From an examination of the dedicatory inscriptions in which an ethnic is given it appears that the Milesians were not the most frequent dedicators and that there is no reason to suppose that the use of a sanctuary was limited to the citizens of the state which founded it. The shrines were rather in common use by visiting traders of various states and by Naukratite citizens. The number of inscriptions in which ethnics were written is very small in proportion to the number of vases dedicated and to those on which only the name appears. Nevertheless, such a sampling should have some value as an index. The result of an examination of the lists published in the excavation reports is: Tean five, Lesbian five, Chian four, Phocaean two, Milesian

two.[62] The evidence is very scanty and might be enlarged by a consideration of names, letter forms, and dialects; since we are concerned with Ionian states, however, the use of the latter would involve considerable controversy and uncertainty. The evidence does, with that of the coins, point to the northern Ionian area and to Teos and Chios in particular. That impression is confirmed when we consider the use of the sanctuaries and the various pottery fabrics.

Among the dedications in the Apollo sanctuary there is one certain and one possible (depending on the restoration) Tean; one Chian; two, to judge from the dialect, are Dorian; Phanes is presumably from Halicarnassus, if he is correctly identified with the man who played the traitor in the Persian conquest of Egypt; there are no inscriptions which specifically state that the dedicator is a Milesian, but conversely, a Milesian appears to have made a dedication in the Hellenion, the joint sanctuary of nine other states.[63] Thus, since the sanctuary was not limited to its own nationals, who sometimes went to other sanctuaries, it would hardly seem justifiable to conclude that the inscriptions without ethnics were necessarily made by Milesians. They might equally well have been made in part by citizens of Naukratis or by visiting traders who did not take the trouble to indicate whence they came.

The same general usage would appear to have been true of the Aphrodite sanctuary, although in its case we do not have any definite information about the founder, although Chios is a likely candidate, and it has been regarded as the sanctuary of the city in distinction to those of the traders.[64] Chians, Teans, Lesbians, and Samians would seem to have used it; to judge by the nature of the cult, that of Aphrodite Pandemos, and the cosmopolitan character of Naukratis it was no doubt extremely popular.[65] Very few dedications were found in the Heraion, since its filling had been largely removed by peasants in the interests of better crops; they preserve no ethnics although there is some reason to connect the type of cup on which some inscriptions were scratched with Samos.[66] The sanctuary of the Dioscuri also yielded few inscriptions, but among them is that of a Phocaean.[67] The Hellenion offers a variety of ethnics both from members and nonmembers.[68]

The same conclusion about the common use made of sanctuaries would seem apparent from the pottery fabrics. While it would be difficult and perhaps impossible, as a result of the incomplete study and wide distribution of the pottery after the excavation, to make a table of the relative quantities of the various wares found in the separate *temene*, it is evident that no one fabric was limited to a specific sanctuary; even if we could identify Milesian ware with certainty, the pottery from the sanctuary of the Milesian Apollo is not all Milesian, and that at the earliest period.[69] Yet there does appear a certain amount of affinity between dedicators and their native pottery. A group of Lesbian dedications to Aphrodite is found on Lesbian bucchero ware; there is some reason to assign to Samos a group of cups with dedications to Hera; a small group of Ionian cylixes may perhaps be Cnidian in manufacture and dedication;[70] Chians use their own pottery, in some cases prepared beforehand in Chios, for dedication upon arrival.[71] This cannot, however, be pressed, for Chians use Attic; Teans, Chiot; Greco-Egyptians, Chiot; Samians, Chiot; and Cyreneans, Laconian, possibly because the ware was brought to Naukratis by way of Cyrene.[72] Evidently, the various fabrics were brought into Naukratis for common sale and the dedicators, visitors and citizens alike, chose according to their fancy, which might be filial or

might prefer a novelty. We can assume reasonably that in the first instance the foundations of the sanctuaries would be due to the filial feelings of the traders and of the early residents. There should also be a tendency among visiting traders and residents of the first and second generations to frequent the sanctuaries of their own gods, but, from the evidence of common usage, these gods seem to have become Naukratite deities at an early date. There does not appear to have been any tendency to maintain the sanctuaries as the separate property of a far away state over a long period of time. It does seem justifiable to see in the great relative proportion of Chiot ware, now regarded as made in Chios and not in Naukratis,[73] the reflection of an early and extensive use of the settlement and residence in the community by Chians. Probably, too, from the predominance of the ware in the sanctuary of Aphrodite and the appropriateness of its shapes for dedication we might infer that Chians were the founders of that shrine,[74] which appears to be as early as the sanctuary of Apollo.

It seems probable that in Naukratis, where many Greeks from different cities were living in a single community in a foreign land, the common elements of their culture overwhelmed the separatist ties with their cities and aided in the formation of the city state of Naukratis. The settlers' ties with Greece were maintained by the traders and the Greek articles which the latter brought and were strengthened by the obstacles to political expansion in Egypt. The community was, so to speak, turned inwards upon itself. Naukratis did not, like later settlements in Hellenistic Egypt, Egyptianize, but acted and was regarded by the rest of the Greek world as a Greek polis. There was from the outset little intermarriage, to judge from the names on the archaic Greek inscriptions[75] and the Greek character of the offerings, despite the existence of an older Egyptian town in the immediate vicinity. This Hellenic character was maintained in the Ptolemaic and Roman periods by a civic ordinance forbidding intermarriage with Egyptians. If this regulation originated in the pre-Ptolemaic city, as Wilcken has suggested,[76] Greek women or Hellenized Thracians must have been brought there in some numbers. Perhaps the hetaerae for which Naukratis was famous

had a more fundamental role in the creation of the city than providing amusement for visiting traders. *Mutatis mutandis*, may we mention the example of some American frontier communities? In the early development of the community the evidence indicates that East Greeks played a leading part, and that among the East Greek states it was Chios, not Miletus, which was most prominent.

UNIVERSITY OF CHICAGO

NOTES

1. My thanks are due to Professor William F. Edgerton of the Oriental Institute for suggestions in connection with this article and, more particularly, with the study of the organization of Naukratis mentioned in note 76.

2. J. Hasebroek, *Trade and Politics in Ancient Greece* (translated by L. M. Fraser and D. C. MacGregor [London, 1933]), pp. 62 f.; *idem, Staat und Handel im alten Griechenland* (Tübingen, 1928), p. 64; J. G. Milne, "Trade Between Greece and Egypt Before Alexander the Great," *JEA*, XXV (1939), 178.

3. See the list in the article by R. M. Cook, "Amasis and the Greeks in Egypt," *JHS*, LVII (1937), 236–37. Greek pottery has been found in small quantities at widely scattered points in the Delta and Thebaid; it apparently represents residence by individual Greeks or occasional purchases by Egyptians. The fabrics are mainly East Greek, dating, like the pottery from Naukratis, from the late seventh century through the course of the sixth; there is no break during the reign of Amasis. Cook has pointed out that the latter is true of the pottery of Tell Defenneh. Thus, the concentration of Greeks in Naukratis by Amasis would scarcely seem to be correct (*ibid.*, pp. 233, 235–36).

4. Herodotus ii. 178.

5. The hoards of particular value for the archaic period are: Demanhur (*ca.* 1900–01) with 165 coins (Noe, "A Bibliography of Greek Coin Hoards," *Numismatic Notes and Monographs*, No. 78 [1937], 94, No. 323); Zagazig (1901) with 84 coins (*ibid.*, p. 309, No. 1178). These two hoards were published in a very useful article by Dressel and Regling, "Zwei ägyptische Funde altgriechischer Silbermünzen," *Zeit. f. Num.*, XXXVII (1927), 1–138. Benha el-Asl (1928) with 71 + coins buried *ca.* 485 B.C. (Noe, *op. cit.*, p. 49, No. 143); Delta (1887) with 24 coins, buried *ca.* 500 B.C. (Noe, *op. cit.*, p. 105, No. 362); Myt-Rahineh (1860) with 23 coins buried in the sixth century B.C. (Noe, *op. cit.*, p. 191, No. 722); Sakha (1897) with 72 + coins (Noe, *op. cit.*, p. 233, No. 888). There are, in addition to these relatively large and at least partially complete hoards, small groups of coins which are apparently from hoards of the same period and help to supplement the picture: Damietta (1899 ?) with Cyrenaic coins (Noe, *op. cit.*, p. 89, No. 299); Egypt (ante 1879) with Thraco-Macedonian coins (Noe, *op. cit.*, p. 104, No. 361); Egypt (1900 ?) with Croesus staters (Noe, *op. cit.*, p. 105, No. 365); Fayoum (ante 1913) with Thraco-Macedonian coins (Noe, *op. cit.*,

p. 115, No. 411). We shall be concerned, however, with the composition of only the six more complete hoards. There are, in the case of each, certain difficulties as to the circumstances of finding and questions of "contamination" and partial break-up before the hoards came to the notice of scholars. These do not affect the use of the hoards to any great degree.

6. Dressel and Regling, *op. cit.*, pp. 23–27; Milne, *op. cit.*, pp. 177–83; C. H. V. Sutherland, "Corn and Coin: A Note on Greek Commercial Monopolies," *AJP*, LXIV (1943), 143–44; "Overstrikes and Hoards," *Num. Chron.*, II (1942), 13–16; the literary evidence for the trade in grain and other commodities is collected by Mallet, "Les premiers établissements des Grecs en Egypte," *Mémoires de la Mission archéologique française au Caire*, XII (1897), 1, 277–364. Milne reduces the quantity trade between Greece and Egypt to an exchange of Egyptian grain for Greek silver, arguing that Egyptian linen was not used for Greek sailcloth, that the export of papyrus and glass was largely Hellenistic and Roman, that Greek wine was not used by the Egyptians, who were beer drinkers, that Greek textiles were hardly fitted for use in the Egyptian climate and that Greek timber was too expensive. This seems a somewhat excessive modification on both the score of Egyptian exports and imports; a large number of objects of faience and alabaster have been found on archaic Greek sites; while they may have been made in large part by Greeks in Naukratis and elsewhere the material is at least Egyptian. Herodotus makes an interesting, if obscure, remark about the importation of Greek wine after the Persian conquest (iii. 6): wine was brought from Greece and Phoenicia in jars which were collected by the authorities and sent to Memphis for use in supplying the desert route to Syria with water. The Naukratis Stele of the fourth century B.C. specifically mentions the importation of timber and worked wood into Egypt through Naukratis (B. Gunn, *JEA*, XXIX [1943], 58, 9a). It may, of course, have been brought from the Lebanon. With respect to other commodities the literary evidence does indicate that linen and papyrus were known and used by the Greeks before the Hellenistic period, but certainly they appear as rarely used or luxury articles. In such a comparison of commodities the question of value should be considered, but unfortunately our evidence scarcely allows it. On the whole, Milne's judgment on the score of quantity would seem correct, for other Egyptian exports than grain would pack into a small space and it is hardly

necessary to stress the need for imported grain in most Greek states at an early date.

7. The most recent discussions of the site with citation of earlier treatments are those of E. Gjerstad, "Studies in Archaic Greek Chronology, I. Naukratis," *LAAA*, XXI (1934), 67–84 and R. M. Cook, *op. cit.*, pp. 227–37. Gjerstad attempted to reconstruct the stratification of the temenos of Apollo from the published reports of the excavation by Petrie and by identification of the latter's pottery classes; his conclusion was in favor of a foundation of the Greek settlement largely in the reign of Amasis. Cook has rightly pointed out that adequate information for such a reconstruction does not exist in Petrie's report (*Naukratis*, I) and that the filling was evidently confused (*op. cit.*, p. 228, n. 6; *BSA*, XXXIV [1933–34], 86, n. 2). Since the literary evidence of Strabo and Herodotus, the chief authorities, is inconclusive as to date, the situation would now seem to be that Naukratis' foundation must be dated from the evidence of the pottery. Cook, largely on the evidence of the Attic and Corinthian pottery, of which the chronology is better established than that of the East Greek wares, favors a date in the last quarter of the seventh century, *ca.* 615–10 B.C.; he further considers that the evidence of the pottery does not suggest any sudden enlargement of the community in the reign of Amasis (see note 3). It seems questionable that Attic and Corinthian ware should be used to furnish a date of settlement in what was obviously an East Greek enterprise; the western pottery should rather mark the beginning of some extensive use of the settlement by western traders. While it is probable that some trade would be carried on before Greek settlement, since there was an Egyptian town on the site of Naukratis (H. Kees, *P.-W.*, XVI, 1957–59), it is likely that its volume would be small (on Greek-Egyptian relations in the seventh century see Ure, *The Origin of Tyranny*, pp. 86–103; Parke, *Greek Mercenary Soldiers*, pp. 4–6). It is possible, of course, that many of the regulations concerning Greeks which Herodotus ascribes to Amasis were not of his own making, but were those of earlier rulers. Since Amasis was the most important of the Saite kings his figure would serve as a crystallization point in tradition.

8. The latter are composed largely of Athenian tetradrachms and, when the supply began to fail in the fourth century, of imitations. They reflect the domination of Athenian currency as a medium of international exchange in the trade of the fifth and fourth centuries. For the tetradrachm hoards see Noe, *op. cit.*, Nos. 144, 673, 729, 730, 957, 1082; add the hoards mentioned in *Naukratis*, I, 66 and a hoard recently found at Tell el-Mushkat (*Num. Chron.*, VII [1947], 115 ff.); for the imitations see also Dressel and Regling, *op. cit.*, p. 3, n. 2 and p. 19, n. 3. The percentages of coins from various mints given by Sutherland (*Num. Chron.*, II [1942], 16) are based on the hoards dated before 400 B.C., which obscures the difference in composition between the archaic and classical hoards, although it well illustrates the general picture of the movement of silver from north to south across the Mediterranean.

9. Dressel and Regling, *op. cit.*, pp. 6–7 and 20–23; one such hoard was found at Tell Defenneh (*Tanis*, II, 76).

10. Herodotus ii. 39, 41; see also Aristagoras of Miletus (fourth century B.C.), *FHG*, II, 98, frag. 5; Greek and Carian quarters in Memphis are mentioned; see Ure, *op. cit.*, p. 96, n. 4.

11. Milesian coins are found in two hoards only:

Demanhur (Dressel and Regling, *op. cit.*, pp. 62–64) and Delta (*Num. Chron.*, X [1890], 4); the maximum weight of these coins is 1.24 gms., which is roughly that of the Athenian one and one half obol pieces of the fifth century, the use of which was primarily local.

12. Dicaea in Chalkidike and Potidaea are represented only in the Zagazig hoard; this hoard is rather later than the others (Dressel and Regling, *op. cit.*, pp. 8 and 10). It contains 34 Athenian coins while the large and earlier Demanhur hoard contains none. The three earliest coins (Nos. 190–92) are dated by Seltman (*Athens, Its History and Coinage*, pp. 172–73) to the period, 546–536 B.C., and attributed to the Paeonian mint of Peisistratus (*ibid.*, pp. 58–60); No. 193 belongs to the same group; the remainder in increasing volume are to be dated in the late sixth and early fifth centuries (Dressel and Regling, *op. cit.*, pp. 120–23). The latest coins, a group of 17, are compared by Regling to the types, *BMC, Athens*, Pl. III, 6–8.

13. Sutherland, *AJP*, LXIV (1943), 136–37; if local production could not satisfy the needs of these cities, the population of which would be small in the sixth century, the grain of Thrace and of the Black Sea region was nearer at hand and presumably cheaper than that from Egypt. See also note 47.

14. Dressel and Regling, *op. cit.*, p. 11, n. 1; 55; there is only one Aeginetan coin in the "Silversmith's Hoard" from Naukratis which was buried *ca.* 439 B.C. (Noe, *op. cit.*, pp. 192–93, No. 729) and one in the hoard found at Naukratis in 1905 (*ibid.*, p. 193, No. 730).

15. Dressel and Regling, *op. cit.*, pp. 56–57; the Zagazig hoard (note 12) contained only one Corinthian coin and the Naukratite hoards, mentioned in the previous note, none.

16. Seltman, *op. cit.*, p. 147 (Sakha); three early coins with the head of Athena are included in the Delta hoard (*Num. Chron.*, X [1890], 12). Milne has ascribed the introduction of Athens to the Egyptian market to the economic sagacity of Solon ("The Economic Policy of Solon," *Hesperia*, XIV [1945], 230–45). He points out that issues which began *ca.* 566 (Head, *HN²*, p. 369) found their way to Africa soon after their minting, for Cyrene began to overstrike them *ca.* 550 B.C. See also note 12 above.

17. Sutherland, *AJP*, LXIV (1943), 143–45; Milne, *Hesperia*, XIV (1945), 232 ff.; the islands of the central Aegean are not very well represented in the hoards; Naxos and Paros have 7 and 6 coins respectively; since we have no evidence to connect them specifically with Egypt they may well have purchased from Aegina.

18. Herodotus ii. 178.

19. For the Corinthian see Payne, *Necrocorinthia*, p. 25, n. 6 and p. 187; R. J. Hopper, *BSA*, XLIV (1949), 177, n. 65. The Corinthian dates from the late seventh century with most of the imports belonging to the first quarter of the sixth. For the Attic see Beazley and Payne, *JHS*, XLIX (1929), 253–72; Cook, *JHS*, LVII (1937), 228. The first Attic imports date from the late seventh century; while there is a decided increase after the middle of the sixth century it does not have the same intrusive force at Naukratis as in the West and the Black Sea.

20. Prinz, "Funde aus Naukratis," *Klio*, Beiheft VII (1908), 75, 77; Price, *JHS*, XLIV (1924), 202.

21. See the remarks of Milne, *Hesperia*, XIV (1945), 232 ff.; the earliest Corinthian and Attic pottery found at Naukratis is dated in the last quarter of the seventh century (see note 19 above).

22. They are as yet unpublished in full; a few early imports are published in Payne, *Perachora*, I, 76–77, 142–43.

23. Milne, *Hesperia*, XIV (1945), 235; *Num. Chron.*, I (1941), 9–15.

24. Dressel and Regling, *op. cit.*, p. 125, No. 233.

25. It seems probable, but not definitely established, that Corinth got silver from the Illyrian-Paeonian region (May, *Coinage of Damastion*, pp. viii–ix). Potidaea may have served as the base of one avenue of approach to this region (Wade-Gery, *CAH*, III, 552–53) as well as the center for Corinthian influence in the Chalkidike. The problem of its foundation is involved, however, with the difficult question of Cypselid chronology (H. R. W. Smith, "The Hearst Hydria," *Univ. of Calif. Publications in Classical Archaeology*, I [1944], 262). The existence of Corinthian *epidemiourgoi* at Potidaea indicates that Corinth tried to maintain very close relations with the colony (Thuc. i. 56. 2).

26. Sutherland, *AJP*, LXIV (1943), 134, n. 17; there was apparently rivalry between Samos and Aegina for Siphnian silver (Herodotus iii. 57–59).

27. It was probably in the form of Athenian coins if Seltman's identifications of the products of a Thracian mint are correct (n. 12 above; Sutherland, *AJP*, LXIV [1943], 142, n. 52).

28. Milne, *JEA*, XXV (1939), 179; Sutherland, *Num. Chron.*, II (1942), 14; see also Dressel and Regling, *op. cit.*, pp. 23–27.

29. Head, *HN²*, p. 253.

30. Herodotus i. 165.

31. Mytilene was a member of the Hellenion (Herodotus ii. 178). There is also the well known story of the interest of Sappho's brother, if not in the wine trade, at least in the courtesan Rhodopis; somewhat more to the point are the finds of Lesbian pottery in Naukratis, some with inscriptions in the Lesbian dialect (*Naukratis*, II, 65, Nos. 786–93).

32. See note 26 above; perhaps a certain amount came from Spain if Colaeus' voyage was not an isolated instance (Herodotus iv. 152; Cary, "The Sources of Silver for the Greek World," *Mélanges Glotz*, I, 138).

33. Samos had a sanctuary of its own at Naukratis as did Aegina and Miletus (Herodotus ii. 178); the excavations yielded little material from the Heraion, but among it was a group of cups dedicated to Hera which are identified as of Samian origin (Prinz, *op. cit.*, p. 83; Lamb, *CVA*, Cambridge, Fasc. ii, p. 35, No. 71). The "floruit" of Fikellura ware, of which a substantial and thoroughly representative amount was found at Naukratis, is placed in the middle of the sixth century with most of the examples from the site falling in the period, 560–525 B.C. It seems probable that Samos was the chief, if not the only center, of this ware (Cook, *BSA*, XXXIV [1933–34], 90 ff.). This would not, of course, preclude the possibility that Samians were active there before the second quarter of the sixth century, but it seems significant that it is in this period they begin to interfere in the established trade routes of the Aegean (Smith, *op. cit.*, pp. 263–66; but see Hopper, *op. cit.*, p. 172, n. 43 on p. 173) and their activity under Polycrates bears a predatory character.

34. Herodotus i. 163.

35. See note 11 above.

36. The passage in Herodotus (i. 17–22) describing the warfare between Miletus and Alyattes would indicate that the Milesians had developed their local agriculture to a high degree and that the raising of grain was an important part of it. It is difficult to determine how great a part imported grain would play normally in their food supply since Herodotus' emphasis is on the sea as an avenue of supply in time of siege and his account may be colored somewhat by a comparison with Athenian efforts to assure their supply in the mid-fifth century.

37. The literary evidence of colonization is assembled by Bilabel, *Philologus, Supp. Band*, XIV (1920), 9–153. A re-examination of the traditional dating and the lowering of the chronology of the East Greek pottery classes has resulted in placing the foundation of the important and "key" colonies of Istrus, Olbia and Apollonia Pontica in the late seventh century, *ca.* 610–600 B.C. (Burn, *JHS*, LV [1935], 130 ff.; Cook, *JHS*, LXVI [1946], 82). A summary of recent Russian approaches to the problem, with bibliography, can be found in K. M. Kolobotha, *Vestnik Drevnii Istorii*, 1949, 2, 130 f.

38. See the references collected by Argenti, *Bibliography of Chios*, pp. 209 (*s.v.* Athenaios), 304 ff.

39. The dating of the Chian archaic coins is disputed. Baldwin (*AJN*, XLVIII [1914], 36 ff.) starts the series after 550 B.C., but admits the difficulty of dating the earliest examples to that period since they are very archaic in appearance; Mavrogordato (*Num. Chron.*, XV [1915], 17 ff.), on the other hand, starts the series in the last quarter of the seventh century. This dating would seem to have found general acceptance (Gardner, "The Financial History of Chios," *JHS*, XL [1920], 160; Seltman, *Greek Coins*, pp. 29 ff.). The majority of the early Chian coins are from Egypt. The archaic series are divided into two groups characterized by the presence of an amphora on the later and its absence on the earlier. Mavrogordato places the series with the amphora as starting *ca.* 545 B.C. There is a group of very early coins with the sphinx on the obverse, but on the Aeginetan standard (Head, *HN²*, p. 599; accepted as Chian); they are rejected by Baldwin (*op. cit.*, p. 55), but accepted by Gardner (*op. cit.*, p. 161) as representative of an early Chian venture to accommodate its trading activity to that of Aegina before its own standard was settled upon; certainly the connection between Aegina and Chios indicated by the finds of Chiot pottery dedicated at the Aphaia temple (see note 71 below) is suggestive of the correctness of this attribution. One of these coins (Head, *HN²*, p. 599) appears to have an amphora or grain of wheat stamped on it as a symbol.

40. Aristotle *Politics* 1259 a. The coupling of Chios and Miletus is interesting in the light of the evidence for their co-operation (Burn, *JHS*, XLIX [1929], 21–22, 36) in the political sphere.

41. Theopompus, *F. Gr. Hist.*, frag. 122 (quoted by Athenaeus vi. 88, 265C); Poseidonios of Apamea, *F. Gr. Hist.*, frag. 38 (quoted by Athenaeus vi. 91, 266EF); Nicolaus of Damascus, *F. Gr. Hist.*, frag. 95 (quoted by Athenaeus vi. 91, 266EF); Steph. Byz., *s.v.* Chios. Of more weight than these late writers are the interesting remarks of Thucydides (viii. 40. 2) that the Chians had the most slaves of any city except Sparta and punished them more severely because of their number; presumably many were used in agriculture, since Thucydides observes that they knew the country well. Westermann (*P.-W.*, *Supp.* VI, 900) connects this literary tradition of the Chians being the first to use non-Greek purchased slaves with the development of a specialized agriculture and industry, but questions the accuracy of Thucydides' assertion about their number (*ibid.*, p. 906).

42. Aristotle *Politics* 1291 b 24.

43. Bilabel, *op. cit.*, p. 214; Beloch suggests that the Chian colonization was earlier than that of Thasos on the mainland (*GG²*, I, 1, p. 254); note the importance of Ismarian wine, from the district of Maroneia, in the Homeric poems (*Il.* ix. 71–72; *Od.* ix. 196–98). We have little information about the city before the fifth century, but its coinage, on the same standard as that of the Thraco-Macedonian district, began before 500 B.C. (Head, *HN²*, p. 248).

44. Casson, *Macedonia, Thrace, and Illyria*, p. 91.

45. Harpokration, *s.v.* Stryme; Harpokration quotes Philochorus, who had cited Archilochus, with respect to a dispute between Thasos and Maroneia over Stryme. Apparently Thasos was successful, since Herodotus mentions Stryme as a Thasian possession (vii. 108). Its precise site is unknown, but it evidently lay to the east of Maroneia (Meritt, Wade-Gery, McGregor, *The Athenian Tribute Lists*, I, 517–19).

46. Archilochus frag. 2 (Diehl).

47. Rostovtzeff (*Social and Economic History of the Hellenistic World*, I, 111 ff.; see also Casson, *op. cit.*, chap. II) has reviewed the archaeological evidence for Greco-Thracian trading, but mainly for eastern Thrace, which is slightly better known; for that area it is suggested that Cyzicus was the distributor of Ionian goods through the medium of Apollonia. Our first glimpse in any detail of conditions in western Thrace and Macedonia is the description given by Herodotus of Xerxes' march; at that time various cities were called upon for supplies and furnished them, albeit with some difficulty. The fertility of Thrace, however, had made an impression as early as the Homeric period (*Il.* xx. 485). Thus Ionian Greeks had been looking to it for some years before it appeared as a potential haven for some of them from Persian control (*e.g.*, the Teans, Histiaeus, and Aristagoras). The Persian occupation of Thrace was followed at no great interval by the Ionian revolt; if economic causes were partly responsible, as is usually assumed, some part of the grievance should lie in that. We do not, however, have any explicit evidence of its use as a grain supply before the Athenian interest in the region for that purpose in the fourth century. It is to be remembered that Methone looked to the Black Sea for its supply, with Athenian permission, in the early part of the Peloponnesian War (Tod, *Greek Historical Inscriptions*, No. 61). It would seem probable, however, that viticulture was early developed in certain regions at least: Ismarian wine from the locality of Maroneia was famous in Homeric times and liked by Archilochus (notes 43 and 46); Thasos would probably have developed its vineyards in the sixth century. There is some evidence, however, that foreign wine was imported into the Pangaeus region and farther west into Illyria for a long period. It seems hardly necessary to cite evidence for an extensive use of wine in this region of Dionysos and reputedly heavy drinkers. Theopompus (*F. Gr. Hist.*, frag. 129; May, *op. cit.*, p. 12, n. 1) observes that sherds of Thasian and Chian jars were found in the River Naro in Illyria; we do not, of course, know their date, but they were probably identified by the stamps, use of which began in the late fifth century. It is also apparent that foreign wine might be imported into the littoral of the Pangaeus region to the detriment of Thasian production and sale in the last quarter of the fifth century. Daux has published an interesting inscription (*BCH*, L (1926), 214–26, No. 2) prohibiting the importation of foreign wine in Thasian ships to the mainland. There was, then, evidently a demand for wine which the Thasians hoped to fill from their own vineyards. The extent of the mainland is interpreted by Daux (pp. 224–25) as extending from Athos, mentioned in the inscription, to the neighborhood of Stryme. It is unlikely, however, that Stryme was the eastern point, if Daux has a continuous strip of coast in mind, for it lay east of Maroneia (see note 45); that would imply Thasian control of Abderan and Maroneian territory. Probably the eastern limit of Thasian control was contiguous with the western boundary of Abdera. The mention of Thasian merchant vessels is the first explicit mention of such a fleet in operation although its growth would have coincided with the expansion of Thasian control of the mainland.

48. Cook, *BSA*, XLIV (1949), 159.

49. Gardner, *JHS*, XL (1920), 161.

50. See note 26; very little Chiot pottery has been found on Siphnos (Cook, *op. cit.*, p. 159).

51. *Ibid.*; here again excavation may change the picture.

52. Seltman, *Greek Coins*, pp. 29 ff.

53. The sphinx, rosette, cock's head, lotus; Svoronos (*JIAN*, 1919, pp. 219–20) was moved to detach these early coins from Chios and assign them to Assoros, but has found no support (Dressel and Regling, *op. cit.*, p. 66); for the significance of the symbols see Lederer, *Zeit. f. Num.*, XLI (1931), 252.

54. Beloch, *GG²*, I, 1, p. 294; on Abdera and the coinage of the Thraco-Macedonian region see May, *op. cit.*, pp. 13–16 and 34.

55. Chiot pottery has been found at Istria, Kertch, Berezan and Olbia (Cook, *op. cit.*, p. 160); for the composition of the Ionian fleet at Lade see Herodotus vi. 8.

56. Burn, *JHS*, XLIX (1929), 22–23.

57. Tod, *Greek Historical Inscriptions*, No. 23.

58. Strabo xvii. 1. 18, 801; the literary evidence for the foundation is summarized by Ure, *Origin of Tyranny*, pp. 103–5.

59. Herodotus (ii. 178) mentions the sanctuary founded by Milesians to Apollo; many of the dedications designate Apollo as Milesian (*Naukratis*, I, 60–62, Nos. 2, 99, 110, 218, 219, 233, 234, 237, 341) and one as Didymaion (No. 164). The bulk of the pottery was found in a trench containing the discarded votives of the sanctuary; the accumulation dates from the late seventh century, well before the reign of Amasis. The sanctuary occupies a central position among those at the north end of Naukratis and is probably the oldest of the group comprising the Heraion, Hellenion and sanctuary of the Dioscuri.

60. Prinz, *op. cit.*, pp. 38 f.; it is no longer maintained, of course, that the pottery published by Prinz as Milesian and used as evidence of its trading activity was all made in Miletus or carried by Milesian traders.

61. *Ibid.*, pp. 118–19.

62. Tean: *Naukratis* I, 61, No. 209 (Apollo Sanctuary); *ibid.*, II, 68, No. 876 (Apollo Sanctuary); *ibid.*, I, 62, No. 700 (Aphrodite Sanctuary); *ibid.*, II, 64, No. 758 (Aphrodite Sanctuary); *ibid.*, II, 65, No. 779 (Aphrodite Sanctuary). Lesbian: *ibid.*, II, 65, Nos. 786, 788–90 (Aphrodite Sanctuary); *JHS*, XXV (1905), 117, No. 40. Chian: *Naukratis*, II, 63, No. 706; 64, No. 757 (Aphrodite Sanctuary); *BSA*, V (1898–99), 55, No. 51 (Apollo Sanctuary); No. 60 (Hellenion). Phocaean: *Naukratis*, I, 62, No. 666 (Dioscuri

Sanctuary); *JHS*, XXV (1905), 117, No. 39. Milesian: *ibid.*, p. 117, Nos. 18, 19 (Hellenion). Rhodian: *ibid.*, p. 117, No. 16 (Hellenion). Naukratite (?): *ibid.*, p. 117, No. 27. Prinz identified three Samian dedications on the evidence of the names (*op. cit.*, p. 118): *Naukratis*, II, 64, No. 778; 65, Nos. 804–5 (Aphrodite Sanctuary); a Cnidian on the basis of the letter forms: *ibid.*, I, 62, No. 237 (Apollo Sanctuary). To judge from the form of the names there are four dedications made by Greco-Egyptians: *ibid.*, II, 63, No. 741 (Aegyptios); 64, No. 754 (Psende. . . .); No. 766 (Negomandros); No. 767 (Philammonos?). All are from the Aphrodite Sanctuary; the last two names are scratched on Laconian ware and thus may be the names of Cyreneans since Laconian ware was probably brought to Naukratis through that medium (Lane, *BSA*, XXXIV [1933–34], 184).

63. Teans: *Naukratis*, I, 61, No. 209; *ibid.*, II, 68, No. 876. Dorian: *ibid.*, I, 61, No. 104; 62, No. 237. Phanes: Herodotus iii. 4, 11 and *Naukratis*, I, 61, No. 218. Chian: *BSA*, V (1898–99), 55, No. 51. Milesian: *JHS*, XXV (1905), 117, No. 19.

64. A literary tradition preserved by Athenaeus (xv. 675F, quoting from Polycharmus of Naukratis) connects the cult, very doubtfully, with the Paphian Aphrodite of Cyprus, but the archaeological evidence suggests that Chians may have been the founders. In Athenaeus' story, Herostratus, a Naukratite, was making a commercial voyage in the 23rd Olympiad (688 B.C.) in the course of which he touched at Paphos and bought a small statuette of Aphrodite. She saved his ship during a storm so that upon his arrival in Naukratis he dedicated the statuette to Aphrodite in her temple there. It is evidently a story attached to some archaic dedication in the temple like those which appear in the Lindian chronicle. The date appears to be much too early although it has recently been taken at its face value. H. L. F. Lutz ("An Attempt to Interpret the Name of the City of Naukratis," *Univ. of Calif. Publications in Semitic Philology*, X [1943], No. 12, 275–76) accepts the connection with the Paphian Aphrodite and suggests that the Aphrodite cult in Naukratis was in existence before the arrival of the Greeks and thus represents an assimilation with a Phoenician cult of Astarte. A similar suggestion is made for the Apollo cult, the result of assimilation with an indigenous or Phoenician god. Unfortunately for the suggestion, there is very little evidence of Phoenician activity at Naukratis, and the evidence of the excavation shows that both the Apollo and Aphrodite sanctuaries were founded as Greek shrines on the basal mud of the site. There is no pre-existent shrine in either case and the offerings found are almost entirely Greek in character from the start. The sanctuary of Aphrodite was located in the southern part of Naukratis at some distance from the group of shrines around the Apollo sanctuary (see note 59) and near the Egyptian community. The pottery found in it indicates that its foundation was as early as that of the Sanctuary of Apollo; a very large proportion of this pottery is Chiot which may indicate the nationality of its founders and chief patrons during the early sixth century. The cult was that of Aphrodite Pandemos and was duplicated in the Hellenion after that sanctuary was founded (*BSA*, V [1898–99], 56, No. 107 and *Naukratis*, II, 66, Nos. 818 and 821). This duplication may represent the formal participation of Chios in the Hellenion (Herodotus ii. 178). Hogarth considered that the Hellenion was probably built at

the time of Amasis' reorganization (*JHS*, XXV [1905], 136; see also Price, *JHS*, XLIV [1924], 192, 204). Herodotus' failure to mention the shrine of Aphrodite and its location apart from the other Greek sanctuaries prompted the suggestion that it might have been that of the city in distinction to those of the traders (Prinz, *op. cit.*, pp. 115, 119).

65. See note 62. Two female names are among the dedications, possibly those of hetaerae: *Naukratis*, II, 63, No. 712 (Iunx); No. 745 (Mikis). Aphrodite was referred to as the Aphrodite in Naukratis (*ibid.*, p. 64, No. 768) or more specifically as Pandemos (see note 64).

66. Prinz, *op. cit.*, p. 83; *Naukratis*, II, 60–61.

67. *Naukratis*, I, 62, No. 666; *ibid.*, II, 30–32 and 67, Nos. 833–38.

68. See note 62. The Hellenion was correctly identified by Hogarth (*BSA*, V [1898–99], 26 ff.; *JHS*, XXV [1905], 105 ff.). It seems to have contained various groups of chambers dedicated to separate deities: Aphrodite, Artemis, Herakles, Athena (?), the Dioscuri (a group of dedications was found in a chamber, but they may be strays from the Dioscuri sanctuary), and Poseidon (?). There were also numerous dedications to the gods of the Hellenes on which the identification rests.

69. Cf. the identifications made by Gjerstad (*LAAA*, XXI [1934], 80) with the classifications of Petrie.

70. Lesbian: *Naukratis*, II, 64, Nos. 786–93; Samian: Prinz, *op. cit.*, p. 83; Cnidian: *ibid.*, pp. 82 f.

71. *Naukratis*, II, 63, No. 706; p. 64, No. 757. The most interesting example, No. 768, is the Chiot vase with the dedication to Aphrodite in Naukratis painted before firing. It was presumably made as the result of a special order placed at the kiln by a merchant before sailing. Dedications on Chiot ware painted before firing were also found at the temple of Aphaia in Aegina (Furtwaengler, *Aegina*, pp. 455–56). The fragments from Naukratis have been used as evidence for the origin in Naukratis of Chiot ware, as it is now called rather than "Naukratite" (see note 73).

72. Chiot on Attic: *BSA*, V (1898–99), 55, No. 60; Tean on Chiot: *Naukratis*, II, 64, No. 758; p. 65, No. 779; Greco-Egyptian on Chiot: *ibid.*, p. 63, No. 741; p. 64, No. 754; Samian on Chiot: *ibid.*, p. 65, No. 778 (Rhoecus, the sculptor); Cyrenaic on Laconian: *ibid.*, p. 64, Nos. 766–67.

73. Since the excavations of Kourouniotes (*Deltion*, II [1916], 190–214) and Lamb (*BSA*, XXXV [1934–35], 138–63) in Chios, the view that "Naukratite" pottery is of Chian rather than local origin would seem to be accepted (Cook, *JHS*, LVII [1937], 228, n. 9: *BSA*, XLIV [1949], 154). The earliest pieces of this fabric in Naukratis are dated by Cook in the last quarter of the seventh century, but the bulk of it belongs to the first half of the sixth. As Cook has already noticed the Chian origin of the ware and the Chian dedications found on the pottery of Naukratis indicate a close connection between the two places.

74. Price, *JHS*, XLIV (1924), 222; see note 64.

75. See note 62.

76. *Papyruskunde*, I, 1, pp. 13, 51; I, 2, pp. 44 f., No. 27. These indications of the development of Naukratis as a Greek polis at an early period rather than a group of trading factories will be discussed in a forthcoming study of the organization and growth of the city.

THE ORGANIZATION OF
NAUKRATIS

IN A previous article concerning the grain trade between Greece and Egypt in the archaic period it was observed that the pottery dedicated in the earliest sanctuaries at Naukratis, those of Apollo and Aphrodite, showed that the sanctuaries were in common use by Greeks of various origins.[1] The suggestion was made that at an early date in the history of the settlement the sanctuaries lost their character as the peculiar possession of special deities of various other city states and came to be regarded as the sanctuaries of the city of Naukratis, a unified community in its own right. These considerations raise doubts about the familiar reconstruction of the settlement as a group of trading factories existing side by side with one another and with a community of Naukratite citizens. In order to see whether this picture can be revised it is necessary to consider carefully the remarks of Herodotus, our chief literary source:[2]

Moreover Amasis became a lover of the Hellenes; and besides other proofs of friendship which he gave to several among them, he also granted the city of Naucratis for those of them who came to Egypt to dwell in; and to those who did not desire to stay, but who made voyages thither, he granted portions of land to set up altars and make sacred enclosures [temene] for their gods. Their greatest enclosure and that one which has most name and is most frequented is called the Hellenion, and this was established by the following cities in common: —of the Ionians Chios, Teos, Phocaia, Clazomenai, of the Dorians Rhodes, Cnidos, Halicarnassos, Phaselis, and of the Aiolians Mytilene alone. To these belongs this enclosure and these are the cities which appoint superintendents of the port [prostatai of the emporion]; and all other cities which claim a share in it, are making a claim without any right. Besides this the Eginetans established on their own account a sacred enclosure dedicated to Zeus, the Samians one to Hera, and the Milesians one to Apollo. Now in old times Naucratis alone was an open trading place [emporion], and no other place in Egypt; and if any one came to other of the Nile mouths, he was compelled to swear that he came not thither of his own will, and when he had thus sworn his own innocence he had to sail with his ship to the Canobic mouth, or if it were not possible to sail by reason of contrary winds, then he had to carry his cargo round the head of the Delta in boats to Naucratis; thus highly was Naucratis privileged.

In their interpretations of this passage Prinz and other scholars[3] have assumed that a very close relationship existed between the individual sanctuaries and trading factories and that such units were separated administratively from the city of Naukratis. The whole settlement was a composite community: each sanctuary had its own emporion, an establishment with docks, warehouses and the like, while, in addition, the city of Naukratis possessed one for its own uses. Each separate trading factory was under the direction of some type of trade official (the prostatai) appointed by the "mother-city." The city of Naukratis formed a separate area of administration with its own magistrates and institutions, of which there may be a survival in the timouchoi mentioned by Hermeias.[4] Hasebroek has suggested some modification in this picture, in accordance with his general view that trade in Greek cities was largely in the hands of noncitizens.[5] He has argued that the community was divided into two parts: citizens and traders (noncitizens), suggesting that Amasis placed the jurisdiction of the port in the hands of the latter, but that these had no separate *emporia*. The officials in charge of the port (the *prostatai*) had functions of policing and jurisdiction such as were possessed by the later Athenian overseers of the port of Peiraeus.

Before discussing the details of these reconstructions there are certain general points in Herodotus' description to be emphasized. In the first place Herodotus' focus of interest is the philhellenism of Amasis and the manner in which it is shown. It is not so much Naukratis *per se* in which he is interested, but Naukratis as an example of privilege granted to Greeks. Thus, the remarks on the organization of the community and on the concentration of trade through Naukratis are incidental. Secondly, Herodotus' observations on Naukratis do not all refer to the period of Amasis, although the general impression created is that Amasis was the architect of Naukratis. Amasis, having become a philhellene, gave Naukratis as a city to those Greeks who came to Egypt for permanent residence; he also gave land to traders, who came intermittently, for the purpose of founding sanctuaries to their own deities. Herodotus' remarks about the Hellenion, however, refer to his own period: it is the most important sanctuary and its founding states furnish the *prostatai* of the *emporion;* other cities claim this right but do so improperly. This relationship between the Hellenion and the administration of the port must have dated from the foundation of the Hellenion, but Herodotus does not tell us specifically when it was founded. There is, perhaps, an implication that it was founded in the time of Amasis. We are next given the information that three cities, Miletus, Aegina, and Samos, founded their own sanctuaries, perhaps in the period of Amasis, but it is not so stated. We might infer that these are excluded from a share in the administration of the port, since they did not participate in the founding of the Hellenion. They, as well as late comers to Naukratis such as Athens, may be among those mentioned by Herodotus who claim a share without justification. Finally we are told that "of old" Naukratis alone in Egypt was an *emporion* and that overseas trade was concentrated in it. Herodotus was presumably looking back from the vantage point of his own period, when conditions were otherwise, but he does not tell us whether this condition was established by Amasis or was that of some other king.

Two difficult problems are raised by a consideration of the passage in connection with the archeological evidence: in the first place, the position of Naukratis with respect to the Egyptian government, and, secondly, the communal organization of Naukratis itself. They are presumably connected, for Naukratis, whatever the exact date of its foundation, was established in an organized, civilized state which had the power to settle the conditions on which foreigners might reside in it; the conditions might be such as to strongly influence the form of the foreign community.

Herodotus certainly had the impression that Amasis II (*ca.* 569–528 B.C.) either was the founder or was responsible for a thorough-going organization of the community. As Cook has cogently argued, the archeological evidence does not accord with either of these views.[6] The date of the pottery found on the site indicates that Naukratis was settled by Greeks in the last quarter of the seventh century; and its uniform quantity throughout the sixth century, that there was no marked increase of population in Amasis' reign. Cook has also pointed out that there is no justification for the modern view that Amasis concentrated the Greeks residing elsewhere in Egypt into Naukratis by recalling the mercenaries from the eastern frontier.[7] Herodotus tells us that Amasis did move the soldiers from Stratopeda to Memphis,[8] but Daphnae, also a garrison town, and seemingly not to be identified as a civilian town near Stratopeda, was apparently left untouched.[9] The greater part of the Greek archaic pottery found at scattered points in Egypt dates from the period of Amasis.[10] Thus, there may have been a rather freer intercourse of Greeks and Egyptians at that time than previously. This supposed concentration of the Greeks already in Egypt to Naukratis might, of course, be considered another facet of the policy of channeling trade through Naukratis. It would enable an easier control to be exercised over the foreign residents and, in the case of the trade, permit import duties to be collected more easily and smuggling to be checked.[11] Herodotus, however, does not specifically connect this regulation with Amasis and there does not seem to be any evidence for the collection of import duties by the Egyptian government before the regulations of the Naukratite stele in the fourth century B.C.[12] Thus, while we may accept the fact of the concentration of trade, another explanation of it is needed. Further, it is apparent that the activity of Amasis in connection with Naukratis has been greatly exaggerated, however firmly such a tradition was fixed by Herodotus' period.

The explanation of this exaggeration is probably to be sought in a combination of the undoubted philhellenism of the latter part of Amasis' reign, when the threat of Persia made overtures to the Greeks a matter of political expediency, and in the usual practice of a Pharaoh of confirming a predecessor's regulations in such terms that they appeared to be of his own making. Thus, it is likely that a predecessor of Amasis—probably Psammetichus I (ca. 663–610 B.C.), to judge from the tradition preserved by Strabo[13]—granted lands for settlement to the Greeks at Naukratis and concentrated the general trading activity of the Greeks to that point. He was apparently the first of the Saite kings to make use of Greek mercenaries in some numbers[14] and, if Diodorus is to be credited, encouraged trading with the Greeks.[15] Since Naukratis was in the neighborhood of Sais it would have been desirable to regulate and keep an eye on his new associates. Probably, too, seventh century Greek trade was so nearly akin to piracy[16] that the regulations were designed to prevent pillaging in the Delta rather than to enable the collection of import duties.

Amasis probably came to the throne on a wave of Egyptian nationalist feeling against his predecessor Apries,[17] but found that Egypt's overseas trade was in the hands of Greeks and that continued use of Greek mercenaries was necessary. He evidently did move some of them to Memphis, possibly very soon after his defeat of Apries. So far as Naukratis was concerned, he probably reconfirmed, in his own name, the original conditions on which settlement had been allowed, but apparently did not try to enforce the regulations for the concentration of trade. The growth of Persian power after the middle of the century made it necessary to cultivate rather than constrain the Greeks. It is significant that the acts of goodwill towards various Greek communities which can be dated were performed in the latter part of his reign[18] so that their tradition was still strong in the fifth century: Amasis appeared the most prominent and most philhellene of the Saite kings in Greek eyes.

If the reconstruction proposed above is correct, Naukratis' history as a Greek town began in the reign of Psammetichus I,[19] to judge from the archeological evidence, in its latter part. At that time some Greeks would have settled for permanent residence on the lands granted by the king; others, from time to time, as their interest grew, would have taken advantage of the privilege of founding their sanctuaries. The pottery dedicated in the sanctuaries indicates that a common use was very soon made of them for purposes of worship. Did the community coalesce in similar fashion, creating an organization for itself and controlling its economic life, or did various Greek cities control it by sending representatives as Herodotus states?

Herodotus remarks that the nine founding states of the Hellenion furnished the *prostatai* of the *emporion*. As we have noticed, these *prostatai* are usually considered to have been some type of official in charge of trade. Prinz, by analogy, suggests that the three states with separate sanctuaries, Samos, Miletus, and Aegina, had separate trading factories for which each supplied its own *prostatai*.[20] In short, the administration of the main activity of Naukratis and the jurisdiction of the numerous questions which would arise from it are considered to have been in the hands of noncitizens appointed by various Greek states. This does not, on the face of it, seem a very happy arrangement either for adjusting relations between the various concessions, between concessions and the Greek city of Naukratis, or between these units and Egypt. On examination, in fact, this interpretation of Herodotus does not seem justified.

Herodotus does not state or imply that there were *emporia* attached to the separate *temene* for purposes of trade. While it is difficult to restore the physical features of archaic Naukratis from the scanty topographical traces discovered in the excavation, the sanctuaries appear to have been only religious establishments with small temples, altars, and open precincts. The Hellenion had various groups of chambers, but these were apparently shrines dedicated to separate deities. There was probably a single dock and warehouse area along the river bank, but its very existence implies the need for a common regulating authority.[21] If the *prostatai* were officials in general charge of the port and responsible to Amasis, as Hasebroek has suggested, there was such an authority. But the meaning of the terms used by Herodotus is open to question. Herodotus uses *emporion* in chapter 179 unmistakably of Naukratis as a whole, not of the *emporion* of a separate sanctuary, or even of the *emporion* of the whole city. Thus, the word is hardly likely to have the more restricted sense assigned to it in chapter 178. In fact, Herodotus normally uses *emporion* to designate whole and independent communities which had an essentially trading and mercantile existence.[22] It would seem reasonable, then, that in chapter 178 he means the whole community of Naukratis by *emporion*. The interpretation of *prostatai* as some type of trade-consul or official in charge of trade is not supported by its other occurrences in Herodotus. Elsewhere, it is used in the sense of political leader of a state or people.[23] It is such a general word, however, that it might include a technical and limited meaning or be rendered by "representative," but it does seem significant that the word, in fifth century usage, does not have either of the suggested connotations.[24] Thus, it is preferable to understand Herodotus in general terms only: he means the chief magistrates or leaders of the whole community of Naukratis. This solution, however, might seem to raise a more difficult question. Was the whole community of Naukratis administered by officials appointed by those Greek states which had founded the Hellenion?

An analogy for such an institution may be found in the *epidemiourgoi* which Corinth appointed for its colony of Potidaea even when Potidaea was a member of the Athenian empire.[25] In that case, however, only one city state, Corinth, was concerned with the administration of its own colony; in Naukratis nine states and possibly twelve, if we include Samos, Miletus, and Aegina, were involved. It would necessitate a most unusual degree of co-operation between states which were, on different occasions, at variance elsewhere in the Aegean. Further, some of them, namely Phocaea, Teos, and Miletus, ceased to exist as important and independent communities in the archaic period. More important than these general objections, however, is the evidence that Lindos, and later Rhodes, when the synoecism of the island had taken place, appointed Naukratite citizens as *proxenoi*.[26] Rhodes, of course, was one of the founders of the Hellenion. It is significant that Rhodes conceived its relationship with Naukratis in the same terms as its relationship with other Greek cities—the interests of Rhodes in Naukratis were looked after by a Naukratite citizen, not by a Rhodian representative from its own citizen body. Athens, too, appointed a Naukratite, Theogenes, as its *proxenos* in the fourth century.[27] The evidence for the Rhodian *proxenoi* is little more than a generation later than Herodotus and we have no reason to believe that the organi-

zation of Naukratis was fundamentally changed in the interval. Further, it is apparent that, while Herodotus speaks of the founders of the Hellenion furnishing *prostatai* in his own period, the institution is conceived by him as dating from the foundation of the Hellenion. Herodotus, then, seems to have misunderstood, or expressed awkwardly, the nature of the situation. Before considering that problem it would be advisable to see if there is other evidence supporting the view that Naukratis had developed into a unified Greek state at an early date with a consequent growth of its own institutions and traditions.

While the evidence is very scanty, it does confirm the impression that Naukratis acted and was recognized by other Greek cities as a normal city state. Literary references are to Naukratis and Naukratites.[28] The latter contributed to the funds of Delphi and are mentioned in the inscriptions recording contributions in the same manner as the citizens from other states.[29] As soon as the city had an opportunity, in the interval between the conquest of Egypt by Alexander and the proclamation of his own kingdom by Ptolemy I, it issued an independent coinage.[30] It seems established that the city retained its Greek character and institutions as a self-governing city under the Ptolemies.[31] Its laws served as a model for those of Antinoupolis when that city was founded, with the significant exception that the citizens of Antinoupolis were allowed to intermarry with Egyptians whereas those of Naukratis were not.[32] It is to be noticed that there is little evidence of intermarriage in the archaic period.[33] What evidence we have is unanimous that Naukratis was a normal Greek community and desired to remain so.

Why, then, if Naukratis was regarded by the Greeks as an independent city state, did Herodotus state that certain Greek cities sent representatives to govern it? He plainly connected the system of administration with the foundation of the Hellenion. Unfortunately there is no very precise indication of that event. Herodotus does not attribute the foundation specifically to Amasis, but probably implies such an act by the statements about the grants of land and the subsequent foundation of the sanctuaries. Yet there is reason to believe that Amasis only reconfirmed the grants of a predecessor, probably Psammetichus I. Thus, the Hellenion may have been founded before the time of Amasis. The archeological evidence is inconclusive. While the larger part of the material from the Hellenion is later in date than that from the sanctuaries of Apollo and Aphrodite, the material is from its period of use; it is not evidence of construction.[34] Probably, however, it was built later than the other two sanctuaries.

One fact of some significance in this connection is that there appears to be a duplication of cult among its shrines. Aphrodite Pandemos was worshipped in both the Aphrodite sanctuary in the southern part of Naukratis and in the Hellenion.[35] It was suggested in a previous article that the Aphrodite sanctuary was probably a Chian foundation, indicative of the prominent part which Chios played in the growth of Naukratis.[36] Chios, too, was one of the founding states of the Hellenion. Thus, it seems probable that we have in this duplication evidence of a reorganization of the early community for the purpose of creating a unified Naukratis. The residents from Chios and other states joined together to pool their interests and administer the community. The Hellenion was founded to accommodate their small shrines in a common sanctuary, possibly incorporating a certain number of preexistent shrines. As Herodotus tells us the

move was effective; the Hellenion became the center of the city. The above mentioned Lindian proxeny decree was set up there. Those individuals who participated in this foundation became the citizens of Naukratis, and it served as the core for the political organization of the state. It is of some significance that in the Ptolemaic period no evidence of an organization by demes or tribes has been found.[37]

The separate sanctuaries of Miletus, Samos, and Aegina presumably remained outside this civic organization—they remained simply religious sanctuaries. Their citizens came to Naukratis to trade, but they had no share in the administration of the city; if they wished to become citizens and reside there, they were confronted with a problem similar to that existing in other Greek states. They had to be accepted by the organization centering in the Hellenion. Presumably they were admitted by some means as individuals and helped to increase the citizen body, but the nucleus of the Greeks of Naukratis must have been the citizens originally from the states mentioned as founding the Hellenion and their descendants. This reconstruction presumes two stages in the early growth of Naukratis: first a group of traders and residents who had taken advantage of the land grants made by the Egyptian king to found their own sanctuaries in filial fashion. They were probably administered by representatives sent out by the "mother-cities," but, as might have been expected in a community isolated in a foreign land which discouraged assimilation with its own citizens, a desire for a unified community of their own soon asserted itself. In creating such a community the citizens of those states most interested in the trade with Naukratis, who were already in residence in the settlement, took the lead. Probably the moving spirits were the citizens from Chios.

The result was the creation of Naukratis as a unified political comm nity through and around the Hellenion. When Herodotus speaks of its founding states as furnishing the magistrates of Naukratis, he is speaking inexactly; it is rather the citizens originally from those states and their descendants, who were still aware of their origin through the continuance of their cults, who furnished the magistrates. It might be objected that Miletus should have had some share in this move, if not taken the lead, by virtue of its claims as the original founder of the settlement at Naukratis. These original Milesians, however, may have been a group of mercenaries, in a somewhat different relation to the Egyptian state from that of the Greeks who came to trade and settle. The trading interests of Miletus do not seem to have been as strong in Egypt as usually supposed. As argued in the previous article the important trading cities, whose business interests might have led their citizens to settle in Naukratis, were the eastern Greeks of the northern Aegean area, particularly Chios, and of the southeastern Aegean, centered around Rhodes.[38] They were the founders of the Hellenion: Chios, Teos, Phocaea, Clazomenae, Mytilene, Rhodes, Cnidus, Halicarnassus, and Phaselis. They were also the political founders of Naukratis and their descendants formed the main element of its population.

UNIVERSITY OF CHICAGO

NOTES

1. C. Roebuck, "The Grain Trade Between Greece and Egypt," *CP*, XLV (1950), 241–42.

2. Herodotus 2. 178–79; translated by G. C. Macaulay, I (Macmillan, 1904), 199–200.

3. H. Prinz, "Funde aus Naukratis," *Klio*, Beiheft VII (1908), 5–6, 115–16; see also G. Glotz, *Ancient Greece at Work*, pp. 107, 113, 119–20; Glotz-Cohen, *Histoire grecque*, I, 204–7; Hall, *CAH*, III, 292.

4. *FHG*, II, 80–81; quoted by Athenaeus 4. 149 F. This Hermeias was the author of a book on the Gryneion Apollo; the *timouchoi* of Naukratis are mentioned as possessing the right to levy fines for certain violations of festivals held in the prytaneion. Müller identified the author with Hermeias of Methymna, of the fourth century B.C., but only on the grounds that it is probable a Methymnaean would be writing of the Gryneion Apollo, since the sanctuary was in that region; the identification was rejected by F. Jacoby in *P.-W.*, VIII, 731. 6, and Müller's reason is certainly not convincing. If Hermeias does belong to the fourth century B.C. it would, of course, be very likely that the *timouchoi* were an early Naukratite institution. It would, however, be difficult to determine from which city it was originally borrowed, for *timouchoi* are known for several cities which were active at Naukratis in the archaic period: Teos, Miletus, and at Massilia, the Phocaean colony (attested at least for the second century B.C.: *Syll.*³, 591; Strabo 4. 1. 5, 179) as well as in other Ionian and Aeolic cities (Busolt-Swoboda, *Griechische Staatskunde*, I, 357; Schulthess, *P.-W.*, VI², 1366–68; Wilhelm, *Jahreshefte*, XII [1909], 137–38; Robert, *BCH*, LII [1928], 167–68). The earliest example is from Teos in the well known inscription in which the *timoucheontes* are required to protect the state from various dangers (Tod, *Greek Historical Inscriptions*, No. 23). Wilcken also identifies *timouchoi* as an institution among the Hellenomemphites (*ca.* 200 B.C.; *Papyruskunde*, I, 2, pp. 48–50, No. 30. 16).

5. Hasebroek, *Trade and Politics in Ancient Greece* (translated by L. M. Fraser and D. C. MacGregor [London, 1933]), pp. 60 ff.; idem, *Griechische Wirtschafts- und Gesellschafts-Geschichte bis zur Perserzeit*, pp. 282–83.

6. R. M. Cook, "Amasis and the Greeks in Egypt," *JHS*, LVII (1937), 227–37.

7. *Ibid.*, pp. 229–30, 233–35.

8. Her. 2. 154.

9. Cook, *op. cit.*, p. 234. From Herodotus' general description Daphnae and Stratopeda were in the same region (2. 154; 2. 30), but, as Cook points out, Herodotus does not identify them as the same place. He does, however, state that Stratopeda was in ruins in his own time, while Daphnae was still garrisoned. It seems probable that Daphnae is to be identified with Tell-Defenneh, excavated by Petrie, but there is no reason to identify Tell-Defenneh, Daphnae and Stratopeda as Petrie did (*Tanis*, II, 48). The Greek pottery found at Tell-Defenneh is to be dated in the period of Amasis.

10. Cook, *op. cit.*, pp. 230, 236–37.

11. Kees, *P.-W.*, XVI, 1960–61.

12. Erman and Wilcken, *Zeitschrift für Ägyptische Sprache und Altertumskunde*, XXXVIII (1900), 127–35; Gunn, *Journal of Egyptian Archaeology*, XXIX (1943), 55–59. The stele, found at Naukratis, indicates that a 10% tax was placed on all imports from the Aegean and on Naukratite production; the proceeds were used as an endowment for the temple of Neith. The stele bears the name of King Nḫt-nb-f (Nektanebos I, *ca.* 380–360 B.C.), the predecessor of Teos. Kees has suggested (*loc. cit.*) that these levies probably go back to the regulations of Amasis, since they reflect the fundamentals of old Pharaonic economic practice (see also Kees, *Kulturgeschichte d. AO: Ägypten*, pp. 105–6). Edgerton, however, objects that there does not appear to be any evidence that import duties were collected by the Egyptian govern-

ment during the Empire ("The Nauri Decree of Seti I," *Journal of Near Eastern Studies*, VI [1947], 229). In a note written to me on this point Professor Edgerton has observed: "In sum: import duties *may* be an old Pharaonic device, but I have not yet seen any affirmative evidence which seems to me to point in that direction."

13. Strabo 17. 1. 18, 801; Strabo assigns the foundation of the Milesian fort to the days of Psammetichus, who is described as a contemporary of Cyaxares (this is usually rejected as a gloss; see Hirschfeld, *Rhein. Mus.*, XLII [1887], 211 and Ure, *Origin of Tyranny*, pp. 90–91); the Milesians are said to have later sailed up into the Saite nome and to have founded Naukratis after defeating Inaros. Inaros is otherwise unknown in this connection. He may have been a rival of Psammetichus against whom the king used Milesian mercenaries, afterwards settling them in Naukratis, or there may be some confusion in Strabo's mind with the Inaros of the fifth century. In any case the earliest Greek pottery found at Naukratis is dated in the period of Psammetichus I or Necho II, in the last quarter of the seventh century.

14. Herodotus 2. 152; Hall, *CAH*, III, 291; Parke, *Greek Mercenary Soldiers*, pp. 4–6.

15. Diodorus 1. 66. 8: "Psammetichus used to provide cargoes for the merchants, and particularly for Phoenicians and Greeks." See Ure, *op. cit.*, p. 89.

16. There is a tradition of a Naukratite foray up the Nile preserved in Aristagoras of Miletus (*FHG*, II, 99, Frag. 6). See also *Odyssey* 14. 257 ff.

17. The stele of the death of Apries states that Apries roused the Greeks in an attempt to recover sovereignty (*Rec. Trav.*, XXII [1900], 1–9). Amasis' policy toward the Greeks is usually interpreted as an example of double-dealing (Glotz, *Histoire grecque*, I, 204 ff.; Kees, *P.-W.*, XVI, 1959; Cook, *op. cit.*, p. 232). Whatever his motives, Amasis was scarcely in a position, after the first few years of his reign, to estrange the Greeks.

18. Cf. Cook, *op. cit.*, p. 232.

19. This solution of the conflict between the archeological and literary evidence is not, of course, new; see, for example, Hall, *CAH*, III, 292.

20. Prinz, *op. cit.*, pp. 5–6.

21. Prinz has printed a composite plan from those published in the successive excavation reports (*ibid.*, Pl. I). Its indications and the reports show the difficulties of restoration. No agora was identified in Naukratis, but Hogarth suggested that it might have been in the Hellenion or in the Heraion (*BSA*, V [1898–99], 44). The former, however, was occupied by the separate shrines and the latter by a temple, like the precincts of Apollo and Aphrodite. The most plausible suggestion is that warehouses, shops, and business district were closely associated with the docks along the river bank (*ibid.*, p. 40; note the revisions made in Naukratite topography by Kees, *op. cit.*, 1955–56).

22. Herodotus (Liddell and Scott cite no examples from earlier writers; see also Buck and Petersen, *A Reverse Index of Greek Nouns and Adjectives*, p. 105, *s.v.* -τόριος) uses the word in the general sense of a community whose main activity was trade, rather than in the restricted sense of "harbor-market," an area distinct from the city which controlled it. Also there does not seem to be any necessary connotation

of control by another city as implied in the translation "trading-factory." Of the examples in Herodotus (Powell, *Lexicon to Herodotus, s.v.*) the passage referring to the Phocaeans' attempt to purchase the Oenussae Islands from Chios is particularly informative (1. 165): the Chians refused to sell for fear that the islands would develop into an *emporion* and Chios would be cut off; that is, the Chians did not wish an independent community living by trade in their immediate neighborhood. The Black Sea cities are also referred to as *emporia* (4. 17. 1; 20. 1; 24; 108) as are Tartessus (4. 152. 3) and the cities of western Sicily (7. 158. 2). The Black Sea cities (4. 24) would hardly be Milesian stations in the fifth century. The proposal of the Laconians to transplant the Ionians to the *emporia* of the Medizing Greek states after the Persian Wars (9. 106. 3) would presumably have entailed setting up independent communities supporting themselves by trade. In Herodotus the *emporion* is essentially a community living by sea trade, but it is interesting to note that Thucydides can envisage such a place arising from land traffic as in the case of Corinth (1. 13. 5). In Thucydides, however, the sense of trading-factory, with its implications of control to the advantage of another state, seems predominant (1. 100. 2; 4. 102–3; 7. 50. 2; see also Aristophanes *Birds* 1523).

23. Herodotus 1. 127. 1; 5. 23. 2. Thucydides (2. 80.5) uses it of the chief official of the Chaeonians.

24. The lexicographers have been more chary of reading a technical meaning into *prostatai* than have the commentators on Herodotus and the historians: Powell translates "magistrate" (*Lexicon to Herodotus, s.v.*) or "officers" (*Translation of Herodotus*, I, 194) and Liddell and Scott (*s.v.* II, 2) "rulers of Greeks in Egypt"; How and Wells, however, explain the *prostatai* as "consuls" (*Commentary on Herodotus*, I, 254) and Stein, "officials in charge of trade" (*Herodotus* [5th ed., Berlin, 1883], on 2. 178). It is regularly used, of course, to denote the leaders of the Athenian demos (Busolt-Swoboda, *op. cit.*, pp. 414 ff.) and to designate the chief civil magistrate or executive committees of the council or assembly (*ibid.*, p. 451, n. 5 and p. 478; see also Swoboda, *Die Griechischen Volksbeschlüsse*, pp. 67, 91–93, 99 ff.). The word also has a more limited technical usage in the fifth century: the representatives of metics in Athens were called *prostatai* and perhaps a similar connotation of legal representative is to be understood in the difficult passage of the law of the Eastern Locrians relative to their colony at Naupactus (*ca.* 460 B.C.; Tod, *op. cit.*, No. 24, VII. 34). To judge by the examples given in Liddell and Scott, *prostates* as the administrative official of some property or institution is met with only in the Hellenistic period.

25. Thucydides 1. 56. 2.

26. *Syll.*³, 110 (*ca.* 410 B.C.). This inscription was used by Prinz (*op. cit.*, p. 119) as confirmation of a separate Aeginetan factory in the fifth century. That interpretation depended, of course, on the reading given in the Sylloge text: Αἰγ[ινάτε ν τ]ὸν ἐγ Ναυκράτ[ιος]. It has been revised to Αἰγ[υπτιον in the Sylloge index, which not only fits the space equally well, but seems confirmed by the Lindian inscription quoted in the commentary. Evidently Naukratite Greeks might be referred to as Egyptians or as residing in Egypt (see the form of reference in *Syll.*³, 239, B. 37). The inscription, No. 110, would pre-

sumably date from soon after the synoecism of the
Rhodian cities (it is rather emphatic about representation of all the Rhodians) and the Lindian inscription
from shortly before the synoecism. In this connection
it is interesting to note that Herodotus (2. 178) in the
middle of the fifth century can refer to Rhodes rather
than to its several cities.

27. *IG*, II², 1, 206.

28. They are collected by E. M. Smith, *Naukratis*
(Diss., Bryn Mawr, 1924), pp. 66 ff.

29. *Syll.*³, 239, A. 1–6; B. 37–39; C. III. 21–24.

30. Head, *HN²*, p. 845; *Num. Chron.*, VI (1886),
10–11.

31. The evidence is discussed by Kees, *op. cit.*,
1964.

32. Mitteis and Wilcken, *Papyruskunde*, I, 1, pp.
13, 51; I, 2, pp. 44–45, No. 27.

33. Roebuck, *op. cit.*, p. 246, n. 62 on p. 247.

34. Hogarth considered that the Hellenion was
probably built at the time of Amasis' supposed reorganization (*JHS*, XXV [1905], 136; see also Price,
JHS, XLIV [1924], 192, 204), but his description of
the excavation shows that no good evidence for the
date of its construction was found.

35. *BSA*, V (1898–99), 56, No. 107; *Naukratis*, II,
66, Nos. 818, 821.

36. Roebuck, *op. cit.*, p. 242.

37. Mitteis and Wilcken, *op. cit.*, I, 1, pp. 13, 51.

38. Strabo's reference to the foundation by the
Milesians (17. 1. 18, 801) perhaps indicates that they
were originally settled there after serving as mercenaries for Psammetichus (see n. 13 above). For
discussion of the Chian and other interests at Naukratis see Roebuck, *op. cit.*, pp. 236–47.

THE EARLY IONIAN LEAGUE

AT AN early date in their history the Ionian Greeks of Asia Minor united their cities into a league, the members of which celebrated a national festival, the Panionia, to Poseidon Helikonios at their religious center, the Panionion, on the peninsula of Mycale. To Herodotus the festival and the unwarranted exclusiveness of the organization, whose members prided themselves on being *The Ionians*, seemed its most interesting characteristics.[1] The league, however, was of some political importance in the history of the Ionians and of the East Greeks in general, unifying their resistance to Persia at the time of Cyrus' conquest (546–540 B.C.) and in the revolt against Darius (499 to 493 B.C.). To an older generation of scholars, notably Wilamowitz and Cary, this political function, seemingly a characteristic of the league from its origin in the period before 700 B.C., was its most striking feature.[2] Certainly this would have been unusual in a period of Greek history when the characteristic form of association was the religious amphictyony or the ethnic group. Recently, however, it has been suggested that the original form of the league was that of a religious amphictyony or of an ethnic group headed by a king,[3] which developed into the union of independent cities known to us from Herodotus. In these various studies of the league the focus of attention has thus been on its original character and purpose rather than on its organization in the historical period.[4] The problem of its origin, of course, is a matter for speculation rather than of

any sure knowledge since it is involved with the difficult questions of the Greek migration to Asia Minor and of their early settlements there. At least the time of that migration (late eleventh or early tenth century B.C.) seems in process of being fixed at a considerably earlier date than has been suggested recently (post 800), thanks to the excavation of Old Smyrna.[5] For the closing years of the league's existence in the archaic period we have the specific information of Herodotus, almost contemporary and written from a viewpoint hostile to the Ionians. Thus in studying the early league, it seems useful to form a picture of its organization from Herodotus and then, using that as a guide, to discuss some of the problems of its origin.

The league of the sixth century B.C.

Herodotus tells us in his description of the Ionian league that its members met at the Panionion to celebrate the festival of the Panionia.[6] To him, and presumably to Greeks in general, this was the regular business and purpose of the league: the citizens of the member-states assembled regularly to celebrate a festival in honor of their national deity, Poseidon Helikonios. It was the expression in religious form of the unity of *The Ionians* as they called themselves.[7] We do not hear of any other business at a Panionia except for a division of the land of the defeated state of Melia reported in the work of a historiographer, Maeandrius of Miletus, and cited at one point in the well-known boundary dispute between Samos

[CLASSICAL PHILOLOGY, L, JANUARY, 1955]   26 and Priene. As argued below this seems to be an anachronism.[8] Yet the league obviously made certain decisions to implement its resistance to Persia: it functioned as a political union as well as for purposes of religious worship. It is significant that Herodotus does not connect any of the meetings at which such political business was carried out with the Panionia itself. Thus, it seems probable that they were special meetings and that the league was beginning to develop institutions to express its political interests.

The first notice of a meeting which we find in Herodotus is of that convened after the capture of Sardis by Cyrus in 546 B.C. At that time Cyrus had rejected the overtures of the Ionians, except for the city of Miletus, so that they were faced with the choice of fighting or surrendering on unknown terms. They met at the Panionion and resolved to send envoys for aid to Sparta. These envoys consulted with those of the Aeolian league which, in its turn, had decided to follow the Ionian lead. The two groups decided upon a joint spokesman, Pythermos of Phocaea.[9] We hear nothing more of league action during the resistance to Persia; but after the occupation of Ionia the Ionians again met at the Panionion, and discussed and rejected the proposal of Bias of Priene to migrate to Sardinia to found an Ionian city there.[10] At some time previous to this, perhaps under the threat of attack by Alyattes or Croesus of Lydia, Thales had made a proposal to the Ionians for a more centralized organization of the league.[11] Nothing more is heard of league activity until the early stages of the Ionian revolt. After the league took over its direction from the hands of Aristagoras of Miletus[12] a meeting was held to decide upon the request for aid from Onesilos of Cyprus. It was de-

termined to send a large fleet which was placed under the joint command of the captains of the contingents of the various members rather than of a single commander.[13] The final meeting described by Herodotus took place when the Ionians were faced with the great concentration of Persian troops and ships in 494 B.C. At that time they sent delegates (*probouloi*) to the Panionion to decide upon the strategy which resulted in the naval battle of Lade.[14]

All these meetings, except perhaps that at which Thales made his proposal,[15] were convened at critical points in the history of the Ionians, when their independence was seriously threatened or when they were actually at war. In the case of the meeting before Lade we are told that delegates were sent by the members to the Panionion so that no general attendance of the Ionians took place. Presumably the same is true of the other meetings, for a general attendance would have been impossible unless the cities were left unguarded. Evidently these were emergency meetings outside the regular pattern of the Panionia and, as such, indicative of the political concern of the member-states. The league organization was such, then, that extraordinary meetings could be called and the attendance of representatives from the member-states be assured. Some central authority must have existed to issue the summons, and some system of representation have been in existence. Was there a federal priesthood existing at the religious center of the league, at the Panionion, like that of Delphi in the Delphic Amphictyony, or was there a leading state, a *hegemon*, like Sparta in the Peloponnesian League? In more technical language, are we to recognize in the league a religious amphictyony with a developing political outlook or a symmachy in which the religious element was subordinate and whose origin is to be found in political necessities ?

It seems clear that the Ionian league was not a symmachy with a single state as its *hegemon*. As pointed out below, it is evident that no one state dominated the league as a *hegemon* and that treaties of alliance, which normally embodied the constitution of a Greek symmachy, did not exist among the members; such political unity as the league attained was the result of common discussion and joint decision at meetings called under the spur of necessity. Yet, some authority had to exist which could call the members together. Since the emergency meetings are recorded as having been held at the Panionion it seems probable that a religious official of the sanctuary of Poseidon convened them. Although we do not have any specific information about the titles and functions of the officials of the shrine it is probable that they were Prienians, for Strabo tells us that in the later league of the Roman period Priene furnished the priesthood.[16] Only tradition could insure for such an unimportant state such a prominent function.

It is not clear whether the delegates for these special meetings were selected by their cities for that purpose only, or whether they were the regularly appointed officials who represented their cities at the Panionia also. On the whole it seems likely that they were the regularly selected officials, for we know that the meeting which decided upon the Cyprus expedition was not a military council since the commanders represent themselves as unable to change its instructions.[17] That is, this council of *probouloi* was not made up of the military commanders of the cities as might perhaps have been expected in the circumstances. Apparently, then, the regular machinery of the league could be used for the direction of its wars as well as for its festivals in peace. As mentioned above we do not have any information about the schedule of business at the Panionia. Thus, it is probable that only matters directly concerning the festival were scheduled for the Panionia unless, by chance, its meeting coincided with a grave crisis in the affairs of Ionia in general. Apparently, then, the political business of the league consisted only of co-operation in military action. It remains to discuss how effectively that co-operation was implemented.

The member-states of the league were moved to joint action only by the threat of loss of independence with the result that their meetings were emergency sessions and the resolutions taken at them, while of grave importance, were mainly of a diplomatic and strategic character. For example, there was the diplomatic decision to send to Sparta for aid in 546; the strategic decision to send a fleet to Cyprus in 497 and to fight a sea battle at Lade in 494. Constitutional reforms, which would have transformed the nature of the league, such as the proposal of Bias and that of Thales, were rejected. The only resolution of such a type which may have been adopted was symbolic in character, the possible issuance of a league coinage made at the end of the league's existence during the Ionian revolt. Yet the federal character of this coinage is very doubtful.[18] Thus, the league experienced only an initial compulsion towards political unity, but did not work out regular institutions which would have knit it closely together into a true federal union, with a strongly centralized government and the power to compel its members to abide by league decisions. The degree of unity was commensurate with the strength of the fear engendered by a particular crisis. No one city controlled the league as a *hegemon* and various cities dropped out of its military activity if they felt their own position secure. In the resistance to Cyrus' conquest, Miletus and the island states of Samos and Chios did not co-operate with the other members.[19] Even in the course of a campaign the tactical decisions were made by joint consultation of the commanders of the contingents from the separate cities rather than by a commander-in-chief. This was the case in Cyprus and eventually, after the fiasco involving Dionysius of Phocaea, at Lade also.[20] Apparently the consciousness of the Ionians of being a single people had chiefly a religious expression in the Panionia. Yet, it did achieve a limited unity to resist Cyrus and, in the Ionian revolt, succeeded in working out a plan of campaign. It is not surprising, then, that the intellectual leaders of Ionia were conscious of the league's defects as a political instrument and made proposals for a closer union.

Cary has remarked on the significance of the proposals of Bias and Thales, both rejected, for the greater centralization of the league.[21] The member-states, however, did not want it and certainly their feeling of unity could hardly have risen to the challenge of Bias' drastic proposal for a complete synoecism and withdrawal from Ionia. Even the civic loyalty of the Phocaeans was not equal to that when the time came for sailing to the west.[22] Thales' proposal foundered on the same feeling for complete autonomy. "He urged (or, "kept urging") that the Ionians have one *bouleuterion*, and that in Teos (for Teos is the center of Ionia), and, while the other cities should continue to be in-habited just the same, they should be considered as demes."[23] There is no question here of transfers of population or of the concentration of the other Ionians to Teos as residents. The proposal is concerned with a centralization of the government and strengthening its powers over against those of the member-states of the league. If our view of the *probouloi* is correct (regularly elected delegates for the Panionia, but functioning as a council in time of crisis) possibly Thales wished to systematize their council by having it hold regular meetings and to enlarge its powers to deal finally with the foreign affairs of the league as a whole. The *probouloi* would then have become the political representatives with plenipotentiary power of their separate states; the states would have become like demes with control of their local affairs only.[24] Such a proposal would, of course, have transformed the league from a loosely knit ethnic and religious union of autonomous cities into a compact and effective state. It would also have entailed a surrender of sovereignty by the individual members; on that rock the proposal grounded.

It seems apparent from this review of the activity of the league that its political and military functions were extraneous to its character and forced upon it by the special circumstances of the latter part of the sixth century B.C. The league began to develop into a political organization under the pressure of conquest by Croesus and the Persians just as Panhellenism, with some political connotation, developed at that time in Ionia[25] and slightly later in Old Greece. The league was, then, little more than a coalition of independent cities using the machinery of an existing organization of nonpolitical type for the needs of defense of its members. There had been no compulsion by the Lydian kings before Croesus to alter the character of the league and later the more rigorous control by Persia would not allow it to change its form and organization.

The view of Wilamowitz that the league was consolidated under Lydian pressure is properly rejected.[26] The Lydian kings until the time of Croesus do not seem to have envisaged any permanent political relationship with the Ionian cities or the creation of an Ionian province. Their warfare was made against single cities and has been well characterized by Hogarth as of the *razzia* type.[27] The first known settlement of a permanent character was made between Miletus and Alyattes. It was in treaty form and apparently involved only pledges of mutual aid.[28] Certainly the treaty was more favorable than those made between Croesus and the other Ionian cities on the mainland, although the island states may have enjoyed the same favorable terms as Miletus. The treaties with the states of the mainland did involve the payment of tribute and probably compulsory military service, but no interference with the internal arrangements of the cities. Under Croesus, then, the Ionian league could hardly have functioned as a free political unit, for the island and mainland members were in different positions of independence. There is, of course, no record of any dealings between Croesus and the league, but only with the cities separately.[29] Since their independence was impaired, however, it is probable that we should assign to this period the first concern about making the league an effective political organization. As might be expected its reform was bruited by the intellectual leaders of Ionia, Bias and Thales, but failed to gain general support. Only when the Ionians were faced with the prospect of further loss of independence at the hands of Persia did the cities begin to use the league for their defense. Yet, at the time of the Persian conquest the league could not achieve any concerted plan of campaign[30] as it did a generation later at the time of the Ionian revolt.

Perhaps for this reason the Persians do not seem to have broken up the league upon the conclusion of the conquest. After its completion, Herodotus records[31] only the meeting which discussed Bias' desperate proposal, but some organization existed forty years later to take over direction of the Ionian revolt. Probably the Ionians continued their celebration of the Panionia throughout this period and thus kept alive the feeling of Ionian religious and ethnic unity and found an opportunity to air their grievances in conversation if not in action. Persia, like Croesus, discriminated among the Ionian cities by the renewal of the favorable treaty with Miletus[32] while its control of the other cities was even tighter. To the obligations of tribute and military service were added the tyrants, who had a lively sense of their self-interest in maintaining Persian authority. To the Persians, then, there would seem no advantage in breaking up a league with slight record of political activity and a predominantly religious and "national" character. The preservation of such entities was thoroughly in the pattern of their empire. The Ionian revolt, however, was a repudiation of this pattern of rule and during it the league became a closer unit. It planned the campaigns and spread the revolt throughout western Asia Minor.[33] Thus, the league would seem a reasonably effective instrument for East Greek independence so that it is probable that the Persian settlement of 493 B.C. dissolved the organization.[34]

The Ionian league of the sixth century appears to have been an essentially religious and ethnic union upon which certain essays toward a closer political bond were forced by the aggression of Croesus and Persia. Its growth toward a federal system was cut short. With this picture in mind let us turn to the problems of the league's earlier history.

Membership

In Herodotus and the other sources there is an almost canonical list of twelve cities which formed the Ionian league: Miletus, Myus, Priene, Ephesus, Colophon, Lebedos, Teos, Clazomenae, Phocaea, Samos, Chios, and Erythrae.[35] This number seems to have been achieved well before the early seventh century B.C. Pausanias tells us that in the twenty-third Olympiad (688 B.C.) a Smyrnean won an Olympic victory and that Smyrna was then Ionian.[36] Such a comment was evidently provoked by the recollection of its capture by the Colophonians from Aeolian hands,[37] i.e., the capture took place a short time before 688 B.C. Herodotus observes that Smyrna was the only state which applied for admittance to the league and was refused, although it was Ionian.[38] This petition for admittance would presumably have been made shortly after Smyrna was captured by the Ionians and certainly made before its almost complete destruction in the early years of Alyattes' reign.[39] We can only conjecture about the grounds for refusal; probably the league had existed for a considerable period before this in its canonical form, so that the members felt that the number was fixed by tradition.[40] A similar feeling existed, of course, among the members of the Delphic Amphictyony. Possibly Colophon retained some control over Smyrna so that it was regarded as a Colophonian dependency rather than as an independent state. A parallel to the case of Smyrna may be found in the nonmembership of Magnesia on the Maeander. It was traditionally of Aeolian, not Ionic origin, and, after its destruction by the Cimmerians, its territory came under the control of Miletus.[41] Thus the membership of the league seems to have been fixed at the canonical number of twelve cities considerably before 688 B.C. and was kept rigidly at this figure. They were *The Ionians* whose pride Herodotus deplored.

Some of the twelve cities, however, were not of Ionian origin and the league attained its full form only by a process of growth. It seems clear that Chios, Phocaea, Clazomenae, Erythrae and possibly Samos were brought into an existing organization. Chios is said to have joined the league in the time of its king Hector after he had effected a consolidation of the island.[42] Phocaea, Clazomenae and Erythrae were traditionally not primary Ionian settlements.[43] The settlement of Samos is traditionally set a generation earlier than the Ionian migration and there are legends of an early war with Ephesus resulting in the temporary conquest of the island so that Samos may have been brought into the league by force.[44] If these states are eliminated from the list we are left with a nucleus of Miletus, Myus, Priene, Ephesus, Colophon, Lebedos, and Teos. To this, Samos was probably added very early. It is significant that these states cluster around the center of the league, the Panionion on the Mycale peninsula. If they formed the nucleus of the league its growth was the result of colonization ventures and warfare against the Aeolian Greeks to the north of the Ionian region proper. Smyrna's capture would have been the last step in this process, but came too late for its inclusion in the league. A *terminus ante quem* for the development of the full league may be furnished by the kingship of Hector of Chios who has recently been dated *ca.* 800 B.C.[45] If so, the growth probably occurred during the ninth century B.C., and the original nucleus of the league would have been in existence in the tenth century. Before turning to this problem, however, it would be advisable to discuss the theory of Wilamowitz according to which the league came into existence *ca.* 700 B.C. as the result of the Melian War.

The Melian War

The Melian War was considered by Wilamowitz to have been the occasion of the league's formation,[46] and the reported division of the land of Melia after the war has been regarded as the first important act of the league of which we have knowledge.[47] Vitruvius states the members of the league, the canonical twelve states, waged a joint war (*communi consilio*) against a thirteenth member, Melite (Melia), and destroyed it.[48] In an inscription of the early second century B.C. recording the arbitration by Rhodes of a territorial dispute between Samos and Priene there is some additional information about the consequences of the war. Although the text is very fragmentary it seems to be satisfactorily restored as indicating that a division of the Melian land was made by the Ionian league at a Panionic festival (Panionia).[49] The war itself is dated by another inscription, in this case a ruling by Lysimachus made in 283/2 B.C. on the same dispute, to the period before the Cimmerian in-

vasion under Lygdamis (*ca.* 650 B.C.).[50] Thus, there seems to be evidence of a league war against a member state which was destroyed and the land of which was parceled out by a formal league action. Wilamowitz suggested that the sanctuary of Poseidon Helikonios lay in the land of Melia and became the center of the league brought into existence by the war.

Upon examination, however, there are difficulties in accepting the Melian war as a league war and the division of its land as carried out by the league. Let us first consider the evidence of the inscription recording the Rhodian arbitration. It is apparent from the inscription that not only did Melia lose its territory, but that Miletus both gained and lost land and that Colophon was a loser.[51] Thus, there is a discrepancy with Vitruvius' account of the war. In his account the war was a league action by all the twelve members against a thirteenth; from the inscription it was a struggle between various states of the league which resulted in losses and compromises for states other than Melia. The states which we know were concerned were Samos, Priene, Miletus and Colophon.[52] It was apparently not a league war, but a struggle between the cities for land, like many others of which we know in early Greek history. This view of the war makes it difficult to accept the supposed action by the league with respect to the land.

The action is cited as a precedent by the Samians in the course of their argument before the Rhodian arbitrators. Its authority was Maeandrius of Miletus, a historiographer, charged with being a *pseudepigraphus*.[53] While that blot on his reputation need not condemn his statement, it does seem important that other historiographers cited by Priene were in contradiction to

Maeandrius about the allocation of the land in this division.[54] The evidence, then, rests on the account of a historiographer of doubtful reputation who is known to have used, invented, or whose name gave currency to one of two traditions. It should not inspire confidence. Further, the circumstances in which the league division of land was supposed to have been made are unreal. The league is represented as strong enough collectively, and in possession of the machinery, to impose its will on such members of its organization as Miletus and Colophon. Not only the language used to describe the action, but the procedure required for such actions belong to the fourth century and the Hellenistic period when arbitrations by leagues are better attested. They can hardly be found, however, before the Hellenic league of Philip II.[55] In such a process there has to be a power of compulsion over the other members either by a single state or by some machinery, and the common will for joint action. The machinery had not been invented in the early archaic period and the will was conspiciously lacking at all times in Greece. In the league of the sixth century no one state was predominant so that we must either assume this earlier league was organized quite differently, or that, like its descendant, it did not function politically except under extreme compulsion for which there is no evidence here. At the date usually given to the Melian War, *ca.* 700 B.C., the league was presumably an association of independent city states, for shortly thereafter we hear of Gyges' attacks on various Ionian cities. It séems conclusive, however, that in all the other precedents cited by Samos and Priene in the course of their long dispute over this land in the Mycale peninsula we do not hear of an action by the league.

The land was fought for and allocated in treaty settlements or in negotiation between the two parties concerned, but the league did not take a hand.[56] Thus the evidence in this inscription concerning the Melian War and the league action should be rejected.

Vitruvius, however, does state that there was a league war against a member state, Melite; since we have no other information about it the usual identification with the Melia of Hecataeus, which he called a Carian city, is probably correct.[57] While we can reject the circumstantial detail of Maeandrius about the settlement after the war, there should have been a Melian War in Ionian tradition to which he and other historians could attach their detail. Perhaps we have a confused record of a war undertaken by the Ionian cities around Mycale, the nucleus of the later league, against and in the case of some, in alliance with a native Carian town, Melia, which was destroyed and whose land was occupied.[58] The Melian War, then, may be an episode of the very early days of Ionian settlement when the league existed only in embryo and struggles with the natives of the region were in process. The league, too, would scarcely have been the association of city states which Vitruvius makes it out to be.

The establishment of the league

In the sixth century the league appeared to be essentially an ethnic organization, claiming for itself the name of *The Ionians*, and expressing its consciousness of being a single people through its religious festival, the Panionia, and through its attempts at union for defense in war. This development in the direction of political unity was cut short by the failure of the Ionian revolt. The league had evidently borne such a

character for a very long time and succeeded in identifying the non-Ionian
states, like Chios, which it had taken
in at an early date, as Ionian also. This
process of absorption had been carried
out by a nucleus of Ionian states around
the Mycale peninsula. How is it that
such a group of states, which we know
as independent cities with their own
character and traditions, had a consciousness of being one people and the
power to establish that belief as a lasting tradition ? It seems apparent from
the archeological evidence as yet known
that the cities began as small, unimportant communities.[59] There is an almost unanimous tradition of conflict
and eventual intermingling with what
must have been a fairly numerous native population. Yet, what we have met
in the Ionian league is characteristically
Greek in its subsequent development
and the patron deity of the league,
Poseidon Helikonios, is evidently a god
brought with the migrants from the
Boeotian area in Old Greece.[60] He remained the "national" god of these
Ionians and had no oracular or international development such as the shrines
at Claros, Branchidae or the Arte-
mision at Ephesus. It seems clear that
the nucleus of the migration into the
Mycale area must have consisted of a
strong group of settlers who had a
coherent organization of their own and
a sense of identity as Ionians. They
maintained this to such effect that other
Greeks in smaller and weaker bands,
who migrated, subscribed to it in large
part and it outweighed the various native influences from intermarriage and
the like. Herodotus, of course, recognized this group as the Athenian element, the true Ionians, among the
migrants; and recent scholarship has
tended to favor this view rather than
to consider Ionian development as a

local growth in Asia Minor from a mixed
selection of settlers from various parts
of Greece, as Wilamowitz suggested.[61]
With the Ionians of Old Greece and the
migration itself we are not presently
concerned, but only with the question
of how an ethnic unity might have been
established and maintained in Asia
Minor.

The developed tradition of the Ionian
migration pictured a well-organized,
large-scale movement from Athens,
which served as a concentration point
for refugees after the collapse of the
Mycenaean kingdoms (except that in
Attica), to the coasts of Asia Minor. It
was led by the sons of King Codrus who
founded the twelve Ionian cities and in
supreme command was either the founder of Ionian Miletus, Neleus, or of Ephesus, Androclus, depending on the respective claims to primacy of these
cities.[62] Thus an Ionian state organized
under a supreme king is represented as
being in existence from the outset. The
towns of its cadet-rulers were the Ionian
cities of the league so that the league
in its original form was a kingdom.
There is much, of course, to object to
in this tradition. The oldest information
we have in the literary sources about
the migration, from Mimnermus, knew
only of a migration directly from Pylos,
not by way of Athens, and Pherekydes
of Athens in the fifth century apparently wrote of Neleus coming to Miletus
directly from Pylos; the Athenian claim
to be the metropolis of all Ionia is exaggerated, and much of the tradition is
demonstrably of Athenian origin in the
period subsequent to the Persian Wars;
the full league of twelve cities could
hardly spring full born from the migration, as the awkward stitchings of local
and Athenian tradition indicate.[63] Yet,
the tradition must have an element of
truth: the coincidence of tribal names

on each side of the Aegean (in Athens and in the Ionian cities and their colonies) should indicate that a part of the Asiatic Ionian population were of Attic origin;[64] Herodotus' notice of the Apaturia in Athens and Ionia;[65] the nature of the cult of Poseidon Helikonios; all these point to a coherent and strong group of migrants from the Boeotian-Attic region, which were hardly to be differentiated at the time of the migration. It was apparently this group which established the tradition of the Ionian ethnos. While the settlers might have preserved this ethnic consciousness since it had a religious expression in the cult of Poseidon Helikonios, yet its expansion and continued existence suggest that the group possessed and maintained political coherence and supremacy in the Mycale area. This is perhaps reflected in the local traditions of Ephesus.

In the scraps of local tradition which Strabo and Pausanias have preserved, Ephesus fares rather better as the chief center of Ionian settlement than Miletus: "The royal seat of the Ionians was established there and still now the descendants of his (Androclus') family are called kings; and they have certain honours...."[66] This kingship evidently had a more than local Ephesian importance in early Ionia. The king of Ephesus is represented as waging war on Samos, which had collaborated with Carians against Ionians, as aiding Priene in its struggles with the native inhabitants of that region and capturing a town, Larisa, near Tmolus, from the Maeonians.[67] It seems significant that these are represented as wars for the Ionians against non-Ionian elements. That may be the coloring of an age which was conscious of the distinction between Greek and barbarian, but it may also reflect the position of the king

of Ephesus as champion of the early Ionian settlers in the area of the Panionion. From their respective geographical locations it might be expected that Ephesus would be more concerned about the Panionion, which possibly marked the landing place of the first settlers, than would Miletus. This primitive league would not, of course, be a league of city-states. Its units in this period would be ruled by kings and the king of Ephesus would head the group of kings whose towns later developed into city-states; perhaps in the *basileus* of the league known in Roman times we have the descendant of the early chief king of the league, his office having devolved into a purely religious function, and no longer being attached to a single family in one particular city.[68] As the towns of this primitive league developed into city-states their kingships, too, would devolve into religious offices and the old quasi-feudal ties with the chief king of the league lose their vigor. The emergence of the Ionian towns as city-states would mark the end of the primitive political unity of the league, but the religious expression of their previous unity remain in the celebration of the Panionia to reinforce and provide the means for mutual defense, as against the Aeolians and later the Persians. Their separateness from the other Ionians, whom they joined in the Delian festival, indicates an earlier and stronger cohesiveness.[69]

Is it not possible that in this early Ionian league we may have the transference of a post-Mycenaean kingship to Ionia, and in the vivid pictures of the uneasy relation of chief king and subordinate kings in the Homeric poems a reflection of the position of the rulers in the Ionian towns in their early political association? In Athens we know that there was an actual cultural continuity from Mycenaean times and probably a kingship surviving from the Mycenaean period until the time of the Ionian migration.[70] Apparently the Ionians of the migration came in large part from this Attic region. The institution of the Mycenaean kingship may have been carried to Ionia to refresh the older memories of it preserved in the epic poetry. It remains to summarize this reconstruction of the league.

As recent excavation indicates, the settlement of the coast of Asia Minor by Greeks seems to have taken place in the tenth or possibly the latter part of the eleventh century B.C. As the tradition indicates, a strong group of settlers from the Boeotian-Attic region of Old Greece settled in the Mycale area. They were the dominant Ionian nucleus, probably joined for several generations by smaller groups from elsewhere in Greece and intermingling with natives to some extent. They came with the organization of a weak post-Mycenaean kingship such as probably existed in Athens at the time of their departure. This was reproduced in the Ionian towns around Mycale with Ephesus as a center. During the tenth and ninth centuries this loose quasi-feudal organization remained in existence with considerable friction among its kings, which we see reflected in the legends of early warfare among the Ionian cities, and, as an institution, in the Homeric poems. This organization preserved its ethnic consciousness by means of the Panionia. In the latter part of this regal period the group of states around Mycale warred with the Aeolian Greeks to the north and took Chios, Erythrae, Phocaea and Clazomenae into their association, probably Ionicizing them by colonization. Toward the end of the ninth and throughout the eighth century the kingships would lose their political character and the towns grow into *poleis* as on the Greek mainland. The league would thus develop into the organization of twelve independent city states which we know from the archaic period. It retained this form until the threat of subjugation by Croesus and Persia forced it to take on a political and military character. Yet since the league had existed for more than a century and a half as a union of city-states, it experienced the same difficulties as other Greek leagues of this type in working out the problems of cooperation. Any development along these lines was cut short by the failure of the Ionian revolt and by the incorporation of the Ionian cities into the Athenian Empire.[71]

NORTHWESTERN UNIVERSITY

NOTES

1. Herod. 1. 142–48.

2. Wilamowitz-Moellendorff, "Panionion," *SB Berlin* 1906, 38–57 (*Kl. Schr.*, V, 1, pp. 128ff.); M. Caspari (Cary), "The Ionian Confederacy," *JHS*, XXXV (1915), 173–88; see also, Wilamowitz, "Über die ionische. Wanderung," *SB Berlin*, 1906, 59–79 (*Kl. Schr.*, V, 1, pp. 152ff.). These studies have remained basic for the study of the league, with most historians following the reconstruction of Wilamowitz (most recently, D. Magie, *Roman Rule in Asia Minor* [1950], I, 65–66; II, 866–67, n. 47). He considered that the league came into existence *ca.*700 B.C. as the result of a war by its members-to-be against the city of Melia in whose territory the Panionion was presumed to lie. Cary considered the war a much more trivial affair in the history of the league which, he suggested, was formed between 900 and 700 B.C. in the course of warfare with the Aeolian Greeks to the north. Cary is followed by Glotz-Cohen (*Histoire grecque*, I, 272) and by W. Judeich

("Zur ionischen Wanderung," *Rh. Mus.*, LXXXII [1933], 307).

3. Judeich (*ibid.*, pp. 307–14), although accepting Cary's view of the time and consolidation of the league, identified it as an amphictyony centering around the cult of Poseidon Helikonios. A. Momigliano ("Il Re degli Ioni nella provincia romana di Asia," *Atti del III Congresso Nazionale di Studi Romani*, 1934, 1, pp. 429–34) has suggested that the league was originally an ethnic-political association headed by a "king of the Ionians" whose title is found in the league of the Roman period. G. de Sanctis (*Riv. fil.*, LXIII [1935], 418–19) is critical of the view, but it has been accepted by H. Bengtson (*Philol.*, XCII [1937], 130 and *Griechische Geschichte*, p. 53).

4. The above-mentioned study of Cary (n. 2) is most useful for the league of the sixth century B.C. and for its revival in the fourth century and Hellenistic periods; cf. also Lenschau, *Klio*, XXXIII (1940), 222–24 and

I. Calabi, *Ricerche sui rapporti fra le poleis* (Florence, 1953), pp. 26–36.

5. J. M. Cook, *JHS*, LXXII (1952), 104ff.; Cook and E. Akurgal, *Illustrated London News*, Feb. 28, 1953, pp. 328–29. The discovery of rich deposits of pottery in the proto-geometric style (tenth century B.C.) and of house remains of *ca.* 900 and the succeding centuries is reported. As the excavators note, this will involve revision of recent views placing the Greek settlement on the coast of Asia Minor after 800 B.C. (*e.g.*, G. Hanfmann, *AJA*, LII [1948], 135–55; for a more cautious appraisal of the material from Smyrna see Hanfmann, *HSCP*, LXI [1953], 6–7, 10, 16–17). Smyrna was apparently an Aeolian foundation rather than Ionian (see below, n. 37), but it is probable that the material culture of the Greek area in western Asia Minor followed a generally similar course of development. That, however, should not lead us to ignore the traditional distinctions between Aeolian, Ionian, and Dorian Greeks, which were obviously felt by the Greeks themselves in the archaic period. The traditional date of the Ionian migration is the early eleventh century B.C. (1086/85 or 1076/75; Jacoby, *Mar. Par.* 27, pp. 151–52 and *FGrH* No. 239, Comm. on 27) or in its third quarter (1044/43 according to Eratosthenes, who placed it four generations after the fall of Troy; 1045/44 for Ephesus and 1039/38 for the other cities according to Eusebius 1. 187. 36). These chronological indications have been accepted by most historians who regard the migration as a consequence of the Dorian invasion of mainland Greece.

6. Herod. 1. 143; 148. For the membership see above, pp. 31 f.

7. The members of the league evidently called themselves *The Ionians*, for Herodotus protests (1. 141. 4–143; 147) against what he felt was an unjustified assumption of a name common to a much wider group: islanders, Athenians and nonleague members like Smyrna in Asia Minor (above, p. 31). The league is also referred to as the *koinon* of the Ionians (5. 109. 3). Herodotus' usage of Ionians and Ionia is rather interesting, for it shows a variation between *The Ionians* of the league, Ionians in their widest ethnic sense, and Ionians and Ionia in official Persian usage to designate the satrapy (see Bengtson, *Philol.*, XCII [1937], 129 ff.).

8. Pp. 32 f.

9. Herod. 1. 141; 151–52.

10. Herod. 1. 170.

11. *Ibid.* Herodotus indicates the time of Thales' proposal as "before Ionia was destroyed (by the Persians)"; his interest, however, was not in the temporal relationship to Bias' proposal but in the quality of Thales' suggestion (χρηστὴ δέ). Thus, it is not specifically connected with the Persian conquest, but is probably to be referred back to the period of Lydian aggression under Alyattes or Croesus. Miletus did not take part in the political deliberations at the time of the Persian conquest, for it had made a special treaty with Alyattes which was renewed by Cyrus (Herod. 1. 22. 4; 141. 4). Thales, of course, was a Milesian. For discussion of Thales' proposal see above, p. 29.

12. The revolt was started by Aristagoras of Miletus who appears as its director until after the burning of Sardis and the withdrawal of the Athenian and Eretrian forces; thereafter (Herod. 5. 104 ff.) Herodotus writes of the Ionians as planning the strategy and carrying on the war. For the activity of the league during the revolt see Calabi, *op. cit.*, pp. 29–33; Calabi apparently considers that a regular symmachy was organized in the revolt; my own interpretation is that the league utilized its existing organization, which was not that of a symmachy.

13. Herod. 5. 108–9.

14. Herod. 6. 7.

15. See above n. 11.

16. Strab. 8. 7. 2 (384); 14. 1. 20 (639); Magie, *op. cit.*, II, 869, n. 52. Momigliano (*op. cit.*, p. 434) has identified the Prienian priest who performed sacrifices at the sanc-tuary of Poseidon Helikonios with the "King of the Ionians," known from inscriptions of the Roman period (below, n. 68) and considered by Momigliano to have been the head of the early league. One difficulty with this identification is that Strabo does not speak of this Prienian official as a "King"; further, if the office of King had a continuous evolution from its original character as a military commander of the Ionian people, it is difficult to see why it should be a Prienian privilege. That city played a minor role in the tradition of early Ionian settlement (n. 67) and could hardly have been the royal seat of the Ionian monarchy. Its part in the administration of the sanctuary is rather to be ascribed to the location of the latter in its territory; the place of Priene is analogous to that of Delphi in the Amphictyonic League.

17. Herod. 5. 108–9.

18. Gardner, *JHS*, XXXI (1911), 151–60; Cary (*JHS*, XXXVI [1916], 102) has pointed out various difficulties to its acceptance as a federal coinage.

19. Miletus did not dominate the league politically, for it did not even participate in some meetings (see n. 11). Naturally, in warfare the more powerful states would have had considerable influence in making decisions so that perhaps the appointment of Phocaeans to executive positions represents a compromise between them or between the Ionian and Aeolian Leagues, for, as I shall discuss elsewhere, Phocaea was the chief port for Aeolian and Lydian trade. There is, however, no hint in the sources of political domination by one city. Presumably, then, representation from each state in the "council" of the *probouloi* was equal. Chios betrayed the Lydian leader of revolt, Pactyes, to the Persians in exchange for Atarneus on the mainland (Herod. 1. 155–60). Samos, of course, remained independent and flourishing under Polycrates, and was not taken over by Persia until the reign of Cambyses.

20. Herod. 5. 108–9 (Cyprus); 6. 11–12 (Lade). In Herodotus' obscure account of the selection of Dionysius as commander-in-chief for a few days there may be a reflection of another institution of the league, proper to it at a much earlier time and revived here by force of circumstance. When the full Ionian levy had assembled, the Ionians met in assemblies (*agorai*) and selected Dionysius to command them. That is, the Ionian people as a whole chose their commander in a sort of armed assembly. If, as suggested above (pp. 35 f.), the original form of the league was like that of the quasi-feudal kingships in Homer, this armed assembly of the people would have been a normal institution. Calabi (*op. cit.*, pp. 32–33) suggests that these *agorai* were meetings of the heads of the new democratic governments. This view seems open to the same objections as the interpretation of the meetings as councils.

21. Cary, *JHS*, XXXV (1915), 178–80.

22. Herod. 1. 164–65.

23. Herod. 1. 170. 3. Thales' proposal may be part of an ideal plan of political reform rather than the answer to any specific aggression. In the plan Teos was to be the capital of the league because of its central position. If this reason is a part of Thales' argument, not Herodotus' observation, it would fit an ideal league better than a specific military crisis, for other cities were more secure strategically.

24. Cf. Cary's discussion, *op. cit.*, pp. 179–80.

25. Herod. 5. 49. 3. Aristagoras made his plea to Sparta "in the name of the Greek gods" and on behalf of the Ionians, "men of the same blood."

26. Wilamowitz, *op. cit.*, pp. 45–46; Cary (*op. cit.*, p. 176) points out that records of league action against Lydia are conspicuous by their absence; see also, Glotz-Cohen, *Histoire grecque*, I, 272.

27. D. G. Hogarth, *CAH*, III, 508–9.

28. Herod. 1. 22. 4. Alyattes, after years of raiding, finally made the Milesians, *xenoi kai symmachoi*; the circumstances in which the treaty was made suggest that

the two parties were on an equal footing. This agreement would probably have been renewed by Croesus and was again renewed by Cyrus (n. 11). See also Diog. Laert. 1. 25.

29. Herod. (1. 27) records that Croesus entered into *xenia* with the islanders since he was unable to capture them; this perhaps indicates that the islanders were put on the same favorable footing as Miletus. The relationship in any case was more favorable than that with the cities of the mainland which became subject allies (Herod. 1. 141). The settlements made with them were apparently in treaty form (*synthekai*; Polyaenus *Strat.* 6. 50); tribute was exacted (Herod. 1. 6; 27. 1); probably military levies could be demanded. After Croesus' return to Sardis from the battle with Cyrus on the Halys River, he dismissed a force described by Herodotus as *xenikos* (foreign, 1. 77) and fought the Persians with his own troops. His *allies*, Egypt, Sparta and Babylonia, are stated to have been absent from both engagements; yet Xenophon mentions that Cyrus settled Egyptians who had been in Croesus' service in Larisa and Cyllene in Aeolis after the war (*Cyr.* 7. 1. 45; *Hell.* 3. 1. 7). Probably they were Greeks who had served in Egypt as mercenaries, returned home to their native states and had been hired by Croesus. Their number was probably small since they were settled in flourishing towns (Schefold, *Larisa*, I, 8, n.3 and 26). It is unlikely that these men made up the force described as *xenikos*, for, if so, their settlement would not have been a problem for Cyrus: they would already have been domiciled in Greek towns at the time of the battle. Presumably, then, the *xenikos* army was made up of contingents levied from the allied Greek cities by Croesus. Further, Herodotus normally uses *epikouroi* of mercenaries (Powell, *Lexicon to Herodotus*, *s.v.*). The various obligations of the Greek cities to Croesus are sufficient to justify Herodotus' statement (1. 6) that he deprived the Greeks of freedom, although he does not seem to have attempted to use tyrants as the Persians did. Strabo (13. 1. 25 [593] and 14. 1. 21 [640]) is sometimes cited as evidence for Lydian garrisons in Ilion and Ephesus: the passages indicate that the populations moved down from the acropolis to low ground during the reign of Croesus so that the inference has been drawn that Lydian troops occupied the high points; these moves, however, as at later periods, may have been the result of population pressure and the regime of peace which prevailed in western Asia Minor during the latter part of the reign of Alyattes and that of Croesus. Santo Mazzarino (*Fra Oriente e Occidente*, pp. 191–252) in a detailed review of the relations between the Greeks and the Lydians develops the theory that Lydian influence was exerted in the Greek cities by intermarriage, "Lydizing" families and priests, rather than by support of tyrants. Certainly, in all the record of relations the Lydian kings dealt with individual Greek cities, not with the league. For example, when Miletus was hard pressed by Alyattes, only Chios came to its aid (Herod. 1. 18. 3). This need not mean, of course, that the league was nonexistent or in abeyance (see Cary, *op. cit.*, p. 176); it was merely not functioning as a political organization throughout this period and no treaties requiring mutual aid existed between its members.

30. Chios, Samos and Miletus did not co-operate with the other members of the league so that its resistance to Persia was seriously impaired (see n. 19). While the league determined to send to Sparta for aid (Herod. 1. 141. 4), it does not seem to have formulated any strategy of general defense, for in Herodotus' account (1. 153ff.) we read only of the actions of Pactyes, the Lydian rebel, and those by Harpagus, the Persian commander, against separate cities.

31. Herod. 1. 170.

32. N. 11. Miletus was evidently in a most flourishing position under the Persian regime (Herod. 5. 28). It is probably to this period that the great trading activity of Miletus with the Black Sea region is to be assigned, for the first colonies seem to have been established only two

generations earlier, *ca.* 610 B.C. Probably, too, Miletus paid no tribute to Persia by virtue of its special treaty.

33. N. 12.

34. Herod. 6. 42. In the report of the settlement, however, there is no mention of the dissolution of the league. The argument of Cary (*op. cit.*, p. 181) that the making of treaties between the Ionian cities for the arbitration of disputes may indicate that the league was dissolved would not be valid if, as argued above (pp. 28 ff.), the league had never arbitrated disputes between its members.

35. Herod. 1. 142–48; the same list is found in *Mar. Par.* 27; Strab. 14. 1. 3 (633); Paus. 7. 2. 5ff.; Ael. *Var. Hist.* 8. 5; Vitruv. (4. 1. 4) adds Melite (above, p. 33) and Vell. Pat. (1. 4. 3) omits Teos, an omission of no apparent significance; see the table in Lenschau, *Klio*, XXXVI (1944), 217.

36. Paus. 5. 8. 7; 4. 21. 4.

37. Herod. 1. 150; Mimnermus Frag. 12 (Diehl); the tradition in Strab. (14. 1. 4 [633] which made Smyrna a colony of Ephesus is probably only an invention to make Smyrna out as an Ionian city (Magie, *op. cit.*, II, 888, n. 91). If, however, it was an Ephesian colony and thus Ionian from the outset, its nonmembership in the nucleus of the league may be explained by its dependent status and subsequent capture by the Aeolians. Presumably the Aeolians were in the process of expanding southward *ca.* 700, for Larisa seems to have been occupied by Greeks about that time. Its occupation would have given the Aeolians control of the road running south to Smyrna as well as easier access to the Hermus valley (*Larisa*, I, 17ff.; Schefold considers that the capture of Larisa facilitated the founding of the Aeolian League; whatever the circumstances of its origin the league seems to have functioned as a unit at the time of Smyrna's loss [Herod. 1. 150]).

38. Herod. 1. 143. 3; the evidence of Strab. (14. 1. 4 [633]) and Paus. (7. 5. 1) which has been interpreted as showing that Smyrna was a member of the early league is ambiguous and should not outweigh Herodotus' positive statement. It is probably a reflection of Smyrna's prominent position in the Hellenistic and Roman leagues (see Cadoux, *Ancient Smyrna*, p. 68, n. 1).

39. Herod. 1. 16; Strab. 14. 1. 37 (646); Hogarth, *CAH*, III, 513; the archeological evidence of the Corinthian pottery, found on the site of the destroyed temple, indicates that Alyattes made his successful attack not later than the end of the seventh century (*Anatolian Studies*, I [1951], 16).

40. A contemporary reflection of this is probably to be found in the *Iliad* (11. 692), where Neleus, the traditional founder of Miletus, is said to have twelve sons (Momigliano, *Studi ital. di fil. cl.*, X [1932], 262ff.).

41. Strab. 14. 1. 40 (647). Magnesia was traditionally of Thessalian (Aeolian) origin which would explain its nonmembership in the nucleus of Ionian cities clustered around Mycale. It was also at war with Ephesus before the Cimmerian invasion (see Magie, *op. cit.*, II, 894, n. 101 for bibliography). Larsen (*CP*, XLVII [1952], 7, 15, n. 6) has pointed out that there is considerable doubt about the Magnesians having been Hellenic originally. Certainly they were non-Ionian and it is difficult to explain an Aeolian colony as far south and inland as Magnesia on the Maeander.

42. Paus. 7. 4. 9–10; Pausanias' remarks are based on Ion of Chios, a writer of the fifth century B.C. Chios was originally an Aeolian rather than an Ionian foundation (Wilamowitz, *op. cit.*, pp. 62–63).

43. Phocaea: Paus. 7. 3. 10. Phocaea was not taken into the league until it received Codrid kings from Erythrae and Teos. Clazomenae: Paus. 7. 3. 8–9. Clazomenae was a Colophonian colony, not one of the original Ionian settlements. Erythrae: Paus. 7. 3. 7. The Ionian settlement in Erythrae is placed after the migration proper; from its location its fortunes would have followed those of Chios closely. See Wilamowitz, *op. cit.*, pp. 55–57; 62–63.

44. Paus. 7. 4. 2. Pausanias has probably drawn his material from Asios of Samos, a poet of the sixth century. Procles of Epidauros made a settlement, apparently a generation before the main Ionian migration, for Androclus, the founder and king of Ephesus, is said to have made an expedition against the son of Procles, driving him from Samos; the alleged cause of the war was Samian co-operation with the Carians against the Ionians.

45. H. T. Wade-Gery, *The Poet of the Iliad* (1952), p. 7. The dating is, of course, conjectural.

46. Wilamowitz, *op. cit.*, pp. 38–46.

47. Busolt-Swoboda, *Griechische Staatskunde*, II, 1282.

48. Vitruv. 4. 1. 4. Vitruvius' Melite is usually regarded as written in error for Melia, mentioned by Hecataeus (*FGrH*, I, Frag. 11). This passage of V. contains numerous mistakes (see Wilamowitz, *op. cit.*, p. 38).

49. *Ins. v. Priene*, No. 37, ll. 53–60; p. 309, No. 37; the restorations of Lenschau (*Klio*, XXXVI [1944], 234) do some violence to the preserved parts of the inscription (cf. l. 49).

50. *OGI*, No. 13; C. B. Welles, *Royal Correspondence in the Hellenistic Period*, No. 7; Cary, *op. cit.*, pp. 174–75. The date usually given to the war is *ca.* 700 B.C., which is conjectural, since the inscription does not refer specifically to the Melian War and merely makes a general reference to events before the invasion of Lygdamis.

51. *Ins. v. Priene*, No. 37, ll. 57–59. Some town or tract of land the name of which began with the letters AI or AK was lost to Miletus, while it gained Thebes and Marathesium. The Colophonians lost the Anaea.

52. See Judeich, *op. cit.*, pp. 307, 309. Judeich notes that the inscription, in itself, is no real evidence for the existence of the league, but considers that the organization was already functioning before the Melian War. It is remarkable that Ephesus is not mentioned in connection with this division of land. That may be the fault of the condition of the stone, for its name could be restored in l. 63.

53. *Ins. v. Priene*, No. 37, ll. 53–54, 122–23; Wilamowitz (*op. cit.*, p. 42, n. 3) attempts to redeem his reputation. See, however, Hiller's doubts in the commentary to l. 59 of the inscription (cf. also Laqueur, *RE*, XIV, 534–35).

54. *Ibid.*, ll. 118ff. The other historiographers mentioned in the inscription did indicate a division of Melian land after the war, but the circumstantial detail of the adjudication by the league is attached only to the account of Maeandrius (ll. 53–59).

55. Roebuck, *CP*, XLIII (1948), 91–92.

56. Welles, *op. cit.*, No. 7, ll. 12ff.; *Ins. v. Priene*, No. 37, ll. 53–54, 102, 105–6. Wilamowitz had considered the *dikaiomata* mentioned in l. 13 of Welles, no. 7 as arbitrated settlements (p. 43, n. 5), but see Welles, *op. cit.*, Appendix, *s.v.* "dikaiomata." Its usual meaning in Hellenistic usage is "document used in evidence" which developed from the Attic connotation of "justification" or "plea of right." As a title for Aristotle's guide to the boundary adjustments made by Philip II of Macedon it evidently had this latter connotation (Roebuck, *loc. cit.*). In this inscription where it is used in conjunction with the phrase, μ[ε]τὰ τῶν ἐξετῶν σ[πον]δῶ[ν, it apparently means the documents in which the treaty settlements were expressed which established a peace of six years' duration (for the events leading up to this see Plut. *Quaest. Gr.* 20).

57. Hecataeus (*FGrH*, I, Frag. 11) calls it Carian, but that, of course, may be merely a geographical reference. H. von Gaertringen (*RE*, XV, 1588–89) has accepted Wilamowitz' reconstruction of the Melian War and connected with it the anecdote about the contention for the throne of Miletus by Leodamas and Phitres in Konon (Frag. 44). This involves identifying the Μηλιεῦσι of Konon's passage as the people of Melia, not of Melos. There is some difficulty in this, for the text refers to Melos specifically. It, too, then, would have to be changed. Yet, the reference should probably refer to Melos and its people,

for this war of Phitres is coupled with that of Leodamas against Karystos, presumably on Euboea. Thus, the anecdote is apparently to be connected with some Milesian raids across the Aegean, or, perhaps with the Lelantine War.

58. The general picture of the Greek settlement in the literary tradition is one of initial conflict with the native population. There was also apparently some active co-operation with them against fellow Greeks (see n. 44).

59. Hanfmann, *AJA*, LII (1948), 135–55; *HSCP*, LXI (1953), 1–37; the evidence, of course, is very scanty and difficult of interpretation, and the publication of the material from Old Smyrna will provide the first adequate picture of an East Greek town in the early years of settlement and the archaic period. Considering the resources and techniques of late eleventh- and tenth-century Greece it is apparent that the colonization of Asia Minor must have been carried out by very small groups. Momigliano (*op. cit.*, pp. 432–33) considers this incompatible with the conception of a single monarchical state in Ionia at the outset and postulates a large-scale movement like that of the expedition to Troy depicted in Homer.

60. Wade-Gery, *op. cit.*, pp. 4–5.

61. See Wilamowitz, *op. cit.*, 59–79, where the picture of the migration as a mixture of various elements from different parts of Greece is developed. On such an assumption there had to be a coalescence and the growth of an "Ionian" culture from new beginnings in Asia Minor; Wade-Gery, *op. cit.*, pp. 4ff. offers a partial revision of this picture. Hanfmann's discussion of the process of settlement based on the archeological evidence tends, of course, to support Wilamowitz' view (*HSCP*, LXI (1953), 10ff.). I hope to discuss the matter further in connection with a study of Ionian trade and economic development.

62. See, in particular: Strab. 14. 1. 3ff. (632); Strabo's account is based mainly on Pherekydes, a fifth-century Athenian writer, but also preserves local traditions; Paus. 7. 2. 5ff. For discussion of the tradition see Jacoby, *Mar. Par.*, pp. 91–92; *idem*, *FGrH*, II, 4, pp. 682–83; Lenschau, *Klio*, XXXVI (1944), 201–19; E. Meyer, *Forsch. z. alten Geschichte*, I, 127–50 (in which the theory of the Mycenaean colonization of the west coast of Asia Minor was advanced; it was fully rejected by Bolkestein, *Klio*, XIII [1913], 429–50 and given up by Meyer in the second edition of his history, *Geschichte d. Alter.*, II², 1, pp. 551–52; the present condition of the archeological evidence indicates only a small amount of Mycenaean trade and few settlements in the Ionian region, Hanfmann, *HSCP*, LXI [1953], 3–5); Wilamowitz, *op. cit.*, pp. 59–79; Hogarth, *CAH*, II, 542–61 (an excellent interpretation of the traditions, using what archeological material was available at the time); Momigliano, *Studi. ital. di fil. cl.*, X (1932), 259–97 (on the foundation legends of Ephesus and Miletus; it demonstrates that the Neleus legend had a different development on each side of the Aegean); J. A. R. Munro, *JHS*, LIV (1934), 109–28 (derives the Ionians on each side of the Aegean from a common Pelasgian group in Thrace). For the archeological commentary which was not available for these studies, see Hanfmann, *AJA*, XLIX (1945), 580–81; LII (1948), 135–55; *HSCP*, LXI (1953), 1–37.

63. Mimnermus Frag. 12 (Diehl). This refers only to Colophon, and it may be another local legend to account for a pre-Ionian Greek settlement there in addition to those mentioned by Pausanias (7. 3. 1–3) from Crete and Thebes with which the Ionians were said to have synoecized. Colophon is one of the sites for which Mycenaean remains are reported (Hanfmann, *AJA*, XLIX [1945], 580–81). Strabo (based on Pherekydes; 14. 1. 2–3) brings Neleus, the founder of Miletus, from Pylos without an Athenian detour; here again there may be some attempt to account for a pre-Ionian, Greek settlement, for there seems to have been a Mycenaean town at Miletus (Hanfmann, *HSCP*, LXI (1953), 4). Lenschau's picture (*RE*, IX, 1874ff.;

Klio, XXXVI [1944], 228–37) of a Pylian migration on a considerable scale from the western Peloponnesus *ca.* 800 B.C. has been rejected by Judeich (*op. cit.*, p. 309). Lenschau argued that the patron deity of the league was originally Apollo, that the Pylian invaders took over control of Colophon, Miletus, Priene and Samos, made war on Melia, divided its land and installed their own deity, Poseidon, as the patron of the league. Such a reconstruction finds little supporting evidence and fails to account for the persistent Ionian tradition in institutions and ethnic feeling. Further, such an effective invasion *ca.* 800 B.C. would probably have left a far greater mark on tradition than Mimnermus' passage; thus, it seems preferable to refer it back to an earlier period.

The tradition of an Athenian origin for the Ionian migration is sometimes asserted to be as old as Solon on the evidence of his line calling Athens the oldest or most renowned (*presbytate*) land of Ionia (Solon Frag. 4. 2, Diehl). The geographical reference of the "Ionia" is not clear, however, for it could be used in its widest sense to mean the whole Ionian ethnos or it might mean only the Athenian and Aegean elements in the Delian *panegyris* (Momigliano, *op. cit.*, pp. 295–96). As we know from the oriental sources, the name, Ionian, was applied to a variety of Greeks before 700 B.C. so that it had a wider extension than merely to the Asiatic Ionians well before that time (Bengtson, *Philol.*, XCII [1937], 148–55; B. Hrozný, *Archiv Orientální*, IV (1932), 169ff.). In Herodotus this tradition of Athenian origin is not yet fully developed, for, although he considers the "true Ionians" to be of Athenian origin, he derives the twelve cities from their numerical counterpart in Achaea and does not mention the Ionian detour through Achaea into Attica (Herod. 1. 145–46; this Achaean origin of the Ionian *dodekapolis* is also mentioned by Timotheos of Miletus, the fourth-century poet, *Pers.* 246–48). The Attic origin, however, appears in full flower after the Persian War (Busolt, *Gr. Ges.*, I², 285, n. 1; see, in particular, Wilamowitz, *op. cit.*, pp. 69–72; Nilsson, *Robinson Studies*, II, 747–48).

64. Nilsson, *Sk. Sv. Ins. i Athen* 1951, pp. 143–49; 1953, pp. 4–6; Bolkestein, *op. cit.*, pp. 429–30, 443–50. Equally significant for the development of the settlements, however, is the evidence of subordination of the Ionian tribes to the place of less important units (e.g., the *chiliastyes* in Ephesus) and of the presence of tribes of non-Ionian and perhaps of non-Greek origin.

65. Herod. 1. 147; cf. Lenschau, *Klio*, XXXVI (1944), 225.

66. Strab. 14. 1. 3 (633); De Sanctis, *Riv. fil.*, LXIII (1935), 418–19; Momigliano (*op. cit.*, p. 434) seems to suggest that the early kingship was established in Priene, but see above (n. 16). His characterization of this early kingship as absolute and anterior to that of Agamemnon depicted in the Iliad (*primus inter pares*) fits an ideal evolution of an ethnic kingship better than any actuality which we can picture from early Greek history or later survivals. In Ionian tradition there seems to have been a strong emphasis on the local independence and individual tradition of the separate cities from the outset, which suggests a quasi-feudal system within a conception of ethnic unity.

67. Paus. 7. 2. 8–9; 4. 2. Strab. 13. 3. 2 (620). If Magnesia was non-Hellenic (n. 41) the Ephesian wars against it would also fall into this category.

68. *OGI*, II, No. 489; *SEG*, I, No. 399; *Ins. v. Priene*, No. 536; see n. 66.

69. Momigliano, *Studi ital. di fil. cl.*, X (1932), 294–95.

70. O. Broneer, *AJA*, LII (1948), 111–14; King Codrus of Athens, whose defense of the city Pausanias describes, was the father of the leaders of the Ionian migration, the Codrid kings of the Ionian cities.

71. This article was written at the Institute for Advanced Study in Princeton during the tenure of a fellowship awarded by the Guggenheim Foundation, enabled by the grant of a leave of absence from Northwestern University. To all these institutions I should like to record my thanks for facilitating work on the problems of East Greek history.

TRIBAL ORGANIZATION IN IONIA

I. INTRODUCTION

In this paper I plan to discuss, in preliminary fashion, the civic organization of the Ionian communities of western Asia Minor before they were taken over by the Persians in the mid-sixth century. Such a study raises, but hardly resolves, some difficult questions of early Greek history. At the outset, we are confronted with the Ionian migration and, through it, with the communal organization of metropolitan Greece in the Dark Ages and Mycenean period. For example, some of the Ionian communities shared the four ethnic tribes of the Ionian people with pre-Cleisthenean Athens: the Geleontes, Hopletes, Aegicoreis and Argadeis. Is this indicative of filiation to Asiatic Ionia from Dark Age Attica, from Mycenean Attica, from metropolitan Greece of the Mycenean period, or, the reverse, from Ionia westward across the Aegean to Attica? These same Ionian communities, however, had two other tribes, the Boreis and Oenopes, which were not found on the west side of the Aegean Sea. Other cities of Ionia had a different set of tribes but were members of the Ionian League and called themselves Ionians. Evidently the process of organization was very complex. In general, however, all the Ionian communities seem to have had a tribal organization, which was typically Greek in its gentile and exclusive character, well before 700 B.C. Some of them, such as Miletus, maintained this into the fifth century, while others, such as Ephesus, modified their original structure to a territorial basis to allow the growth of a more politically integrated community. We can see the traces of adjustments made to include groups of Greek metics and of Anatolian natives in response to the pressures of urbanization as Ionia changed from an agrarian to a mixed economy. Our evidence is scanty and all of it later than the event, but, when the scraps of information are pieced together, they seem to reflect the process of growth in Ionia which I have reconstructed in previous studies.[1]   For convenience I summarize it briefly.

There does not seem to have been large-scale migration to the west coast of Asia Minor by Mycenean Greeks,[2] although some descendants of such settlers may have survived at Miletus, Colophon and elsewhere until the time of the Ionian migration in the eleventh century.   This migration was made by a cohesive group of Greeks from Attica and Boeotia over a relatively short period of time.   The migrants settled around the Gulfs of Ephesus and Miletus to develop the primary towns of Samos, Miletus, Myus, Priene, Ephesus, Colophon, Lebedus, and Teos.   A conscious recognition of their ethnic affiliation led to the establishment of a common religious center for the worship of Poseidon Heliconius at the Panionium in Mycale.   Some cooperation in war was achieved under the leadership of the king of Ephesus. In the tenth and ninth centuries other migrants came from Greece and the Aegean islands to settle in this new Ionia and northwards along the coast.   Some Ionians and Aeolians also moved within the new land to find better homes.   For example, Clazomenae was colonized by Colophon and, presumably, individual Ionians from the primary settlements began to infiltrate beyond the Gulf of Smyrna into northern Ionia.   In that region, however, the towns of Old Smyrna, Phocaea, Chios and, perhaps, Erythrae were probably established originally by non-Ionians.   Their traditions of early settlement indicate a strong Aeolian element and, as discussed below, their tribal organization differed from that of the primary settlements.   The dominant political group on the coast, however, was the Ionian League around the Panionium.   By ca. 800 B.C. the League had extended north to include the northern towns as members.   Old Smyrna, however, predominantly Aeolian at first, was refused admission to the League, although captured by Colophonian exiles.[3] Perhaps the last steps in the League's expansion were the inclusion of Phocaea, the northernmost town, and of Chios, which is said to have joined the League under its king, Hector.

---

[1] Carl Roebuck, "The Early Ionian League," *CP* 50 (1955) 26–40; *idem, Ionian Trade and Colonization* (New York 1959) 24–41.

[2] For discussion of recent views of the Mycenean settlement in Ionia and of the dating and character of the Ionian migration, see J. M. Cook, "Greek Archaeology in Western Asia Minor," *JHS* 78 (1958) 39–40.   For the evidence from Old Smyrna, *idem,* "Old Smyrna, 1948–51," *BSA* 53–54 (1958–59) 10–14.

[3] Cook (above, note 2, *BSA*) 13–14.

II. THE EARLY ORGANIZATION OF THE PRIMARY IONIAN TOWNS

Among the primary settlements there is information about only Miletus, Ephesus, Samos, and Teos,[4] all of which seem to have had six tribes: the four Ionian ethnic tribes, Geleontes, Hopletes, Aegicoreis, Argadeis and the two Asiatic Ionian tribes, Boreis and Oenopes. These are attested, wholly or in part, by evidence from the cities themselves and from colonies in the Propontis and Black Sea, where the tribes were established presumably at the time of foundation. Their presence in Cyzicus reasonably, if indirectly, provides a *terminus ante quem* of ca. 700 B.C. for their existence in the mother-city, Miletus, and in Perinthus of ca. 600 B.C. for their existence in Samos. None of these tribes is attested for the northern towns of the Ionian League, although tradition and, for Phocaea, at least, archaeological evidence indicate that they, too, were founded in the Dark Ages. Evidently their original non-Ionian character was sufficiently well established and the Ionian expansion of such a nature, as discussed below, that the tribal organization of the primary towns was not introduced. Its absence, however, hardly demonstrates that the six tribes did not originally exist in the primary towns, and we can reasonably assume that the co-existence of the four ethnic tribes in Ionia and in Attica (Her. 5.66,69) has some significance for the character of the Ionian migration and would reflect the organization of the first few generations of settlement in southern Ionia.

[4] Miletus: the Hopletes, Oenopes and Boreis are named in *SIG*[3] 57, lines 1–3 (450/49 B.C.) and the Argadeis in an inscription of the early fifth century (*SBBerl* [1904] 85). All six tribes are named in inscriptions from Cyzicus (F. Bilabel, "Die ionische Kolonisation," *Philologus*, *Supp.* 14 [1920] 120–21), while the Oenopes, Argadeis, and Aegicoreis are known from Tomis (Bilabel, *op. cit.*, 123–24) and the Aegicoreis from Istrus (Bilabel, *op. cit.*, 123–24). For the foundation date of Cyzicus see Roebuck (above, note 1, *Ionian Trade*) 112–13.

Ephesus: the Geleontes, Argadeis, Oenopes, and Boreis are known as subdivisions (*chiliastyes*) of a tribe, Ephesians (J. Keil, *JOAI* 16 [1913] 245–48; *idem, Forschungen in Ephesos* 4.284, Nos. 31–32). The Ephesians and other tribes are mentioned by Ephorus (*FGrH* 70, F 116; Steph. Byz., s.v. "Benna"), which affords a *terminus ante quem* in the mid-fourth century for the reorganization (see below, 504).

Samos: the Geleontes, Aegicoreis, and Boreis are named, along with four local Thracian tribes, in an inscription of Perinthus. It was reported by Cyriac of Ancona (Bilabel, *op. cit.* [above, note 4] 173–76). Perinthus was founded *ca.* 600 B.C. (see Roebuck [above, note 1, *Ionian Trade*] 111). For the tribal reorganization in Samos see below, note 22.

Teos: only the tribe, Geleontes, is known (W. Ruge, *RE* 5[2] (1934) 553; *CIG* 3078–79).

The co-existence of the tribes on both sides of the Aegean has been considered usually to indicate filiation from Attica, which implies the existence of *Ionians* there before the migration.[5] Despite recent attempts at revision by Sakellariou and Cassola, this standard view still seems preferable. Sakellariou, who has minimized the Athenian element among the settlers of Ionia, has argued[6] that the four ethnic tribes were common to Greece in Mycenean times. Their presence in Ionia would reflect migration from various parts of Greece in that period. Aside from the difficulty of finding archaeological evidence of extensive Mycenean settlement in Ionia, the Linear B tablets of Pylus and Cnossus do not mention the names of the four tribes. Further, there seems to have been no survival of the names except in Athens, the primary towns of Ionia and in Delos.[7] The presence of the tribes on the latter island may be explained by early migration from Attica or as later Athenian political influence. If the tribes were Mycenean Greek in origin, they were apparently confined to Attica, and their survival to be explained as part of the cultural continuity attested by the pottery from the Ceramicus cemetery and the tradition of indigenous origin cherished by the Athenians. Cassola, however, who prefers to link the origin of the tribes with the development of the communities in Asiatic Ionia itself, has revived the theory that the tribes were transferred from Ionia to Attica.[8] It is difficult to envisage the transfer of such basic social institutions without considerable emigration from Ionia into Attica and even more difficult to conjecture the historical circumstances which would cause such migration. The traditions of settlement in Ionia and of continuous habitation in Attica point in the opposite direction. It is also pertinent to ask why the Boreis and Oenopes were not transferred.

The names of the tribes can scarcely clarify their character at the time of the migration and later. The standard identification[9] as

---

[5] Busolt-Swoboda, *Griechische Staatskunde* 1.120; 2.768–70; K. J. Beloch, *Griechische Geschichte* 1.2².98–100.

[6] M. B. Sakellariou, *La migration grecque en Ionie* (Athens 1958) 47, 255. M. P. Nilsson considers that the four tribes existed in Pylus, whence they were taken to Athens ("Das frühe Griechenland, von innen gesehen," *Historia* 3 [1954–55] 264).

[7] Argadeis: Szanto, *SBWien* 144 (1901) 47; F. Cassola, *La Ionia nel mondo miceneo* (Naples 1957) 249.

[8] F. Cassola (above, note 7) 246–56; for criticism, see Sakellariou (above, note 6) 502–3 and Beloch (above, note 5) 99.

[9] Busolt-Swoboda (above, note 5) 2.769.

original social classes is plausible: nobles (Geleontes), warriors (Hopletes), shepherds (Aegicoreis) and farmers (Argadeis). Yet, in both Attica and Ionia the tribes seem to be associated primarily with kinship groups, and there is no perceptible difference of status among them. The festival of the Apaturia, associated with the phratries, was common to Attica and Ionia, except, in the time of Herodotus, at Ephesus and Colophon (Her. 1.147), and, we may suspect, in the northern towns. At an earlier date tribes and phratries were linked, as Nestor's exhortation to Agamemnon before Troy indicates (Il. 2.362–63). The tribes, of course, may have represented social divisions in the early years of Ionian settlement in Attica, but lost their coherence in the development of a palace-centered economy in the Mycenean period. The names could survive and the tribes acquire their new character of kinship groups in the troubled conditions of the early Dark Ages. The migration to Ionia and the difficulties of early settlement would emphasize the usefulness of closely knit groups, such as the household, clan, and phratry, for survival. These considerations, however, are part of the larger question of the origin of Greek tribal institutions and lead us far from Ionia. While the origin of the four ethnic tribes is obscure, it is at least probable that the Boreis and Oenopes were formed in Asiatic Ionia. They, too, seem to have existed in the Ionian mother-cities before the foundation of colonies in the Propontis and before the incorporation of the northern towns into the Ionian League.[10] They would, then, have been made up of one or more of the following elements: descendants of the Mycenean settlers, Greeks of non-Ionian origin who came to Ionia in the tenth and ninth centuries, or, from Anatolian natives. On the whole, it seems probable that they represent the inclusion of the second element, the early Greek metics.

It is likely that the Ionian colonists made no discrimination between the descendants of the Mycenean settlers and the Anatolian natives, but took the land and subordinated its owners where they could. Where they could not, we might expect intermarriage and the survival of strong pre-Ionian family groups. The latter adjustment is perhaps indicated by the names in the *pyrgoi* list of Teos, while subordination of the natives is revealed by

---

[10] Cassola (above, note 7) 255; see above, note 4.

the evidence of a serf population in some of the Ionian towns.[11]
On the other hand, new Greek settlers, who came after the Ionian
migration to make their home in the new settlements, would have
strengthened the Ionians. Devices could be found, when the
number of metics justified it, to incorporate them into the communities. While the barriers of kinship in the four ethnic tribes
could not be breached, the creation of new tribes was a characteristic Greek device. The names, Boreis and Oenopes, seem
artificial, for they can be connected with heroes, Borus and
Oenopion, whose legends may be localized to Thessaly, Boeotia
and Crete. These connections should mark the tribes as Greek,
although Sakellariou regards the Oenopes as native Anatolians,
dark-complexioned men.[12] With the incorporation of these non-
Ionian (by ethnos) groups, we may begin to speak of Ionians and
Ionia with a political connotation, rather than with the purely
ethnic designation which would apply to the four older tribes.

III. THE EARLY ORGANIZATION OF THE NORTHERN TOWNS

Although the evidence is very scanty, it is apparent that the
northern Ionian communities had a different organization from
that of the primary towns. Clazomenae, about which there is no
information, may well have had some or all of the six Ionian
tribes, for it was a colony of Colophon; but Phocaea, Erythrae
and Chios apparently were communities in their own right
before becoming members of the League. The case of Phocaea is
clearest. It was founded at least as early as the Dark Ages, for
Protogeometric pottery is reported.[13] There were three tribes:
the Pericleidae, Teutheadae and Abarneis, whose existence in the

[11] On the *pyrgoi* inscription, see Hunt, *JHS* 67 (1947) 71, 76; for serfs, see below,
note 29.

[12] Boreis: there seems to be general agreement that this name indicates a Thessalian
(Aeolian) element and that the tribe was formed in Ionia of non-Ionian Greeks
(Busolt-Swoboda [above, note 5] 1.118, note 8; Sakellariou [above, note 6] 74;
Cassola [above, note 7] 250).
Oenopes: there is dispute about the meaning of the name. It has been explained
as indicating a link to Boeotia or to Crete (Busolt-Swoboda [above, note 5] 1.118,
note 8), but Sakellariou ([above, note 6] 67–8) insists on the meaning, "dark-
complexioned." The Oenopes would have been the "blacks" at first and, then, a
tribe of native origin. Cassola (above, note 7) 250 tentatively suggests a Bacchic
connection. Neither view seems particularly cogent and the onus of proof lies on
those rejecting the obvious connections with metropolitan Greece.

[13] J. M. Cook, *JHS* 78 (1958) 41; see Pausanias 7.3.10.

Phocaean colony of Lampsacus provides a *terminus ante quem* of *ca.* 615 B.C. for their existence in the mother city.[14] The name, Pericleidae, has the ring of a Greek *genos* and may well have been made up of the followers of Pericles, the first Ionian king of Phocaea, and their descendants. In origin, then, the Pericleidae were a relatively small gentilic group, not a tribe of the type found in the primary Ionian towns. The names, Teutheadae and Abarneis seem non-Ionian, perhaps non-Greek, although they are sometimes connected with King Deoetes and King Abartus, who were said to have come from Teos and Erythrae respectively. Perhaps tradition gave an Ionian origin to the "founders" of these groups after Phocaea had become a member of the Ionian League. The names may well indicate that the non-Ionian founders of Phocaea were too strong to be denied social recognition when the town became politically Ionian. If these conjectures are correct, we may have a clue to the manner in which Phocaea was taken into the League and why the six old Ionian tribes were not introduced into it. To judge from the case of Old Smyrna, there was a steady increase of Ionian influence in the area north of the Gulf of Smyrna in the tenth and ninth centuries. This is marked primarily, of course, by the Ionicizing of pottery decoration and shapes, but reflects the effects of trade, infiltration of individual Ionians from the south and the attraction exercised by the politically dominant power of the coast, the Ionian League. Ionian political affiliation, however, would have been the product of successful military attack or the eventual fruit of an alliance sought by the northern towns. For example, Old Smyrna was captured by Colophonian exiles and Chios' own king, Hector, brought his state into the League. In the case of Phocaea, we might conjecture that an Ionian chieftain, Pericles, made a successful raid and settled with his followers to rule the town. The new ruling group formed the gentilic organization of the Pericleidae, in effect a new tribe, alongside the existing groups of the Teutheadae and the Abarneis. There would be no occasion or need to introduce the six Ionian tribes to Phocaea, for no regular

---

[14] Pericleidae: *IGRR* 4.1326; 181 (Lampsacus); Teutheadae: *IGRR* 4.1325; Abarneis: Hesychius, s.v. Probably the colony, Abarnus, in the Hellespont owes its name to colonists of this tribe. Sakellariou (above, note 6) 411–12 considers that the tribal names, Abarneis and Teutheadae, may be Greek; and Keil connects them specifically with the names of the kings, Deoetes and Abartus, who were sent to Phocaea from Teos and Erythrae (*RE* 20 (1950) 444; Pausanias 7.3.10).

colonization nor any joint action by the members of the League as a whole had been involved. Pericles, by virtue of his Ionian origin, could bring his newly acquired town into the League. In the Dark Ages, of course, warfare was essentially raiding by clan chieftains, and political ties a matter of their personal relationships. This reconstruction is, of course, frankly conjectural and, unfortunately, there is no information about the circumstances of the adherence of Chios and Erythrae to the League to amplify the picture. We do, however, know a little about their tribal organization.

Erythrae, like Phocaea, had three tribes. Pausanias records that one was called Chalcis.[15] The name may indicate a group of colonists from Euboea who retained their coherence in a synoecism of Erythrae, but when they came, or whether this synoecism was early, we do not know.

The tribes of Chios are obscure. Although the so-called "Constitution of Chios," now dated 575–50 B.C.,[16] shows that a tribal organization was basic and presumably pre-existent to the "constitution," it does not give the names or the number of the tribes. Beloch has suggested that the tribe, Oenopes, was present, for Oenopion from Crete was the traditional founder of Chios.[17] If so, this may point to early, non-Ionian, Greek migration as in the case of the primary towns.

These early tribes of all the Ionian towns seem to have been Hellenic in character, representing a predominantly Greek element, an aristocracy of landowners and a lower class of free farmers with a few craftsmen. But the Greek settlements were made in well-populated, native areas and, at the outset, a cultural fusion began which is apparent in the craft products and religious practices. We may ask how the political fusion was accomplished, for, in the course of time, the Greek tribal organization would have become an increasingly intolerable strait-jacket, preventing the extension of political participation to Anatolian natives and to later Greek metics. Intermarriage would have accomplished

---

[15] Pausanias 7.5.12. A locality, Chalcis, is attested epigraphically (*SGDI* 5610). It was on the isthmus connecting the Mimas peninsula to the territory of Clazomenae.

[16] M. N. Tod, *GHI* 1².1; L. H. Jeffery, "The Courts of Justice in Archaic Chios," *BSA* 51 (1956) 157–67; J. H. Oliver, "Text of the So-Called Constitution of Chios from the First Half of the Sixth Century B.C.," *AJP* 80 (1959) 296–301.

[17] Plutarch, *Theseus* 20 (from Ion of Chios); Theopompus (*FGrH* 115, F 276); Beloch, *Gr. Gesch.* 1.2².100.

something, for the union of Ionian men with native and metic women would have brought the children into the Ionian community, but the reverse would have set the child among the aliens. Perhaps this, along with the growing cultural fusion, established an environment conducive to ideas of political assimilation, but it is more likely that the first steps were taken to satisfy the needs of military defense. In Ionia the towns had not only to reckon with native groups on their own territory, as it grew, but to defend themselves from Anatolian and, at times, neighborly Greek pressure. In the warlike conditions of life in early Ionia, it is probable that all elements of the community were needed for military service, even if the brunt of the fighting fell on the nobles and their clansmen. For such a purpose it seems that a decadic organization of the population into nominal groups of 1,000, *chiliastyes*, and of 100, *hekatostyes*, was devised at an early date.

IV. THE CHILIASTYES

There is a hint in the *Iliad* of such decadic organization, probably as a means for military levy rather than as an actual battle order. Achilles' 50 ships and their crews were divided into 5 *stiches* under 5 separate leaders, each in command of 10 ships and 500 men (*Il.* 16.168–72). Combats, of course, were settled by individual heroes, but their following comprised nameless oarsmen and fighters, who swarmed like bees around their chieftains. The potential usefulness of such a system in Ionia is suggested by analogies in early Germany[18] and England. In Germany the terms "hundred" and "thousand" were applied to the inhabitants of a locality who had hung together in migration and settlement and formed a military unit of the settled community. In England a "hundred" seems to have designated a group of householders forming an agricultural village. It may have served as a military levy, or as a fiscal unit paying one hundred lamb's hides. Ultimately it became a juridical district. In Ionia, as the communities developed into city-states, the military *chiliastys* would have acquired a traditional coherency which enabled it to become the means for political reorganization. We find it as a subdivision of new tribes in several Ionian communities, most clearly in Ephesus.

[18] Busolt-Swoboda (above, note 5) 560–61.

At some time prior to the mid-fourth century, for our earliest
notice is from the historian, Ephorus, the citizens of Ephesus were
reorganized into 5 tribes; the Ephesians, Bennaei, or Bembinaei,
Teans, Euonymi and Carenians.[19] Each of these was sub-
divided into at least six *chiliastyes*, for that number is known for
the tribe, Ephesians. They were the Boreis, Oenopes, Argadeis,
Geleontes, Lebedii, and Salaminii. Evidently the older Ionian
element in the population of Ephesus had been formed into a new
tribe, most properly called Ephesians, and the former tribes
demoted to make up its subdivisions. Greek metics from Lebedus
and Salamis (which Salamis is unknown) were included. Names
of the other tribes and of their *chiliastyes* have been identified as
from Greek and native ethnic groups, *genê* and local toponyms.[20]
At the time of the reorganization there was a very decided
weakening of the older Ionian element and extension of political
participation in the state to alien groups. For the change the
chiliastyes were made the instrument. It is probable that they
were pre-existent and not invented for the occasion.

Ephorus sets the reorganization in the legendary past of Ephesus,
and the term, *chiliastys*, was widely used in Ionia and in the
Ionian colonies.[21] Although our notices are late, the institution

[19] See above, note 4; for discussion, see Sakellariou (above, note 6) 132, note 7 on
133–34 and *Hellenika* 15 (1957) 220–31. The Ephesians are considered to be composed
mainly of the Ionian element in the population, since the *chiliastyes* bear the names of
the old Ionian tribes. The Bennaei or Bembinaei are identified as Anatolian natives
resident in the territory of Ephesus. The Teans would have been originally refugees
or migrants from Teos (at the time of the Persian conquest ?). The Carenians are
identified as migrants from the area of Carene on the coast of Asia Minor opposite to
Lesbos, but it seems unlikely that there would have been a large enough number from
this small place to make up a whole tribe. The Euonymi are sometimes connected
with Athens because of the coincidence with an Attic deme name, but a Carian origin
seems more plausible (e.g. Euonymia). Sakellariou allocates eight *chiliastyes* of 1,000
members each to each tribe and estimates the population of Ephesus at 40,000 citizens.
It is reasonable to assume that the tribe, Ephesians, had eight *chiliastyes*, for the missing
Argadeis and Hopletes should probably be included with the other Ionian tribes; but
the population estimate can hardly be correct. If the *chiliastyes* were pre-existing
territorial units, they must have long since lost their exact numerical significance.
The number of 40,000 citizens implies a free population of about 120,000, which is
very high for this period of the sixth century (see Roebuck [above, note 1, *Ionian
Trade*] 21–23).

[20] Sakellariou (above, note 6) 132–37 discusses the difficult problems of identification. A list of the *chiliastyes* is given by J. Keil, *JOAI* 16 (1913) 245–48.

[21] See, in addition to the instances noted above, *CIG* 3641b (Lampsacus); Aeneas
Tacticus 11.10 (Heraclea Pontica); *SGDI* 3059 (Byzantium); *SGDI* 276–78 (Methymna
on Lesbos). A similar decadic arrangement was used on Cos where it was gentilic in
character and linked with the three Doric tribes (Busolt-Swoboda [above, note 5] 258).

should be prior to the founding of the colonies. Perhaps we should recognize in the *chilioi* of Colophon, whom Xenophanes criticized (Frag. 3, Diehl), an aristocratic *chiliastys*. Samos, too, experienced a tribal reorganization,[22] dated by Beloch to the time of Polycrates, in which two, or perhaps three, new tribes were established and the older Ionian tribes subordinated into *chiliastyes*: a new tribe, the Astypalaeans, was made up of the older Ionian inhabitants of the city of Samos, while the Chesians were formed from the Carian town of Chesia in west Samos; a third tribe, Aeschrionia, is dubious. It is mentioned only by Herodotus and, if it existed at all, may have been short-lived.[23] The old Ionian tribe, Oenopes, became a *chiliastys* of the new tribe, the Chesians.[24] In Miletus, however, there was no similar reorganization, for inscriptions of the first half of the fifth century reveal that the six, old Ionian tribes were still basic for the government. Yet, significantly, a *chiliastys* of the tribe, Argadeis, designated as the first, *prôtê*, is identified.[25]

[22] Two tribes are known for the second century B.C. from an inscription regulating the distribution of grain (*SIG*³ 976, line 40). Their names are given by Themistagoras of Ephesus (*FHG* 4, page 512, No. 1; *Et. Mag.*, s.v. "Astypalaea") as the Astypalaeans and the Chesians. Since Astypalaea was the name of the Samian acropolis (Polyaenus, *Strat.* 1.23) and Chesia the name of a Carian town, the tribal names probably reflect an organization in which Greeks and Carians were given equal place in the state. The time is controversial, but the view of Beloch (*Gr. Gesch.* 1.1².375) seems most acceptable, that it was the work of Polycrates; if not of Polycrates himself, perhaps in the troubled years following his death. Themistagoras had related it to the early years of settlement as the work of the kings, Procles and Tembrion, which was accepted by Wilamowitz (*SBBerl* [1904] 931), but should be rejected because of the evidence of the existence of the Ionian tribes (above, note 4). Bürchner's view (*RE* 1² [1920] 2214) that the coup of the leaders of the expedition sent to defend Perinthus against the Megarians in the early sixth century was made the occasion to establish the new tribes, seems most unlikely. The Samian generals utilized the Megarians to unseat the oligarchical government in Samos (Plutarch, *Moralia* 303E–304C), but the struggle is best regarded as a quarrel between factions of the Samian *geomoroi*. A *terminus ante quem* for the *chiliastyes* and the *hekatostyes* is afforded by references in late fourth century inscriptions (*SIG*³ 312, line 30; *SEG* 1.362, lines 19–20).

[23] Herodotus (3.26) casually mentions a Samian tribe, Aeschrionia, as furnishing the settlers for the city of Oasis in Libya. This has been considered as an inexact reference to a smaller gentilic group (Busolt-Swoboda [above, note 5] 260, note 2). The derogatory name (?) perhaps refers to a new tribe of slaves, some members of which later emigrated for military service in Egypt. Many Samians were killed at the time of Syloson's tyranny (Her. 3.149; Duris [*FGrH* 76, F 66]) and slaves were enfranchised.

[24] *SEG* 1.362, line 35.

[25] See above, note 4; for the *chiliastys*, *SBBerl* (1904) 85 and Bilabel (above, note 4) 123.

V. POLITICAL REORGANIZATION IN IONIA

It is probable that these political reorganizations, the traces of which are visible in the new function of the *chiliastys*, are to be connected with the activity of the tyrants and the stasis of the sixth century. By that time, the economic growth of Ionia, fostered by its trade and colonizing, had brought new economic groups into existence in many Ionian cities and produced a high level of prosperity in which metics and Anatolians, as well as Ionian Greeks, shared. In a recent discussion of the tribes of Ephesus, Sakellariou has argued that their reorganization was a gradual process beginning in the first half of the sixth century under the tyrant, Pythagoras.[26] This seems very plausible, if we can trust the traditions of the tyranny. They stress the bitter enmity of the tyrants, Pythagoras and Pindarus, to the Basilidae, the descendants of the Ionian kings, and to the other men of standing and power in the city. Perhaps the tyrants sought support among the Anatolians and Greek metics and paid for it by the creation of new tribes which converted their *chiliastyes* into political units. If so, this recognition of the Anatolian element may well be reflected in the acceptance of their goddess, Artemis, as the patron deity of the city. The earliest altar basis of the Artemisium is now dated *ca.* 600 B.C.,[27] coincident with the tyranny of Pythagoras. The monumental building of the temple was partly subsidized by Croesus in the middle of the century. At the time of his attack on Ephesus the citizens dedicated their city as a suppliant to Artemis by attaching it to the Artemisium with a rope (Her. 1.26). In effect, the city gave itself to the native goddess. Perhaps the old Ionian festival of the Apaturia was discarded shortly after this time.[28]

In Miletus, however, despite the civil strife of the early sixth century, the old tribes were retained. The tyranny of Thrasybulus and his would-be successors was followed by stasis between the two groups described as the *Ploutis* and the *Cheiromacha* (Plutarch, *Moralia* 298c) who were ridiculed by the name, Gergithes.[29]

[26] For Pythagoras see Baton of Sinope *FHG* 4, page 348, No. 2; for Pindarus, Aelian, *Var. hist.* 3.26.

[27] P. Jacobsthal, "The Date of the Ephesian Foundation-Deposit," *JHS* 71 (1951) 85–95.

[28] Her. 1.147; Sakellariou (above, note 6) 278, note 1.

[29] Heracleides Ponticus in Athenaeus 524A. In this context the term is applicable to all those opposed to the wealthy, and indicates contempt, but Gergithes has

Were not these "hand-fighters" the troops of the lower-class military *chiliastyes*, while the wealthy landowners supplied the hoplites and the ship captains? This stasis was arbitrated by Parian judges (Her. 5.28–29), who placed the government in the hands of the landowners, those with well-kept fields as Herodotus put it. Presumably a moderate oligarchy was established which restricted citizenship to the wealthy and middle groups in the state, who were members of the six, old Ionian tribes.

Unfortunately the evidence for Chios is obscure. The "constitution" does reveal a new council with 50 members selected from each tribe, thus giving more power to the *dêmos*, but we do not know whether the circle of citizenship was enlarged.

This background of Ionian political development in the sixth century at least makes it easier to understand the sophisticated proposal of Thales for centralization of the Ionian League (Her. 1.170.3), which seems so far in advance of his time. As some of its member states became more fully integrated communities, he envisaged an Ionian League with a plenary council, to which members would send representatives, while the states themselves sank into the position of demes,[30] somewhat like the *chiliastyes* of the tribes. Herodotus drew his analogy from the Athenian reorganization made by Cleisthenes, but, before Cleisthenes, there lay almost a century of Ionian experience in political integration.

evidently been borrowed from the name of some group in Miletus. The Gergithes are usually identified as serfs formed from the pre-Ionian population. Perhaps, as the state urbanized, the name was extended to ridicule all the lower classes. The Gergithes may have been Anatolian natives, for the name was used also for the remnants of the Teucri in the Troad and Aeolis (Her. 5.122; 7.43; Strabo 589 [13.1.19]). Miletus, however, is very far from the Troad.

In Priene the former serfs were called *Pedieis*, "Plainsmen," (*OGIS* 11; C. B. Welles, *Royal Correspondence in the Hellenistic Period*, Nos. 6, 8). They are mentioned in Hellenistic inscriptions as former dependents and, their freedom obtained, foes of the state. The name, "plainsmen," is probably to be explained by their residence in the plain of the Maeander River between Mycale and Latmus, where they would have worked the land of the Prienians until winning their freedom.

[30] Roebuck (above, note 1, *Ionian League*) 29.

THREE CLASSES (?) IN EARLY ATTICA

IN the traditions of early Athenian history there are references to an ordering of society different from the familiar classification by agricultural production defined by Solon: Pentakosiomedimnoi, Hippeis, Zeugitai and Thetes. Instead of these names we hear in several connections of Eupatridai, Agroikoi (or Geomoroi or Georgoi) and Demiourgoi. These groups appear in a political context after the usurpation of the archonship by Damasias, 582/1–580/79 B.C. Damasias, according to the *Athenaion Politeia* (13, 2), was removed from office and replaced by 10 archons for the remainder, 10 months, of the year 580/79 B.C.: 5 from the Eupatridai, 3 from the Agroikoi and 2 from the Demiourgoi. Although this notice seems to have the validity of official record,[1] the situation itself is difficult to accept: 10, instead of the usual 9, archons, representing groups which, in name at least, have no connection with those established by the Solonian classification.[2] The names at first sight suggest that the 10 archons were representatives of a cross-section of Athenian society, of aristocrats, farmers, craftsmen and laborers. While the vesting of governmental power in the board of archons apparently has a precedent in the crisis of Kylon's conspiracy (Thuc., I, 126, 8), the number 10 should hardly apply to the archonships. We might suspect that this is a special commission, in effect suspending the Solonian constitution until the latter was put to work again in the following year. Perhaps the commissioners were formally designated as reconcilers and archons, to act without reference to the assembly as had the 9 archons of 632 B.C. Yet a governing commission with representation from craftsmen and laborers seems very surprising in an archaic Greek state.

As has been suspected, of course, such an arrangement is more at home in the political theorizing of the late fifth and fourth centuries.[3] But if the action is historical, there were in Athens *ca.* 580 B.C. three defined groups of sufficient coherence and standing in the state that it was desirable to have recourse to them at a time of political crisis. Their existence at that time would give support to the tradition that the groups had existed for some time, even if we suspect their identification as social classes.

---

[1] F. Jacoby, *Atthis*, p. 175. I am grateful to Evelyn Smithson of the University of New York at Buffalo for her helpful suggestions and information about the archaeological material of Dark Age Attica; agreement on the conclusions expressed below, of course, is not necessarily implied.

[2] Presumably we should infer that the three groups, whatever their nature, were not property classes. Accordingly, I have not tried to bring them into specific connection with Solon's reorganization or with his property classes. For discussion see C. Hignett, *The Athenian Constitution*, Oxford, 1958, pp. 319-321.

[3] J. Day and M. Chambers, *Aristotle's History of Athenian Democracy*, Berkeley, 1962, p. 173.

Tradition ascribes such an ordering of Athenian society to the organization of Athenian government by Theseus. Plutarch (*Theseus*, 25) credits him with separating out the Eupatridai among the Athenians and investing them with privilege: they were to know divine matters, to furnish archons, to be teachers of the laws and exegetai of holy and secret things: in short, to be the governing group in Athens in whose favor Theseus renounced the monarchy. As distinct from the Eupatridai the Geomoroi and the Demiourgoi were to form the people, equal in themselves and each group of general benefit to the state. The Geomoroi were reckoned as useful and the Demiourgoi numerous. Other late sources [4] indicate a twofold division of Athenian society into Georgoi and Demiourgoi before Theseus privileged the Eupatridai to make Athens an aristocratic state. Can we determine the nature of the groups?

Recently two explanations have been suggested. R. Sealey [5] has argued that the groups were, *ca.* 580 B.C., regional parties, while F. Wüst and J. Oliver [6] have preferred to regard them as old, hereditary classes or castes submerged in the Solonian reorganization but familiar and usable in the crisis of 580/79 B.C. It is difficult to accept the identification as regional parties. Sketchy as the account of the years between Solon and Peisistratos is in the *Athenaion Politeia*, creation of the governing commission of 580/79 is presented as a stabilizing move after the deposition of the would-be "tyrant," Damasias. The measure was anti-revolutionary in intent, presumably designed to preserve the Solonian system. Perhaps this could have been the purpose of a coalition of regional factions, but it is pertinent to ask why, if these were the names of the factions of *ca.* 580 B.C., those of a decade or so later at the time of Peisistratos' rise were entirely different. The latter do seem to designate proper regional groups, but it is difficult to explain the Eupatridai, Geomoroi and Demiourgoi as such. Perhaps the Eupatridai, as the governing class of aristocratic Athens, with their holdings mainly in the Athenian plain, had a regional interest, but were all the Eupatridai located there? The seat of the Alkmaionidai has been placed with some plausability in the district of Anavyssos near the southwest coast, and the Peisistratidai were apparently in Brauron. [7] But what of the Geomoroi and Demiourgoi? How could magistrates' titles, as Sealey explains the terms, which were presumably ubiquitous in Attica, become labels for regional parties?

[4] Schol. Plato, *Axioch.*, p. 465; *Lex. Dem. Pat.*, p. 182 (*Gennetai*) indicates that the two groups, Georgoi and Demiourgoi, remained in existence until the reorganization of Kleisthenes. Strabo (VIII, 7, 1) has the names of four Estates: Georgoi, Demiourgoi, Hieropoioi, Phylakes; possibly this is a speculative identification of the four old Athenian tribes by function. Diodoros (I, 28, 5) indicates three *mere* in early Athens. All this seems part of the political theorizing referred to in note 3.

[5] R. Sealey, *Historia*, IX, 1960, pp. 178-180; X, 1961, pp. 512-514.

[6] F. Wüst, *Historia*, VI, 1957, pp. 180-182; VIII, 1959, pp. 1-10. J. Oliver, *Demokratia*, p. 30, note 30; *Historia*, IX, 1960, pp. 506 ff.

[7] W. Eliot, *Historia*, XVI, 1967, pp. 279-286; see, in particular, R. J. Hopper, *B.S.A.*, LVI, 1961, pp. 189-219; D. M. Lewis, *Historia*, XII, 1963, pp. 22-26.

The other line of explanation, which recognizes the groups as hereditary classes or castes, seems more satisfactory at first sight, but it, too, involves considerable difficulties. As Oliver and Wüst have pointed out,[8] the respective representation of the three groups in the commission should indicate an order of importance. Eupatridai were the most prestigious, Geomoroi in second place and Demiourgoi in third. But was this a hierarchic ordering by class or caste? In a situation of political crisis the prestige of power and position was needed, not that based on some old shadowy form of class distinction which Solon felt could be overlooked. Indeed, to interpret the groups as classes or castes in any formal and legally defined sense is dangerous, for, like the Greek tradition itself, such a view assumes a definitive ordering of society at some specific time. The members of the commission would have been recognized leaders of some type from their groups but how can we assume that craftsmen and laborers, who may have had no place in the Athenian assembly,[9] would have had leaders acceptable to the assembly when the commission was selected? We should seek the nature of the groups in the process of social evolution in Attica in the Dark Age and recognize that they were still potent in the early sixth century, even if disguised under the new Solonian classification.

Eupatridai

The traditional criterion for a Eupatrid was membership by descent in a great family, with the nexus of wealth, privilege, birth and prestige attached to it. No one would deny that there were such families in seventh-century Athens and there seems no reason to deny them the collective name of Eupatridai,[10] although it is interesting that Solon does not use the term. Yet we can scarcely assume that their position of social primacy and the name, which emphasizes only the aspect of good birth, originated on a single occasion, either by the act of Theseus or with the creation of the archonship. The latter was the first reservation of political privilege. It is historically more significant to see if some estimate can be made of the time and manner in which a group of great families came into existence in Attica. For the seventh century we

---

[8] Wüst, *Historia*, VI, 1957, p. 187; Oliver, *Historia*, IX, 1960, p. 506.

[9] Hignett, *op. cit.* (note 2), p. 101.

[10] Day and Chambers, *op. cit.* (note 3), p. 173 and the articles cited in notes 5 and 6. The name Eupatrid, which stresses good birth, presumably would have been applied after the great families had become recognizable by wealth and privilege, but at a time when reaction to aristocratic rule had set in. The word is laudatory, probably coined by aristocrats to stress the one qualification which " equalizing " farmers and parvenu merchants could not obtain. The time of such reaction was in the late seventh and early sixth centuries; see W. Donlan, *Agathos-Kakos; A Study of Social Attitudes in Archaic Greece* (Dissertation, Northwestern University, 1968), pp. 120-121, 208, 210 ff. and *idem*, " The Role of Eugeneia in the Aristocratic Self-Image During the Fifth Century B. C.," *Classics and the Classical Tradition*, p. 64, note 2. Pentakosiomedimnoi seems to be specifically coined for a property qualification, presumably that of Solon, to separate the very wealthy out of the Hippeis. It is the only such specifically quantitative word in the rating list.

do have some specific evidence but for the period before that only inference from the archaeological record.

The seventh century saw the consolidation of political and economic power by the wealthy families of Attica, but towards its close there was also increasingly effective reaction against their hold on government when the concept of the polis became stronger. Without pressing the statement (*Ath. Pol.*, 3, 5) that archons were chosen ἀριστίνδην καὶ πλουτίνδην as a legal qualification, it is reasonable that in practice they were. Throughout the seventh century the archonships grew to a college of 9 by the time of Kylon's conspiracy in 632 B.C. The administration of the law was firmly in their hands and those of their peers on the Council of the Areopagus and in the various special courts. Extension of the hold by the wealthy on land and agricultural production in Attica brought the peasants close to revolt by the end of the century. Solon could see only two classes in Attica, the wealthy and the poor, and endeavored to reconcile them by setting up a scale by which individuals might participate in the government. It has been reasonably suggested [11] that in this period of reaction against the aristocracy the latter began to seek other justifications for their position than wealth and privilege. Perhaps the term, Eupatrid, was coined to emphasize that birth was the unbreakable barrier which closed their ranks. Obviously in the seventh century the great families had consolidated their leading position by multiplying specific forms of privilege reserved to themselves and had acquired the consciousness of class. But as great families they had existed before this and won acceptance of their primacy. Can we detect this in the archaeological record of the Dark Age?

Both tradition and the evidence of archaeology [12] attest that there was some continuity of habitation in Attica beyond the collapse of the Mycenaean organization at the end of the Bronze Age. Yet that organization was shattered, much of Attica depopulated and only Athens and a few other points became the sites of survival and refugee settlement. Perhaps a few important Mycenaean families were able to maintain themselves by holding some of their land, even acquiring more, but presumably the elaborate Mycenaean system of landholding perished. In short, we should scarcely look for the origins of many of the great Athenian families in survival from the Mycenaean Age. Nor apparently should we identify them as a conquest-aristocracy which had taken over land by occupation and was able to support itself by native labor on large estates, for there was no serf group in Attica as in Thessaly, Sparta and some of the colonial regions. In brief summary the archaeological evidence of the Dark Age seems to indicate that at the outset there was a concentration of habitation at Athens with, perhaps, a scattering on the east coast. Then, as population increased

---

[11] W. Donlan, note 10 above.

[12] For the end of the Mycenaean era in Athens see O. Broneer, " The Dorian Invasion. What Happened at Athens," *A.J.A.*, LII, 1948, pp. 111-114; for the archaeological record in Dark Age Attica, J. N. Coldstream, *Greek Geometric Pottery*, London, 1968, pp. 336, 341, 344, 348, 360.

and land became scarcer, there was a diffusion throughout Attica—first to sites near Athens, then to Eleusis, Marathon and the interior. By 800 B.C. at least, population was increasing rapidly on the east coast and settlement had started on the Saronic shore on the west. This process of internal colonization in Attica seems to have extended into the eighth century when the numbers of the rural population in Attica rose sharply. Of course the picture may be illusory, simply from scarcity of evidence from the countryside, but, if it is correct, there are some useful implications for understanding the nature of the three groups with which we are concerned.

As noticed above, the Eupatridai were said to have had religious and political privilege. Their land holdings were concentrated, although not exclusively, in Athens and its plain. For example, the clan of the Medontidai still owned a plot of land below the Acropolis in the fifth century.[13] They had grown to primacy in and near the later city. Presumably at the outset of the Dark Age land for farming, which was necessary for survival, was available, so that certain families were able to settle in desirable locations and by industry and proliferation of their members to extend their holdings. While we can scarcely assume that Attica enjoyed an idyllic absence of internal friction, the land does seem to have been free from invasion and great disturbance over the eleventh and tenth centuries. Generations of agrarian life enabled the survival of families and recognition of the primacy of some of them in terms of land ownership and agricultural wealth. There was no need of specific designation of such primacy, for its recognition would have been automatic and gradually extensive. We can, of course, hardly trace the rise of such families either individually or for the group as a whole, but their wealth has been recognized in grave furnishings and burial practice in the ninth and eighth centuries.

We should be cautious of identifying by its rich contents alone a particular grave as the grave of a " noble," for wealth might be won or lost in a single generation through a raid; cautious, too, of recognizing in a particular symbol a badge of class status. For example, the suggestion that the representation of a horse on certain Protogeometric amphoras marked a noble's burial is countered with the observation that the horse has a chthonic significance.[14] It is a religious rather than a class symbol. Similarly the representation in terracotta of five small granaries for grain storage found in a wealthy woman's burial need not mark her as a member of one of the Five-hundred-busheler families.[15] She may have been, but logic would compel us to recognize Zeugitai in those graves containing similar representations but with only two granaries

---

[13] *I.G.*, I², 871 ; Lewis, *Historia*, XII, 1963, pp. 22-26.

[14] C. G. Styrenius, *Submycenean Pottery*, Lund, 1967, pp. 113-114.

[15] E. Smithson, *Hesperia*, XXXVII, 1968, pp. 83, 96. The suggestion that the term, Penta-kosiomedimnos, had the legal sense of qualifying for the archonship in the ninth century (the burial is dated *ca.* 850 B.C.) raises very considerable difficulty about the time of the establishment of the aristocratic government in Athens, for the latter is usually placed in the latter part of the eighth century (Hignett, *op. cit.* [note 2], pp. 42-45).

or wine jars. Rather, these seem to be symbols of wealth. More significant for such identification would be the indications in the funerary practices of regard, as well as the ability to pay, for the continuity of the family: continuous use and safe-guarding of a rich family plot over generations, provision of special apparatus for libation and the like. Thus it seems reasonable to see in the large libation vessels appearing over some of the rich cremation graves in the Kerameikos in the late Protogeometric period [16] the beginning of such family consciousness and, more certainly, in the elaborate furniture of the Dipylon graves of *ca.* 800-750 B.C. its full fruition [17]—the pride and assertion of membership in a great house. In short, the Eupatridai, although they may not have been called that, were fully established in the early eighth century and able to assert their political privilege throughout the seventh. Presumably they had risen to prominence in Athens and had fixed their main seats of residence and estates in the Athenian plain from the outset. They had brought the state of Athens into existence.

Geomoroi

Of the three words used to describe the second group in the sources, Geomoroi, Agroikoi and Georgoi, the latter two are descriptive but Geomoroi, land-sharers, is specifically designative. It identifies a group which had been assigned shares in land and probably is the oldest of the terms. At least Aeschylus (*Supp.*, 613) used *gamoroi* to designate Athenian citizens. The term is, of course, known from other Greek states, Syracuse and Samos, where it referred to the oligarchs, but originally the word must have indicated the original settlers who shared the land of these colonies.[18] Presumably they retained and enlarged their lots, becoming an oligarchical, governing class in the Archaic period. Some of them would have been magistrates, but there is no reason, with Sealey,[19] to assign that meaning to the Geomoroi of early Athens. In Athens the Eupatridai became the oligarchical, governing group. In the Geomoroi of Athens, then, should we not recognize the ordinary farmers, substantial landholders, whom Solon classified as Zeugitai and restored to well being, as distinguished from the great families? At an early date, when legal definitions did not exist, some may have risen to " great family " status; in the seventh century many declined to the Hektemorate and to slavery, sinking in the social scale. But why should they be called land-sharers? The poor farmers of Solon's time and the landless men apparently

[16] Styrenius, *op. cit.* (note 14), pp. 114-115, 121.

[17] Coldstream, *op. cit.* (note 12), pp. 349 ff.

[18] Oliver, *Historia*, IX, 1960, pp. 560 ff.; *Demokratia*, p. 30. While Oliver properly stresses the significance of the meaning, land-sharers, he explains both Geomoroi and Demiourgoi as surviving from the Mycenaean system of land tenure; this is very difficult to accept in the light of the archaeological record. Wüst identifies the Geomoroi as private, free landholders, the Zeugitai of Solon's classification (*Historia*, VI, 1957, p. 190).

[19] Sealey, *Historia*, IX, 1960, pp. 178-180.

voiced demands for a redistribution of the land, but there is no hint in tradition that the land of Attica had been formally divided among its people as in a colonial or conquest settlement.

Perhaps, however, we can envisage the origin of the Geomoroi in connection with the process of internal colonization. We do not know how the diffusion of population from Athens was carried out in the ninth and eighth centuries but there are a few hints. In Greek political speculation the clan village was held to be the kernel of the ultimate polis; some Athenian clan names were identified with demes.[20] Such a settlement has been recognized, at least in the physical form of its cemetery, at Vari.[21] We might picture the establishment of a village and the sharing of the land around it as the venture of a cadet member of a clan from the main family seat on the Athenian plain; the head of the group established a manor and distributed the land in substantial plots among his followers. As the village acquired a sense of local identity and increased in size, its own excess population and the landless men attracted to it might find plots of land to farm out in the *eschatia* or a living as shepherds, laborers and craftsmen. We might recognize the Geomoroi in the substantially found, original settlers and their descendants, and the Thetes in the newcomers and in the community's own excess. Who, then, were the Demiourgoi?

Demiourgoi

Murakawa, in his study of Demiourgoi,[22] accepts both the reality of the governing commission of 580/79 B.C. and the existence of the three groups in Dark Age Attica, explaining the Demiourgoi as common people of various occupations. He ascribes the place of the latter in the governing commission to the high development which trade and industry had reached by 580 B.C. However, to judge by Athenian pottery production and export, trade and industry were only beginning to rise in the first quarter of the sixth century; the community was still agrarian, so that craftsmen and laborers would hardly have had political weight. Murakawa, despite his thorough study of the Demiourgoi in the capacity of magistrates, does not explore the possibility that they may have formed such a group in pre-Kleisthenean Attica. Generally speaking, Demiourgoi were important officials of the whole state in some Doric communities, as in Argos, or promoted to that status from local office when the state synoecized, as in Elis. But in Arcadia and Achaea they seem to have remained local officials, while in Phocis they are known as the officials of a phratry.[23] In Classical Athens, of course, the name applied to such local officials was Demarch, not Demi-

---

[20] Lewis, *Historia*, XII, 1963, p. 26.
[21] Eliot, *Phoenix*, Suppl. V, *Coastal Demes of Attica*, Toronto, 1962, p. 39.
[22] K. Murakawa, *Historia*, VI, 1957, pp. 385-415.
[23] Murakawa, *op. cit.* (note 22), pp. 390-391.

ourgos. Hesychius [24] explains that Dorian Demiourgoi were equivalent to Demarchs in Athens but there is no documentary evidence that the former term was used there for a local official who may have been the predecessor of a Demarch. Yet Kleisthenes did create new demes in his reorganization, as well as using those which existed, so perhaps he felt that a remodeled label would have been helpful.

There are some general indications that Demiourgoi may have designated local officials, village heads, in the pre-Kleisthenean state. As noticed above,[25] one tradition indicates that the Demiourgoi, along with the Geomoroi, were in existence until the time of Kleisthenes. The same tradition defines both groups as Gennetai. Presumably, then, the Demiourgoi were clansmen and landholders, hardly to be identified as workers at various occupations. Murakawa, however, does seem to be correct in trying to account for the Demiourgoi as a product of various local conditions in the Dark Age rather than as survivals of some Mycenaean institution, e.g., workers on the *damos'* land or officials of the *damos*. If the archaeological record in Attica of breakdown and diffusion of population, which would have involved a change in the system of land tenure, is correct, we should hardly try to explain the institution in terms of survival. Logically Homeric usage of the term might contain some hint, but perhaps Homeric Demiourgoi were more at home in trans-Aegean Ionia than in Ionian Attica. In any case, the Demiourgoi were few in number in the Homeric community and are hard to define as a homogeneous group. Some, like the heralds, were members of the community, while others, like bards, were strangers to it. All may have shared the sense of availability to the Homeric public, but in post-Homeric times, some, like the Kerykes of Athens and the Talthybiadai of Sparta, emerged among the notables, while others became magistrates, and still others, craftsmen and laborers. Presumably explanation of the different lines of development lies in the local conditioning factors which shaped institutions in separate parts of Dark Age Greece.

We might suggest that in Attica the Demiourgoi appeared in connection with the internal colonization and the establishment of village and town life. As villages and towns were formed, the interests of their inhabitants would begin to focus on local concerns and gradually become a community interest. In some degree this might be directed by a clan leader, but what if there were two or more clan groups in a locality? The substantial landholders, the Geomoroi, would have a common local interest and the same social status. This could be expressed by the selection of a local official in a common assembly—of a Demiourgos. That is, all Demiourgoi were probably Geomoroi but not all Geomoroi would become Demiourgoi. All the Geomoroi of Attica would be members of the assembly of Athens when the localities coalesced into a single state and would select their state officials from the Eupatridai but the

---

[24] Hesychius, *s.v.* Demiourgos. Lewis notes that the earliest occurrence of Demarch seems to be in Demosthenes, XXI, 182 (*Historia*, XII, 1963, p. 26, note 48).

[25] Above, note 4.

Demiourgoi would remain local officials and so be properly representative of a local interest. The time for the appearance of the Demiourgoi thus seems to be the several centuries of internal colonization, culminating in the eighth century, while the pressure to maintain them would have been generated in the egalitarian movement of the seventh century, when the Geomoroi were being depressed and the reaction to the Eupatridai mounted.

As Wüst and Oliver have noticed,[26] there does seem a balance in the commission of 10: 5 were Eupatridai, while the other 5 had a homogeneous, non-Eupatrid character. Collectively the whole commission represented the landholders of Attica and continued, if not in Solonian terms, at least the Solonian intent of the reorganization of 594 B.C. It is hardly surprising that the state reverted to a more even keel and that it was a full generation, not until 546 B.C., before Peisistratos was able to found his tyranny firmly.

CARL ROEBUCK

NORTHWESTERN UNIVERSITY

[26] Above, note 6.

SOME ASPECTS OF URBANIZATION
IN CORINTH

66 CORINTH was now (c. 750-700 B.C., in the Late Geometric Period) a thriving commercial *polis*, rapidly increasing in size. The nucleus of the Geometric town seems to have been in the neighborhood of the future Agora, where a sequence of pottery from graves and wells covers the whole Geometric Period . . . The wide circulation of Corinthian wares is a symptom of the rapid expansion of Corinthian trade . . . this was a natural consequence of the decline of Attic exports, and the seizure of the commercial initiative by Corinth." Coldstream.[2]

" Jusqu' à la fin du viii e s., Corinthe ne semble donc avoir différé en rien des autres cités du point de vue de l'organisation sociale et de l'activité économique " . . . And of Corinth in the seventh century: " Ne parlons pas d'organisation rationelle: on n'en est encore qu' au stade où l'état de fait économique commence à se dégager de la confusion des improvisations collectives . . . Cette évolution dans la sens d'une production artisanale accrue et d'un négoce naissant et sans doute anarchique n'affecte pas les fondements agricoles primitifs de la cité, si elle affecte certes son équilibre général. On n'a en particulier aucune raison de penser que les oligarchiques Bacchiades se détournèrent de leur existence de grandes propriétaires fonciers pour se consacrer aux " affaires " et transformer consciemment leur cité en un centre industriel et commerçant." Will.[3]

" The fact that both Archias (oekist of Syracuse) and Chersicrates (oekist of Corcyra) were probably Bacchiads was taken to suggest the state organization which the theory (commercial motivation in the Corinthian colonization of the eighth century) requires . . . a member of the ruling clan could clearly be required as oikist without the expedition necessarily being a planned act of state . . ." Graham.[4]

[1] This article was written during the tenure of a Senior Fellowship from the National Endowment for the Humanities. I wish to thank the Endowment, Northwestern University, which granted leave of absence, and the American School of Classical Studies at Athens, which enabled me to use its facilities for work in both Athens and Corinth. Professor Oscar Broneer and Mr. Charles K. Williams, Director of the Corinth Excavation, read the mss. in first draft and made many helpful suggestions. In addition, Mr. Williams sent me the mss. of his report on the excavations of 1970 before its publication and discussed topographical matters with me in Corinth and by letter. I very much appreciate their advice and information, given generously, and assure them that any departures from it should be ascribed to the author's perversity.

[2] J. N. Coldstream, *Greek Geometric Pottery*, London, 1968, pp. 365-366.

[3] Édouard Will, *Korinthiaka*, Paris, 1955, pp. 337-338. Will, while denying any commercial motivation to the Corinthian colonization of the eighth century and any commercial policy to the Bacchiads, does stress the opportunities for trade opened up by colonization and sets the beginning of the process of urbanization in Corinth in the seventh century.

[4] A. J. Graham, *Colony and Mother City in Ancient Greece*, Manchester, 1964, p. 220. Graham is arguing against the theory of pre-colonization trade in the West and against commercial motivation in eighth-century colonization, as developed a generation ago by Blakeway and Dunbabin.

These three quotations from recent, and excellent, books reveal some of the difficulties which beset the historian of Dark Age and Archaic Greece. Coldstream characterizes Corinth in the latter part of the eighth century as " commercial," " seizing commercial initiative," while Will describes it as agricultural and envisages the economic factor as beginning to emerge only in the following (seventh) century. Coldstream calls Corinth a polis, Graham, by implication, a clan community. For the latter regards the colonization of Syracuse in 733 B.C. and of Corcyra in the same year (or in 709 B.C.) as carried out without state planning; that is, the community did not officially designate an oekist, determine which citizens were to migrate and arrange for the distribution of lots to them in the new colony.

Perhaps these characterizations of Corinthian society are not to be pressed too far as reflecting the respective frames of reference of their authors. For example, Coldstream, on the basis of the excavational evidence at Corinth, conceives of the community physically as a city in embryo, its nucleus near the future Agora, with clusters of villages forming on the plateau near by; perhaps, when considering the wide distribution of pottery in the late eighth century, he means by " Corinth " not so much the deliberate action of the state as certain Corinthian potters and traders acting on private initiative. But the " seizure of . . . initiative," striking in a hitherto rural state, remains. Corinth rapidly did become the chief trading city of Greece, notorious at a later date for holding its artisans in some regard: " Least of all do Corinthians scorn artisans " (Herodotos, II, 167).

The important question for Corinth, as for other Greek states in their infinite variety, is when and how we may recognize the appearance of elements which are characteristic of Greek urbanization; of urbanization in the sense of a complex division of labor by function and the resultant development of a class structure; Greek, in the sense of the integration of the social, political and moral community. Obviously the question cannot be answered from the scanty evidence available for any one city state, nor can the experience of one Greek city be extended to the whole of Aegean Greece, let alone to the colonial areas. Corinth, however, provides a generally useful example in the sphere of economic development. Apparently it was rural, relatively poor, obscure and even isolated in the Dark Age, but very rapidly became the most prominent state of Aegean Greece from the late eighth to the early sixth century.

What particular aspects of urbanization may be discussed from the evidence available for early Corinth? First, there is the physical growth of the city into a community. How early was there an urban center? When did governmental direction and organization of the resources of the community become apparent—for building monumental temples, fortifications, provision of a water supply, in the allocation of land for public uses, as for an agora, or by the relegation of cemeteries to the outskirts of the city. Second, there is the political aspect—when did Corinth begin to act as a community in foreign affairs, not through the personal diplomacy of its leaders' guest friendships and gift-giving and by raids for personal gain, but by deliberate policy to acquire and to organize territory or to colonize, be it for commercial reasons or to send some of its excess population abroad? Internally, when was the older kinship structure of society replaced by a territorial structure to integrate the individual into the community on a new basis? Third, there is the economic aspect—when, for example, did the pottery industry begin to specialize its production for a home market or for export? When did the city begin to regulate trade and take a fiscal interest in commerce? a political interest? All these aspects are, of course, interrelated, and we can hardly expect that the early Greeks separated them out as sharply as do modern historians. There is good evidence for discussion of some of these questions, little or none for others; all aspects do not appear at the same time, for some are cause and others effect, but all are involved in the formation of Corinth as a city state, of its synoecism in the broad sense of that term.

CORINTH IN THE DARK AGE

Today the most conspicuous landmarks of ancient Corinth are the cluster of Doric columns standing in the archaic " Temple of Apollo," to use its conventional name, and, rising above them to the south, the sheer mass of the city's acropolis, Acrocorinth. Below Acrocorinth stretch two broad terraces, well-watered and fertile in themselves, overlooking the rich coastal plain bordering the Gulf of Corinth. Ultimately classical Corinth, enclosed by its lengthy fortification wall, spread over much of the terraces from its center in the area of the Temple Hill. But both in the Bronze and Early Iron Ages the pattern of settlement seems to have been that of scattered villages, widely separated and presumably linked to one another by a network of paths. Their inhabitants were attracted to the site both by its strategic position at one of the crossroads of Greek communication and by the tempting natural advantages of cultivable land and an ample water supply.[5] The pattern of settlement was dictated by the terrain. From the upper to the lower terraces and from the latter to the coastal plain, ravines break through the shelves of conglomerate which form the floors of the terraces. The course of the ravines provided natural paths, and their sides and the edges of the terraces gave access to the water held by the beds of clay underlying the conglomerate. At the edges of the terraces beside the ravines were desirable sites for settlement—high ground with commanding views, copious water supplies and access to the fields. In time of dire need, though the climb was long and steep, Acrocorinth offered refuge.

It seems probable that from the outset the area around the Temple Hill, now the site of the modern village of Ancient Corinth, was the most advantageous place for settlement and exerted the attraction of a nodal point for a community of Corin-

[5] H. S. Robinson, *The Urban Development of Ancient Corinth*, Athens, 1965, pp. 1-6.

thians. Here the hill, commanding the adjacent region, offered a focal point. Its top has been cut level to bed the temple, and rock has been quarried from the west end, with the exception of the cube left for the Fountain of Glauke. These alterations and the Greek and Roman building, particularly the monumental layout of the Roman Forum, make it difficult to envisage the original form of the region. Apparently the Temple Hill was the highest point of a rim of high ground extending in an arc to enclose a hollow from the modern museum on the west to the Fountain of Peirene and the Lechaion Road on the east. The hollow is now covered with the paving of the Roman Forum and bounded on the south by the South Stoa of the late fourth century B.C. At the foot of the south slope of the Temple Hill was the natural source of water which became the Sacred Spring and at the east end of the hollow the more copious supply of Peirene. The Sacred Spring drained eastward to join the stream flowing north from Peirene near what is now the course of the Lechaion Road. The site, then, offered both high, healthy ground for residence on the west, the natural protection of the hollow, a lookout at the edge of the upper terrace and abundant water.

Presumably the paths, which ultimately became roads, followed the natural lines of communication offered by the terrain. The earliest road discovered, closed *ca.* 575 B.C., when the first monumental temple on Temple Hill was destroyed, ran along the north side of the Temple Hill from east to west, roughly parallel to the modern road leading westward from Ancient Corinth.[6] Apparently it linked the predecessor of the Lechaion Road, giving access to the hollow from the northeast, to the later road to Sikyon, leading into the hollow from the northwest. Presumably, too, this early road continued along the upper terrace to the west, as does the modern road, and from it paths led up to Acrocorinth. Thus the high ground of the Temple Hill and the modern museum served by these routes was an important focal point.

While Mycenean Corinth is known only by some fragmentary pottery[7] and by slight reference in Homer's *Iliad* (II, 570), the pottery finds at least indicate that the Mycenean town was situated in the same general area as the historical city. At the

[6] We do not know when the road came into use, but perhaps its conversion from a path to a more regular roadway is to be associated with the building of the earliest monumental temple on the hill, the predecessor of the so-called " Temple of Apollo." Professor Henry Robinson, who is currently investigating the archaic temples, has generously informed me of new evidence for their dating: the earliest building was constructed *ca.* 700 B.C. and was destroyed about the end of the first quarter of the sixth century; the temple, some of whose columns are presently standing, seems to have been built *ca.* 560-540 B.C. The roadway, then, was evidently an important thoroughfare from *ca.* 700 to 575 B.C. For the traces of the road see R. L. Scranton, *Corinth,* I, iii, pp. 156-157; Mary C. Roebuck, *Hesperia,* XXIV, 1955, pp. 148-150; for the early roads in the hollow to the south of Temple Hill see C. K. Williams, *Hesperia,* XXXIX, 1970, pp. 37-38 and for a contour plan of the area, p. 32, fig. 10.

[7] S. Weinberg, *Hesperia,* XVIII, 1949, pp. 156-157; R. Hope Simpson, " A Gazetteer and Atlas of Mycenaean Sites," *Bulletin Supplement of the Institute of Classical Studies, Univ. of London,* No. 16, 1955, p. 30.

east end of the Roman Forum, behind the Julian Basilica, a deposit of Late Mycenean vases, LH III b, c (one, a large krater with a chariot scene) was found. Some Mycenean sherds were discovered also on the Temple Hill and a few at Mylos Cheliotou to the northwest of the Temple Hill at the edge of the lower terrace. But survivals and the literary tradition offer some hints of the transformation from Bronze-Age to Iron-Age Corinth. The name itself, Korinthos, survived. Religious traditions, apparently predating Dorian Corinth, persisted and, indeed, the lack of impact made on Corinth by specifically Dorian cults and institutions may indicate continuity of habitation by a larger pre-Dorian population than previously suggested.[8]

However that may be, historical Corinth was traditionally a Dorian city. Its " foundation " was connected with the return of the Herakleidai or set a generation later than that event. In tradition the Dorian take-over is represented as violent and abrupt. Thucydides recalled the coming of the Dorians in his statement about the fighting between the first Dorian settlers at Solygeia (Galataki) and the Aeolians at the city of Corinth (IV, 42).[9] The Dorian seizure of the town perhaps provided the historical incident from which the myth of Hellotis sets out. This daughter of Timandros of Corinth, identified as a pre-Dorian goddess whose name appears later as an epithet of Athena, is said to have thrown herself and her sister (there are some variations) into the flaming ruins of the temple of Athena. The Dorian leader, Aletes, made expiation for her death by establishing the festival of the Hellotia.[10] Lists of the Dorian kings after Aletes were worked out which traced the descent of the royal family to the oligarchy of the Bacchiads who ruled Corinth throughout the eighth and much of the seventh century B.C.[11] No archaeological traces of this violent occupation by the Dorians have been discovered, however, so that probably we should

---

[8] T. J. Dunbabin, *J.H.S.*, LXVIII, 1948, p. 62; Will, *op. cit.*, pp. 288-289, 293. Although Will noticed the implications of cult survival, he followed the archaeological evidence then available that the region of Corinth was virtually deserted. Perhaps it is useful to recall the analogy offered by Roman Corinth. The Hellenistic city was destroyed in 146 B.C., but, when the Roman colony was founded a century later, the tradition of the sanctuaries and cults of the time before the destruction was potent, so that many sanctuaries were repaired or rebuilt to honor the same deity as previously. Presumably the ruined shrines had been used by the rural population living in the region.

[9] Solygeia is identified with Galataki, to the southeast of Corinth, where a Late Geometric and Archaic sanctuary (of Hera ?) has been excavated. While tombs of the Bronze Age were found there, Submycenean and Protogeometric pottery are not reported (N. M. Verdelis, *Archaeology*, XV, 1962, pp. 184-192).

[10] For the myth see the scholia to Pindar, *Olymp.*, XIII, 56 and *Etym. Mag., s.v.* Hellotis. The myth and the historical cult are discussed by O. Broneer, *Hesperia*, XI, 1942, pp. 140 ff. and Will, *op. cit.*, pp. 130 ff.

[11] For a very thorough study of the king lists, *ibid.*, pp. 259-295. Despite the obscurity of the kings in tradition and some disagreement on the beginning of the Dorian epoch in Corinth, the genealogies give a tradition of a continuous hereditary kingship in a single ruling family, that of the Bacchiads.

think in terms of gradual, but substantial, infiltration of migrants, who formed a stable community in which they predominated by *ca.* 900 B.C.[12] There seems now to be enough excavational evidence to identify a Protogeometric settlement in the western part of the original hollow and the high ground above it, and the continuous series of Geometric pottery from graves and wells enables at least a ceramic tradition to be worked out.[13]

It is tempting to see the nucleus of historical, Dorian, Corinth in this settlement. The earliest and most numerous traces of habitation in the region have been found here: remains of a Submycenean hut and pottery from burials west of the modern museum; in 1969 more Submycenean and Protogeometric graves were excavated at the west end of the Roman Forum, and in 1970 Protogeometric sherds were found in the filling dumped over the bedrock floor of the hollow at the end of that period.[14] A series of graves and wells on the high ground at the west extending from the Early Geometric period into the sixth century B.C. indicate that residence was continuous there.[15] In the west end of the hollow the excavation of 1970 south of the Sacred Spring revealed Geometric terrace walls and remains of two Protocorinthian houses—the latter used for smelting as well as residence. Early in the Protocorinthian Period, too, the Sacred Spring itself was improved by tunneling out a supply chamber into the clay and sealing its walls and floor. As the excavator has concluded,[16] the whole west end of the hollow was evidently a growing village in the Archaic Period, at first squeezing out the Geometric burial area at the extreme west end by the road entering the hollow, then, in turn, itself being curtailed by the growth of sanctuaries. It is pertinent to note also that the cults of this western area were early and important: the sanctuary of Medea has been localized on the top of the cube of rock which forms Glauke;[17] the earliest monumental temple in Corinth was built

[12] T. J. Dunbabin, *op. cit.*, p. 62; Will, *op. cit.*, pp. 288-289. Presumably the incoming settlers from the Argolid (or more directly from the northwest?) were a mixture of newcomers and the surviving Bronze Age population (V. Desborough, *The Last Mycenaeans and Their Successors,* pp. 231-232, 251-252, 259).

[13] The main studies of Corinthian Geometric pottery are: S. Weinberg, *Corinth,* VII, i, pp. 9-32 (pottery from the main excavations through 1939); R. Young, *Corinth,* XIII, pp. 13-49 (from the North Cemetery); J. N. Coldstream, *Greek Geometric Pottery,* pp. 91-111 (a general study of Corinthian Geometric in the context of Greek Geometric production). Notice of the finds since Weinberg's publication may be found in the excavation reports in *Hesperia.*

[14] Weinberg, *op. cit.*, p. 3 (also, G. G. Styrenius, *Submycenean Studies,* p. 138); Williams, *Hesperia,* XXXIX, 1970, pp. 12-20; XL, 1971, p. 3.

[15] Geometric: Weinberg, *Corinth,* VII, i, Nos. 103-115; *Hesperia,* XVII, 1948, pp. 204-208; Williams, *Hesperia,* XXXIX, 1970, pp. 12, 20.

EPC Linear: *Hesperia,* XVII, 1948, pp. 208-214 (Well C).

EC: *Hesperia,* XVII, 1948, pp. 214-229 (Well D); C. Boulter, *A.J.A.,* XLI, 1937, pp. 217-236; Weinberg, *Corinth,* VII, i, pp. 60 ff. (Well north of Temple E).

[16] C. K. Williams, *Hesperia,* XL, 1971, pp. 23-24.

[17] R. L. Scranton, *Corinth,* I, ii, pp. 149 ff.

on the Temple Hill early in the seventh century,[18] while to the north, at the foot of the hill, apparently lay the sanctuary of Athena Chalinitis.[19]

Presumably the settlement of the Geometric Period spread across the hollow from the Sacred Spring to the southern side. The thorough preparation of the ground on the south for the construction of the South Stoa in the late fourth century has removed much of the evidence, but traces of residential occupation from Proto-geometric sherds, Geometric graves and wells to house remains of the fifth century B.C. were discovered.[20]

Another cluster of Geometric habitation was along the stream bed north of Peirene. There an Early Geometric retaining wall has been found, and occupational debris, graves and wells attest continuous residence to the early sixth century B.C. Apparently at that time the area became industrial, for remains of a dyeworks have been excavated.[21]

The hollow and its entrances along the roads from the northeast and the north-west, then, were the site of a continuously growing settlement from the traditional epoch of Dorian settlement in Corinth. The earliest and most significant remains, so far discovered, were towards the west end, but nowhere in the region does there seem to be any indication of utilization of the ground for an early agora. As suggested by the excavator, perhaps the early agora of Corinth is to be sought to the north of the Temple Hill, near the main east-west road and the important early sanctuaries.[22]

While population was concentrating in the hollow and near the Temple Hill other clusters of habitation were springing up on the terraces and at their edges. Again, there seems to have been a favoring of the western part of the region, probably the result of the gravitational pull of the nucleus near Temple Hill. Along the north edge of the lower terrace below the modern village of Ancient Corinth, several graves of the Early Geometric Period, containing a large amount of pottery, were found near the descent of the Lechaion Road to the coastal plain. But to the west burials

---

[18] See note 6.

[19] T. L. Shear, *A.J.A.*, XXXII, 1928, pp. 489-490; for the cult see note 10.

[20] Submycenean and Protogeometric sherds: *Hesperia*, XX, 1951, p. 293. Geometric: *Corinth*, VII, i, Nos. 73-77 (MG graves); *Hesperia*, XVIII, 1949, pp. 153-154 (LG well); *Hesperia*, XX, 1951, pp. 293-294 (MG II well); *A.J.A.*, XLI, 1937, pp. 544-545 (LG graves).

EPC Linear: *Corinth*, VII, i, Nos. 116-134 (well).

See also Williams, *Hesperia*, XXXIX, 1970, pp. 33 ff.

[21] Protogeometric: unpublished sherds from the fill in which the Early Geometric wall was set. Geometric: *Corinth*, I, ii, p. 4; *Corinth*, VII, i, No. 68 (EG, near the Baths of Aphrodite), Nos. 54-66 (MG I, Coldstream, *Greek Geometric Pottery*, p. 94); habitational debris from the late eighth century onwards (Weinberg, *Hesperia*, XXIX, 1960, pp. 245-246, 252).

Archaic dyeworks (under the Peribolos of Apollo): *Archaeological Reports*, 1966-67, p. 7; 1967-68, p. 7; Δελτ., XXIII, 1968, pp. 134-135.

[22] Williams, *Hesperia*, XXXIX, 1970, p. 35.

were more numerous: an Early Geometric grave near the later Asklepieion, the large group in the North Cemetery (Middle and Late Geometric), a small group in the Potters' Quarter (Late Geometric) and an Early Geometric burial at Mavrospelaies, near the Roman Villa.[23] A Geometric settlement west of the Temple Hill, near the modern village of Anaploga, is marked by the discovery of a cemetery and a house well (Middle and Late Geometric).[24] Each of these groups of graves is near a good water supply and each of those at the edge of the terrace near a path which led up from the coastal plain. Although remains of houses have not been found near the graves, it seems reasonable to see the burials as evidence of family groups or small villages forming by the paths and water supplies. The fact that burials were made in the central settlement throughout the Geometric Period, just as outside it, precludes the view that the latter were the result of the establishment of a recognized urban center from which it seemed desirable to exclude burials.[25]

The picture of Corinth in the Geometric Period, drawn from this brief review, is remarkably similar to that of the settlement of the present day: a large village at Ancient Corinth, a smaller one at Anaploga, groups of houses, family clusters, near the edge of the lower terrace. Probably other clusters of Geometric habitation will emerge at scattered points near the water supplies and roads as chance finds and excavation continue. The earliest and most intensive settlement does seem to have been near the Temple Hill, revealed by the Submycenean and Protogeometric pottery finds. Continuous growth made it in effect an urban center for the whole region, but recognition of it as such would have been continuous and automatic, marked, in particular, by the development of sanctuaries and shrines, rather than by deliberate planning and organization of its space. Perhaps it is fair to say that the earliest landmark of monumentalization was the construction of the big temple on Temple Hill in the early seventh century B.C.[26]

Presumably the growing community at Corinth drew some of its population from the Corinthians living in the hills and the remoter parts of the Corinthia, as well as by natural increase of its original settlers. There has been little investigation of Geometric habitation in the region, but, even so, some pattern is discernible. Most of the graves known are in the hilly region to the southeast, on the way to the Argolid. While some Early Geometric burials have been found at Zygouries and habitation

[23] Graves east of the Lechaion Road: *Corinth*, VII, i, Nos. 22-53.
Asklepieion: *Corinth*, VII, i, Nos. 20-21.
Potters' Quarter: *Corinth*, XV, i, pp. 7-9(LG).
North Cemetery: *Corinth*, XIII, pp. 13-49 (MG II and LG).
Mavrospelaies: *Hesperia*, XXXIII, 1964, pp. 89-91 (EG).
[24] Robinson, *Hesperia*, XXXVIII, 1969, p. 35; *B.C.H.*, LXXXVIII, 1964, p. 705.
[25] R. Young, *Corinth*, XIII, pp. 13-14.
[26] For the archaic city see Robinson, *The Urban Development of Ancient Corinth*, pp. 7-12; Williams, *Hesperia*, XXXIX, 1970, pp. 33-35, 38; also note 6 above.

debris in the later sanctuary of Poseidon at Isthmia,[27] there are three graves of the Middle Geometric Period at Tenea (Athikia), one at Clenia, and a Late Geometric sanctuary at Solygeia (Galataki).[28] Perhaps these indicate a concentration of population at an early date in this neighborhood resulting from the Dorian spread northwards from the Argolid. Such a concentration, too, is indicated by the tradition that the settlers for the colony at Syracuse were drawn from Tenea.[29] Perhaps, as Will has suggested,[30] there is a hint here that the hill country of the Corinthia was overpopulated by *ca.* 733 B.C. The terraces and coastal plain of Corinth, too, may have been overpopulated, not in the sense that available land was overbuilt, but by the system of land tenure. Large-scale holdings by the great families—we are told that there were over two hundred Bacchiads in that group (see below, p. 106)—and the smaller holdings of the peasants living in the villages may have blocked further agricultural exploitation. Such a condition could have led to political discontent at home and colonization abroad for relief. Also, of course, it might have stimulated urbanization by increasing craft production for the Corinthian community and for export. There is, in fact, some indication in the pottery production of Corinth in the Middle Geometric II phase (*ca.* 800-750 B.C.) that such was the case.

At Corinth the ceramic tradition of the Geometric Period was continuous and individual. Coldstream has characterized it succinctly: " Fine, pale clay; plump, rotund vase-forms; austerely simple ornament, painted with fastidious neatness. . . . Its internal development . . . is logical and consistent." [31] This Geometric production seems to have developed naturally from Corinthian Protogeometric and upon it, *ca.* 725 B.C., came the impact of the Orientalizing influences from which developed the Early Protocorinthian style. There was influence on the shapes and decoration of Corinthian Geometric from Athens, the major center of pottery production through the Protogeometric and Geometric Periods, but Corinthian potters were selective, and the Athenian influence is by no means so pronounced as in the Argolid. In fact, the Athenian influences were discarded in the Middle Geometric II phase. As Coldstream has suggested, trade, if that was the source of the Athenian influence, was stronger across the Saronic Gulf by sea to the Argolid than by the land route through the Isthmus and the Corinthia.[32] Evidently, then, Corinth was relatively isolated in a

[27] Zygouries: *Zygouries*, pp. 174-176 (EG).
Isthmia: habitation debris, O. Broneer, *Hesperia*, XXVII, 1958, p. 27.
[28] Athikia: *Corinth*, VII, i, Nos. 69-72; *A.J.A.*, LXI, 1957, pp. 169-71; *Hesperia*, XXXIII, 1964, pp. 91-93. All the pottery is Middle Geometric.
Clenia: *A.J.A.*, LIX, 1955, pp. 125-128 (MG I).
Solygeia: see note 9 above.
[29] Strabo 380 (VI, 6, 22).
[30] Will, *op. cit.*, pp. 319-321.
[31] Coldstream, *op. cit.*, p. 91.
[32] Coldstream, *op. cit.*, pp. 91, 95-97, 341, 352.

cultural sense and rural in character. The region received no large influx of foreign population and did not attract foreign craftsmen to settle. Its population was poor, or conservative in taste, for throughout the Geometric Period the graves did not contain exotic articles. In most cases, too, they contained little metalware or jewelry of local origin.[33]

The types of pottery found in the graves of the North Cemetery, in particular, may reflect the rural character of Corinth before 800 B.C. The dead were buried with the same types of pottery used in their households during life, often coarse and handmade, seldom a speciality; popular shapes were oinochoai, pitchers for pouring, and skyphoi, small cups for drinking. There were a few aryballoi and pyxides for cosmetics, a few small kraters and hydriai, but very few amphoras. However, some change is apparent in the Middle Geometric II pottery after 800 B.C. Coldstream has noted the rejection of Athenian influences and the emergence of a purely Corinthian style in that period.[34] While handmade vessels of a traditional type were still used, large kraters for libation to the dead were placed near the graves, and a few specialties set in them. Local marketing conditions, then, seem to have been more favorable for the potter, stimulating to his interest and his inventiveness. In this period, also, pottery was exported beyond the Corinthia and the Megarid, to which exports had been largely confined in the ninth century. In the first half of the eighth trade was evidently developing in the Gulf of Corinth. The people of Delphi bought Corinthian pottery for use, as well as dedication, and a Corinthian trading post was established on Ithaka ca. 780 B.C.[35] There the colonists preferred to import Corinthian pottery for dedication in the local shrine at Aetos and presumably, too, for their own use. Thus archaeological evidence indicates a change in Corinth on the eve of the traditional date usually accepted for the establishment of the Bacchiad oligarchy, ca. 750 B.C., and the planting of colonies in Syracuse and Corcyra. Is there any hint of this in the historical traditions?

THE POLITICAL COMMUNITY

To judge from tradition, Dorian Corinth was united from the outset into a political and social community of the Corinthians under a single ruling dynasty. The only notice of internal conflict between different communities in the Corinthia is

[33] On the pottery from the North Cemetery, R. Young, *Corinth,* XIII, pp. 14, 40-49. It might, of course, be argued that the North Cemetery contains only the burials of poor peasants from near-by villages, not a cross-section of the whole population which would include the wealthy; the latter, of course, may well have been buried in family plots on their own estates, as yet undiscovered or plundered long ago. It is true, however, that while some Geometric burials found elsewhere contained much pottery, few were " rich " in the sense of having exotics and costly jewelry (cf. C. H. Morgan, *A.J.A.,* XLI, 1937, p. 545—a " rich " grave).

[34] See notes 31 and 32 above.

[35] Coldstream, *op. cit.,* pp. 352-353.

Thucydides' reminiscence of the Dorian settlers at Solygeia warring against Aeolians at Corinth. That implies a successful conclusion to these hostilities by the establishment of a Dorian regime over the Corinthia at the former Mycenean town. Evidently a cultural community, at least in the ceramic sense, existed throughout the Corinthia, for the Geometric pottery from the whole region is homogeneous in style; presumably the fine ware was made at Corinth itself. While we should be chary of equating ceramic community with political community, for Megara, too, seems to have used fine Corinthian pottery and did not develop an individual local style,[36] no evidence points to the existence of several small independent kingships in the Corinthia. The Bacchiads, as kings and then as ruling aristocrats, have almost completely obscured other noble families.[37]

While the image of the early Corinthian kings is shadowy,[38] the genealogies picture the kingship descending in a hereditary line through the Bacchiad family, descended from the Heraklids. Bacchis was not the first name on the lists, but there seems no reason to suppose that its appearance marks a change in dynasty. Apparently, too, the change from monarchy to family oligarchy in 777 or 747 b.c. was in the framework of dynastic continuity.[39] The change from hereditary to elective office in the whole genos was presumably a concession to the continuous extension of the clan both by descent and probably, too, by intermarriage with other noble families of the Corinthia. For example, the mother of Kypselos, herself a Bacchiad, was married to Aetion, a non-Bacchiad (Herodotos, V, 92, 2), but Kypselos is said to have become polemarch and then to have used that office as a springboard to tyranny (Nikolaos Dam., frag. 57, 5). While factional strife among the Bacchiad families was not removed, enlargement of the circle of office was significant of a feeling for the need of greater political unity and strength within the community. Three elected officials—prytanis, basileus and polemarch—replaced the single basileus; a large council, for there are said to have been over two hundred Bacchiads (Diodorus, VII, frag. 9), was constituted, in which elective power was vested, and an assembly of the Corinthian demos continued to exist.[40] It is likely that general concern for a stronger state, expressed in the form of aristocratic cohesion, was felt in Corinth at the time of the establishment of the Bacchiad aristocracy. The half-century between 750 and 700 b.c. seems to mark the appearance of Corinth as a polis. Its government

[36] Coldstream, op. cit., p. 353, note 3. See also, Hammond, B.S.A., XLIX, 1954, pp. 99-100.

[37] The Corinthian oekist of Epidamnos, Phaleas, is identified by Thucydides as a descendant of Herakles (I, 24), but not as a Bacchiad or a Kypselid. While Kypselos' mother was a Bacchiad, his father was from a different family group (Herodotos, V, 92, 2).

[38] Dunbabin, op. cit., pp. 62-63.

[39] The establishment of the Bacchiad oligarchy is set in 777 b.c. by the Eusebian tradition, but in 747 by the Apollodoran. For the chronology see note 11 above.

[40] I have followed the reconstruction of Will, op. cit., pp. 298-306. See, most recently, S. I. Oost, " Cypselus, the Bacchiad," Cl. Phil., LXVII, 1972, pp. 10-30.

was broadly based, at least for the period; its rulers' aims were expansive in an effort to better the condition of the whole community, and Corinth began to experience the changes symptomatic of urbanization.

By 750 B.C., as noticed above, regular navigation was starting on the Gulf of Corinth; the pottery industry had begun to expand its production, and a trading post had been established on Ithaka. Presumably none of these was the result of deliberate political action by the rulers of Corinth, but all were signs of change and expansion. Overpopulation evidently was pressing, for in 733 B.C. Syracuse was colonized. This venture, organized under a Bacchiad oekist, indicates that the government both was concerned about the problem and had the power to direct the people of the Corinthia. That concern and power seem apparent in other actions of Corinth in this same period: the Perachora peninsula and land north of the Isthmus seem to have been seized and a successful stand made against Pheidon of Argos.

FOREIGN RELATIONS

The territories bordering on the Corinthia were Sikyonia to the west along the coastal plain, the Argolid to the south beyond the hills, and the Megarid to the north across the Isthmus. Relations with the Sicyonians in this early period are completely obscure; perhaps we should assume that they were in the nature of neighborly squabbles over sheep and cattle. In any case there is no hint of a Corinthian attempt to expand to the west. The Argives are usually recognized as the early " great power " of the northeastern Peloponnesus, exercising cultural suzerainty and perhaps a form of control through filial relations over the Corinthia and the Megarid. As discussed below, there is some reason to doubt this state of affairs, but perhaps personal relations among the great families of the northeastern Peloponnesus were generally harmonious, cemented by guest-friendships and intermarriage before their communities developed into city states. In any case relations between Corinthians and Argives seem to have been cordial until the ambition of Pheidon provoked a rift.

With Megara relations were apparently different. From the Corinthia relatively level and cultivable land stretched to Geraneia and the promontory of Perachora.[41] On Perachora were not only the lookout and cove at the tip of the promontory but cultivable land east of Lake Vouliagmeni and in the area of the modern village of Perachora. While the lookout and harborage would not have been of interest until navigation became regular on the Gulf of Corinth, the cultivable land of the Isthmus and of Perachora would have seemed desirable to both Corinthians and Megarians.

---

[41] For a recent sketch map of the Corinthia see P. Wallace, *Hesperia*, XXXVIII, 1969, p. 497. Evidence of Bronze Age and Geometric habitation in the area of the later (early seventh century B.C.) sanctuary of Poseidon at Isthmia is reported by O. Broneer, *Hesperia*, XXVII, 1958, pp. 27-28. Late Geometric and EPC pottery has been found in graves in the Isthmus and the region to the north, *Ath. Mitt.*, LXXI, 1956, pp. 51 ff.

It was accessible to both and a bone of contention. A tradition reported by Plutarch (*Quaest. Gr.*, 17) recalls the conflict, and excavational evidence of the sanctuary at Perachora perhaps enables us to see its culmination in the take-over of the territory by the Corinthians about the mid-eighth century.

The earlier phases of this fighting, conducted in a quaintly chivalrous fashion, were marked by forays of small groups from either side, raids between Corinthian and Megarian villagers and their leaders. Hammond has interpreted the continuous pressure as resulting both in the Corinthian conquest of the territory and in the synoecism of the five original *komai* of Megara.[42] Perhaps, too, stress in the Megarid, resulting from harrassment and loss of territory, prompted the colonization of Megara Hyblaea in Sicily, dated in the mid-eighth century, prior to Syracuse, by its excavators.[43] Should we not also connect the Corinthian take-over with the indications of overpopulation in the Corinthia, with the beginnings of regular Corinthian use of the Gulf for navigation and trade (the colony on Ithaka and the trade to Delphi) and ascribe the Corinthian victory to the greater unity and centralized direction which the Bacchiad reorganization had given to Corinth? The evidence from the sanctuary of Hera at Perachora provides some basis for these suggestions.

Establishment of a sanctuary at the tip of the Perachora promontory was marked by the construction of the little temple of Hera Akraia, currently dated *ca.* 800 B.C. While this temple went out of use toward the end of the eighth century, *ca.* 750-720 B.C., in the meantime, *ca.* 750 B.C., the temple of Hera Limenaia had been built and continued to be the chief shrine of the sanctuary throughout the Archaic Period.[44] There is a marked difference in the type of votive offerings made to Hera Limenaia from those in the earlier shrine. The latter are simple, local in origin and relatively few in number, but from Hera Limenaia came the mass of exotic and unusual offerings which are associated with Perachora: fine pottery, ivories, small bronzes, objects from the east, from as far afield as Luristan. These were evidently a product of the Greek, or more specifically Corinthian, trade with the Levant which began *ca.* 725 B.C.

[42] N. Hammond, *B.S.A.*, XLIX, 1954, pp. 93-102 and *A History of Greece to 322 B.C.*, 2d ed., p. 107. Hammond dates the Corinthian take-over to 750-700 B.C. and sets the synoecism of both Megara and Corinth earlier. As discussed below, pp. 114-116, the synoecism of Corinth seems to have had a different form and to have followed the absorption of the territory. Will (*op. cit.*, pp. 358-359) characterizes the Corinthia as organized, like the Megarid, κατὰ κώμας, at the time of this sporadic fighting. He notes the tradition of a temporary domination of the Megarid by Bacchiad Corinth (pp. 359-360); this might, of course, refer to a Corinthian victory and the subsequent organization of the Geraneia and of Perachora.

[43] G. Vallet and F. Villard, *B.C.H.*, LXXVI, 1952, pp. 343 ff.; the archaic pottery from Megara Hyblaea is published in *Mégara Hyblaea, 2, La céramique archaïque*, Paris, 1964. Coldstream argues against the early dates for Naxos (757) and Megara Hyblaea (750) in *Greek Geometric Pottery*, pp. 324-325. The traditional date for Megara Hyblaea is 728 B.C.

[44] Hera Akraia: *Perachora*, I, pp. 30 ff.; the dating is revised downward by Coldstream, *op. cit.*, pp. 352-353, 404.

Hera Limenaia: *Perachora*, I, pp. 113; Coldstream, *op. cit.*, pp. 353, 404.

and was reinvigorated from *ca.* 625 B.C. The earliest pottery from the sanctuary of Hera Akraia has been classified most recently as Corinthian, rather than Argive.[45] Thus, the view of the excavators, which had considered the pottery indicative of an Argive foundation of the sanctuary and, by extension, of an early Argive " domination " of the Corinthia and of the Megarid, should be revised. Argive pottery there was at Perachora, but apparently it is to be placed after 750 B.C. and thus its presence need indicate no more than the interest of a wealthy, neighboring state in a growing sanctuary of the goddess Hera. She was common to all the Dorians of the northeast Peloponnesus, even if originally at home in the Argolid. To bring this archaeological evidence into connection with the historical event of a Corinthian take-over of the sanctuary is a delicate matter.

Hammond, in his study of early Megara,[46] noted that among the five *komai* which synoecised to form the city state of Megara were two districts named Heraia and Piraia. Presumably these were situated on the promontory of Perachora. He suggested that the Corinthian occupation of the promontory was marked by the establishment of the cult of Hera Limenaia and so dated the occupation about the middle of the eighth century. In effect, Hera Limenaia replaced Hera Akraia. At the same time, it is suggested, Corinth also took over Krommyon along the shore of the Saronic Gulf, thus establishing its control north of the Isthmus in the Geraneia. Coldstream finds some support for Hammond's view in the distinctive character of the votive offerings from the shrine of Limenaia [47] and in the identification of the earliest pottery from the Akraia shrine as Corinthian. While on the evidence of the pottery the sanctuary of Akraia might have been either a Megarian or a Corinthian foundation, for Megarians too used fine Corinthian pottery, it seems preferable to regard it as Megarian. It is difficult to see why Corinthians would found a new cult to Hera Limenaia little more than a generation after establishing that to Akraia. It is preferable to regard the founding of the cult of Limenaia as marking the Corinthian seizure of the sanctuary from the Megarians at a time when the former wished to emphasize that aspect of Hera's worship which accorded with Perachora's function as a lookout for Gulf navigation. If we may take the trade to Delphi as indicative of the inception of regular Corinthian use of the Gulf in the first part of the eighth century, this well explains Corinthian interest in seeking to acquire the rocky promontory tip as well as cultivable land. There was evidently concern both to improve the safety of navigation in the Gulf and to relieve the pressure of population in Corinth. Both actions accord with the vigorous colonizing action of Corinth in the last half of the eighth century as the new polis developed. Before discussing that, however, it would be useful to

[45] Coldstream, *op. cit.*, p. 353, note 2; Hammond (*B.S.A.*, XLIX, 1954, p. 101) had suggested that the early pottery of the Akraia shrine was local Megarian, imitative of Argive.

[46] See note 42 above.

[47] See notes 36, 45 above.

review Corinth's relations with Argos, the great power of the eighth century in the northeastern Peloponnesus.

The Argives, to judge from their place in tradition and from the evidence of excavation in Argos, were the most important people in the northeastern Peloponnesus during the first part of the Early Iron Age.[48] They attained their acme of prosperity in the last half of the eighth century, but, before that, Dorians of the Argolid are considered to have spread northward across the Isthmus to the border of Attica. While the Corinthia and the Megarid were scarcely members of an Argive " empire " in a political sense, historians have assumed that the Argives exerted cultural domination of the region and that close ties existed between the Argives and their " colonies " to the north. Will, for example, pictures a small group of Dorian kingdoms, gravitating around Argos, the kings of which were in more or less close personal dependency on the Temenids.[49]

That picture was based partly on the presumed control of Perachora by Argos, an assumption which seems no longer tenable, and partly on the view that the ceramic region of the northeastern Peloponnesus was dominated by Argos. But, as noticed above, Corinthian Geometric pottery followed its own course of development, although at times reflecting strong Athenian influence. There is no reason to assume that this influence was exercised through the medium of Argive imports. In fact, there seems to be no imported Argive ware in Corinth until after 750 B.C. Then Corinthian, in its turn, was imported into the Argolid.[50]

By the late eighth century Bacchiad Corinth seems to have been independent of Argos and, indeed, was moved to open hostility by the ambitions of Pheidon. The relationship is revealed by Plutarch (*Am. Narr.* 2) in the story of the dismemberment of Actaeon and by a scholiast on Apollonius of Rhodes (IV, 1212). However difficult of interpretation the story may be, both Will and Huxley accept its picture of Argive-Corinthian relations in the time of Pheidon.[51] Leaving aside discussion of his date,[52] we may use the setting of the story as a source of information about Corinth's early years as a polis.

[48] G. Huxley, *B.C.H.*, LXXXII, 1958, pp. 588-601; Coldstream, *op. cit.*, pp. 362-363.

[49] Will, *op. cit.*, pp. 36-37, 289-291, 339-341. Will considered the presumed Argive control of Perachora as indicative of Argive suzerainty over the Corinthia.

[50] Coldstream, *op. cit.*, pp. 91-104. Coldstream recognizes one LG Argive krater among the pottery from the North Cemetery in Corinth (p. 140).

[51] See note 48 above and Will, *op. cit.*, pp. 344-357.

[52] The dating of Pheidon's regime is one of the most difficult chronological problems of early Greek history, and the traditions of his relations with Corinth indicate only that it coincided with the general period of the Bacchiad aristocracy. Huxley and Coldstream (note 48 above) regard Pheidon as a mid-eighth century figure, while Will (*op. cit.*, pp. 352-357) argues for the mid-seventh century in accordance with his lowering of the inception of the Kypselid tyranny to *ca.* 620 B.C. Others prefer to place Pheidon in the early seventh century; for bibliography see H. Berve, *Die Tyrannis bei den Griechen*, II, pp. 518-519; Berve prefers a mid-eighth century date.

Throughout the story Corinth is presented as a unified state under a centralized Bacchiad government, although some opposition to the Bacchiads is apparent. When Pheidon, with intent to weaken Corinth, asked the Corinthians for a contingent of 1,000 men to aid him, the force was dispatched by Corinth as an equal and trusting ally. When an Argive noble, Actaeon's father (or grandfather), revealed that Corinth's trust was misplaced, Corinth offered him political asylum and the privilege of residing in Melissos, a Corinthian village. When a Bacchiad, Archias, made the attempt to kidnap Actaeon, the latter's father appealed in the market-place of Corinth to the Corinthians for help. He received only an expression of sympathy (like Telamachos in Ithaka), as might have been expected in a city ruled by the Bacchiads. Therefore he had recourse to Poseidon at the Isthmian sanctuary, where he made a sacrifice of his own life. In reprisal Poseidon brought famine to Corinth, until, to expiate the curse, Archias went off to colonize Syracuse (or the Bacchiad, Chersikrates, was expelled to colonize Corcyra). Nikolaos of Damascus (frag. 35) adds a sequel: Pheidon found a pretext for attacking Corinth by coming to the aid of an anti-Bacchiad faction, failed and was killed in fighting near Corinth. Without pressing into the difficulties of historicity and chronology, it is apparent that throughout the episode Corinth is represented as a state which has drawn the Corinthia into a unity and whose government controls the villages and the people. It is hardly surprising to discover some faction among the two hundred odd members of the family of the Bacchiads. It is tempting to set the situation, and Pheidon, in the third quarter of the eighth century and to bring the notice of famine into connection with the colonization of Syracuse. If so, Corinth's ability to defeat Pheidon falls into the pattern of vigorous activity displayed by its take-over of Perachora and the land north of the Isthmus.

EARLY COLONIZATION

During the eighth century B.C. the Corinthians founded three overseas colonies: on Ithaka, at Syracuse and on Corcyra. To understand the motivation and organization of these ventures would be highly important for our knowledge of the community of eighth-century Corinth, but the foundations lie before or at the beginning of recorded history in Greece. For Ithaka there is no literary tradition, but the evidence from the sanctuary of Aetos indicates that a small group of Corinthians settled on the island and began to use the shrine, already in existence, ca. 780 B.C.[53] The traditional date of Syracuse, 733 B.C., is usually accepted.[54] The synchronization of Corcyra, however, with Syracuse is perhaps incorrect, for the present archaeological evidence points rather to the alternative date of 709 B.C.[55] In any case Ithaka was colonized well before the earliest colonies in Italy and Sicily, although perhaps not

[53] Coldstream, *op. cit.,* pp. 353, 409.
[54] For a recent discussion of the dating of the western colonies see *ibid.,* pp. 322-327.
[55] Graham, *op. cit.,* pp. 218-220.

before some voyaging to the region had started, while Syracuse and Corcyra were settled after Greeks were sailing westwards with some regularity. Ithaka hardly falls into the pattern of western colonization and trade but rather into that of use of the Corinthian Gulf.

Corinthian interest in the Gulf, however, seems to have been confined largely to its east end—pottery and bronzes were traded to Delphi [56] and the safety of navigation facilitated by the occupation of Perachora. We can only conjecture about the attraction of Ithaka, outside the Gulf, for a group of Corinthian traders. The settlement seems plausibly identified as a trading post, for Ithaka, already peopled, hardly provided land for agricultural settlement. Also, Coldstream has noted that the Corinthian pottery from its shrine was too great in quantity to be the product of exchange with Ithakans or a testimony to the piety of passing Corinthian traders. Even if one of these explanations should be correct, it is still necessary to account for the trade. Evidently there was profit and/or strategic advantage in settling on the island. While Ithaka could control entrance to the Gulf of Corinth, such a strategic motive at this early date is surely anachronistic—it implies regular navigation in and out of the Gulf, a developed political interest by Corinth and the stationing of warships at Ithaka. Perhaps the settlers were concerned only to provide safe harborage for their own and occasional other craft, not only from weather, but from pirates, whose activity remained endemic in Western Greek waters and presumably was as early as trade itself.[57] Trade, then, there seems to have been, and if it was not to Italy, ships were making their way among the islands and up the coast into the Adriatic.[58] At least the identification of the post as Corinthian indicates that for some Corinthians trading was a means of livelihood in the early eighth century. We need not ascribe a commercial motive for the foundation to Corinth as a state, but regard the settlement as the venture of a few private individuals. Corinthian interest in Ithaka remained strong as navigation to the west developed. Imports to Ithaka from Corinth were numerous and Corinthian pottery began to exert a strong influence on the local production.

With the colonization of Syracuse we are on firmer ground than in the case of Ithaka, although the traditions raise some difficulties. The motive was apparently to ease overpopulation in the Corinthia,[59] for the settlers are said to have come from the hill country of Tenea and there is mention of famine in Corinth about the time of the venture. Despite Graham's argument to the contrary,[60] the whole enterprise has

[56] Coldstream, *op. cit.*, pp. 353, 366, 411. On the relations between Bacchiad Corinth and Delphi, see Forrest, *Historia*, VI, 1957, pp. 172-175.

[57] See the treaty between Oianthea and Chaleion (M. N. Tod, *Greek Historical Inscriptions*, I, No. 34; *I.G.*, IX², 1, 717).

[58] Will, *op. cit.*, pp. 38 ff., 321-322.

[59] *Ibid.*, pp. 319 ff.; notes 29 and 30 above.

[60] Graham, *op. cit.*, p. 220. I do not understand the objection of Graham to the colonization

the character of a regularly organized action by the Corinthian state. There was an oekist, Archias the Bacchiad, and the settlers had been assured of grants of land to be given them on arrival in Syracuse; if some desire to get rid of political malcontents by the Bacchiad government was present at the start, feelings of hostility were speedily lost, for relations between Corinth and Syracuse remained cordial throughout their history. To judge from the rapid and successful growth of the colony the vanguard of settlers was followed by other colonists from Corinth.

The founding of a colony on Corcyra, however, seems to reveal a conscious recognition of the island's importance as a port of call on the route to Italy, as well as of its capacity to offer a livelihood for settlers from its soil. The port could provide harborage and exact tolls from visiting ships. Presumably Corinthian realization of the latter is shown by the tradition that Eretrians were ejected to make way for the Corinthian settlers.[61] Even if the foundations of Naxos and of Megara Hyblaea about the middle of the eighth century, prior to that of Syracuse, not be accepted, there was evidently by 733, and certainly by 709 B.C., regular voyaging to Italy. Fiscal and possibly strategic motives seem to be present in the colonizing of Corcyra, which foreshadow the colonial policy of the Kypselids in the following century. Perhaps from the outset the Corcyreans showed a disposition to collect tolls from Corinthian ships. At least by 664 B.C. Corcyra challenged Corinth at sea (Thuc., I, 13) and began to establish its traditional isolation.

It is hardly necessary for our purposes to discuss the colonial policy of the tyrants. Will has characterized it as systematic, motivated in some cases (Leukas, Ambrakia, Anaktorion) to relieve overpopulation in the Corinthia, in others, as strategic, to police the entrances to the Gulf of Corinth and to the Adriatic.[62] Policing, no doubt, was against piracy, but it should be observed that the effect of the effort was to ensure the safety of navigation; that is, a commercial motive is apparent. While the precise relationship between Corinth and these later colonies is not clear, the oekists were usually members of the Kypselid family and the colonies dependent

as a planned act of state. How could a member of the *ruling* clan (Bacchiads) be *required* as oekist without the process being an act of state? Also, while Graham argues that Corinth was not sufficiently organized as a state to have a planned mercantile colony (i.e. to have a commercial policy?)—which is probably true—did not agricultural colonies need to be planned? In this case the colonists knew where they were going, to the east coast of Sicily, if not precisely to the site of Syracuse; they were led by an oekist, a government official, who had consulted Delphi; they took men from the hills, farmers not sailors, and arranged to allocate lots to them. The whole process seems to have been a calculated and organized venture by the state. Will (*op. cit.*, p. 320) considers that the Corinthian land-tenure system of large holdings was transferred to Syracuse and that the lots were not alienable, despite Archilochos' reference (frag. 145b) to one of the settlers selling his land for a cake on the way out. Be the size of the lots as it may, the hungry colonist had something to sell before he got there (cf. M. I. Finley, *Eirene*, VII, 1968, pp. 29, 32).

[61] Strabo, 269 (VI, 2, 4); Plutarch, *Quaest. Gr.*, 11.

[62] Will, *op. cit.*, pp. 517 ff.; Graham, *op. cit.*, chapters III and VII, particularly p. 151, "founded with imperial intentions and remained in close connection with Corinth and under her domination."

on Corinth in some fashion, remaining under Corinthian control. By the latter part of the seventh century, then, Corinth had evidently developed deliberate policies and intentions for trade as well as for the relief of population pressure. The state was using colonization as a deliberate instrument of policy in both respects. How important the trade might be is indicated by the construction of the *diolkos* across the Isthmus *ca.* 600 B.C.[63] and by the establishment of a developed system of tolls by the Kypselids.[64] There seems to be a mixture of political, commercial and fiscal purposes in the Kypselid attitude to trade and colonization. The Bacchiads, who also used members of their own family as oekists, had set a model—by taking land north of the Isthmus and by colonizing Syracuse for the relief of the overpopulation at home, and by seizing the lookout at Perachora and colonizing Corcyra to facilitate trade and the collection of tolls.

SYNOECISM

An obscure definition in Suidas refers to a synoecism of Corinth (*s.v. πάντα ὀκτώ*): "Aletes (the first Dorian king of Corinth), according to an oracle, synoecizing the Corinthians, made eight tribes of the citizens and divided the city into eight parts." Historians are unanimous in dissociating Aletes from any such reform, but, as a result of the obscurity which veils Corinthian tribal organization, there is little agreement as to when the reorganization was made. What evidence there is points to the time between the foundation of Syracuse in 733 B.C. and the establishment of the oligarchy after the fall of the Kypselid tyranny *ca.* 580 B.C. (or *ca.* 550 B.C.?). The upper limit may be set by tenuous inference. The three ethnic Doric tribes, which we would expect to find at Corinth, are attested for Corcyra Nigra (*S.I.G.*,[3] I, 141), a secondary colony by way of Issa, itself a colony of Syracuse. Presumably, then, they existed in Syracuse, where they would have been established at the time of the colonization by Corinthians. A statement by Nikolaos of Damascus (frag. 60, 2) refers to an *ὀκτὰς προβούλων*, set up after the fall of the tyranny. While interpretation of the passage is difficult,[65] the statement seems to indicate that some organization of the Corinthians into eight parts already existed *at that time*. Presumably the older tripartite tribal division had been replaced by an eight-part division—recognized in tradition as the synoecism of Corinth—by the Bacchiads, by the Kypselids or, with less probability in view of the wording of Nikolaos' statement, at the time of the establishment of the classical oligarchy. Most historians have preferred the Kypselids as the agents,[66] for under the tyranny, particularly at its inception or in the reign of

[63] O. Broneer, *Antiquity*, XXXII, 1958, p. 80.

[64] Herakleides Pont., V, 2 (Müller).

[65] Will, *op. cit.*, pp. 609 ff.

[66] Will, *op. cit.*, p. 612, note 2; T. J. Dunbabin, *The Western Greeks*, p. 55; Busolt-Swoboda, *Gr. St.*, I, p. 363 (at the fall of the tyranny).

Periander, there would have been exilings, confiscation and presumably redistribution of land. At Corinth, as in other Greek states, a reorganization of the citizen body might well have accompanied such political and social turmoil.

But an equally good case might be made for the Bacchiads as the authors of the reorganization. First, such a new organization would have included the whole of the Corinthia, not merely the terraces and region adjacent to the " city." [67] As discussed above (pp. 101-103), Corinth of the Geometric Period was a group of villages and there is no evidence that a coalescence was obtained, either in Geometric or Archaic times, other than by a natural process of growth and filling up around the node of the Temple Hill and adjacent hollow. We need not associate synoecism in the physical sense of creation of an urban center with synoecism in the sense of political and social organization. It seems clear that the Bacchiads controlled the whole of the Corinthia, for colonists were sent to Syracuse from Tenea. If our argument about the occupation of land north of the Isthmus and of the Perachora peninsula is correct, we might say that the Bacchiads created the Corinthia as a territorial and political entity about the middle of the eighth century. The take-over of land north of the Isthmus would have involved a distribution of lots for settlers and the incorporation of the region into the existing state of Corinth. Perhaps, too, the success against Pheidon was followed by a redrawing of the Corinthia's borders to the south. The occasion seems proper for a reorganization of the citizen body at some time in the latter part of the eighth century—in effect, a founding, a synoecism, of the polis of Corinth. [68] Such an enlargement and constituting of the state fits into the picture of

---

[67] On the constitution of the Classical Period, for which some epigraphical evidence exists, see R. Stroud, *Cal. Studies Cl. Ant.*, I, 1968, pp. 233-242. We know the abbreviated titles of four of the Corinthian tribes: ΣΙ, ΛΕ, ΚΥ, ΣΥ, and Hesychius names one as the Κυνόφαλοι (*s.v.*). There were at least three groups in each tribe, so that Stroud suggests that a trittys organization on a regional basis, somewhat in the manner of Kleisthenean Athens, existed. While it is scarcely possible to identify any of the subdivisions, his regional areas for the trittyes seem reasonable: the city, north of Isthmus, and south of Isthmus. If the Bacchiads did take over the land north of the Isthmus, it is reasonable to ascribe this basic regional division to them, although, of course, modifications would have been elaborated at various periods after that time. Hammond identifies the Kynophaloi as a tribe of non-Dorians established alongside the original Dorian three (*A History of Greece to 322 B.C.*, p. 107); he interprets the synoecism as pre-Bacchiad and a union of eight villages in the region of the later city. See also S. Dow, *H.S.C.P.*, LIII, 1942, pp. 98 ff. Dow reconstructs the tribal development from the original Dorian ethnic tribes in successive stages: 1) creation of a fourth tribe from non-Dorians with perhaps changes of name for all four by the tyrants; 2) a change from kinship to territorial tribes in the post-tyrannical period; 3) division of each of the four tribes into two parts to make eight as a result of population growth, probably in the fifth century B.C. However, the lack of tradition for the three Dorian tribes in Corinth, along with the relative weakness of Dorian traditions there, indicates that their dissolution was very early. The occasion for the fundamental change to a territorial basis would be most appropriate in a period when the basis of government (the 200 Bacchiads) was substantially enlarged and new territory was taken over.

[68] A certain Pheidon (not the Argive king) is mentioned by Aristotle (*Politics*, 1265b) as a

growth and change in eighth-century Corinth suggested by the archaeological evidence, by the colonizing activity and by the advent of the new aristocratic regime itself. We should not, of course, think of the development of a tribal community and of village settlements into a polis, as ancient Greek theorists did, all accomplished at one time by a single person. Rather it was a process, the stages of which may be identified by symptoms of change and the appearance of new activities. The only continuous record of Corinthian activity throughout this early period is provided by the pottery production. Can we use it as an index of the growth of the community?

POTTERY PRODUCTION AND THE GROWTH OF CORINTH

Among the various craft industries which made Corinth a center of production and trade in the Archaic Period—bronze-working, the manufacture of architectural terracottas, of textiles, of cosmetics and pottery, the latter is the most useful for the purpose of studying economic growth in the community. The amount of pottery discovered in Corinth and throughout the Mediterranean area is large and extensively published.[69] While problems of chronology and classification in detail remain controversial, there is enough general agreement for the historian, at least, to use the material as an index of industrialization. Already in the Geometric Period, pottery making was largely an independent not a household craft, serving the needs of the community and, to a small degree, exported as a commodity, or a package for other commodities, of trade. For our purposes it will be significant to note the points in time and the manner in which the production was expanded. For example, when special types were developed for export; to what degree these also served a local market, and when the local market was enlarged by the production of special types of vases for purely funerary use or for dedication in sanctuaries. This internal market is perhaps a better index of urbanization than production for export. Purchase of pottery for his household needs was within the reach of the ordinary Corinthian and enlargement of that market would indicate a growing margin of wealth. The wealthy, of course, at any period might acquire fine and exotic articles by some means, but their presence is scarcely an index for the whole community.

lawgiver in Corinth. His legislation was directed to keep the number of *kleroi* the same, apparently to prevent their alienation and to restrict the extension of citizenship. It seems proper to connect this freezing of the system of land-tenure with the synoecism. Usually such a measure is cited as made to bolster the position of the aristocracy, but, of course, it would guarantee possession to any landholder, thus bolstering the substantial " middle class " farmers also. Perhaps the growth of Corinthian crafts and continued colonization were fostered by the creation of a pool of landless and poor landholders as population increased. I plan to discuss this at length, however, in a study of early Greek land tenure now in preparation.

[69] One important group of material, the pottery from the Potters' Quarter in Corinth, is being prepared for publication at the present time. Production in that workshop, however, seems to have been in great volume only after 650 B.C., so that its evidence applies only in part to the period discussed below.

While the distribution of pottery abroad is not our main concern, it would be useful to sketch the expansion of export before considering the production in more detail. Before 800 B.C. Corinthian production served only local needs: the villages of the Corinthia, the region of the Isthmus and Megara. By 750 B.C. this area was broadened to include Delphi and Ithaka and the general region of the Corinthian Gulf. Such a distribution implies carriage by sea, so that we may conclude that Corinthian seafaring, at least in the Gulf of Corinth, began with some regularity in this period. Between 750 and 700 B.C. the circle of export widened greatly: to Messenia in the Peloponnesus, to Old Smyrna across the Aegean, to Dodona in Northwestern Greece, to the new colonies in South Italy and Sicily. This great spurt, as usually pointed out, coincided with the colonization of Syracuse and Corcyra and with the emergence of the Linear and Orientalizing style of decoration in Early Protocorinthian production. Thereafter, almost wherever Greek colonists and traders went in the Mediterranean and Black Seas, Corinthian pottery followed them. In the last quarter of the seventh century, three generations after the first major widening, another spurt became apparent. Technically this was marked by the appearance of the Corinthian style of decoration; historically, it seems to have been spurred by renewed contacts with the Near East and by the penetration of the Black Sea. Until *ca.* 575 B.C. Corinth remained the chief exporter of pottery in the Greek world, but then eclipse was rapid and within a generation the foreign markets were largely lost to Athenian wares. In Corinth itself Athenian pottery began to take over the local market, to judge from the contents of the house wells. Explanation for the Corinthian decline is usually found in the better quality of Athenian pottery and the inventiveness of Athenian potters. How are we to explain the rise and expansion of Corinthian production?

To judge from the types of Corinthian pottery found in Corinth in contrast to those exported abroad, the stimulation to greater production was provided largely by the export market. The earliest example is the group of pottery known as the Thapsos group, if we may follow Coldstream in his attribution of it to a Corinthian workshop.[70] The vases assigned to this group, while distinctive in shapes and decoration from other Late Geometric pottery made in Corinth, are homogeneous within themselves, thus produced apparently in a single workshop. None have been found as yet in Corinth, but some were dedicated at Perachora and the rest widely distributed: to Delphi and Thebes in Central Greece, to Ithaka, Naxos, Syracuse, Leontini, Megara Hyblaea, Thapsos (in Lamis' grave) and Pithekoussai in the west and to Thera in the Aegean. In short, the vases were distributed for the new western trade and to an entrepôt for the new eastern trade. Their manufacture seems to have been a deliberate response by one particular shop to an opportunity for export. It seems to have been the vases themselves, new and pleasing in shapes and decoration, which were desirable.

[70] Coldstream, *op. cit.,* pp. 102-104.

The next Corinthian innovation for the export trade, however, coupled a particular vase shape with a special product, the globular aryballos containing perfume or scented oil. The popularity of the latter is usually considered a result of the trade with the Near East, but whether the scent exported from Corinth was made there from local herbs or imported in bulk to be repackaged in Corinth we do not know.[71] If the latter, it demonstrates specialization in the organization of trade as well as in the pottery industry. In any case, some Corinthians again saw an opportunity for an export product and refined an old vase shape, out of use for a generation, to package it. Small aryballoi, globular, ovoid and pointed, in their turn, rapidly became almost a hallmark of Corinthian export. Refinement of other shapes and the invention of new styles of decoration characterized the expanded production: the Linear Style, which surpasses anything Corinth had yet produced,[72] and *ca.* 725 B.C. the first Orientalizing experiments.

The degree to which this innovation was for export is striking. For example, in the graves of the Geometric Period in the North Cemetery at Corinth (800-700 B.C.) there were only one globular aryballos, in a child's grave, and one pomegranate vase, a special shape.[73] There were no Early Protocorinthian vases at all in the graves. Should we conclude that Corinthian potters could not find a local market for their specialties? that this cemetery was only a peasants' burial ground and so is not generally representative? or that Corinthians were very conservative in their burial practices? Similarly the graves lacked imports, jewelry and metal objects. Instead they held ordinary household pottery—skyphoi for drinking, coarse, handmade hydriai for storing water, oinochoai for pouring (MG only), kraters for mixing (they replace the oinochoai in LG). These, of course, in some cases had ritual uses in the cemetery, but they were not special funerary types. On the available evidence no special "burial market" existed in Corinth and the stimulation to expand production came from the developing market abroad.

This initial stimulation resulted in the establishment of new workshops in Corinth in the early part of the seventh century, to judge from the excavation of the Potters' Quarter, as it is called. This is the earliest pottery factory of which we know, but presumably it was only one among others which developed with the growing market. In the Late Geometric Period there was apparently a family group, known from their burials,[74] on the projecting tongue of land about one mile west of the Temple Hill, which was to be the site of the pottery's development. Perhaps the inhabitants made pottery in the Geometric Period, as the excavator suggests, but the evidence of the

[71] H. Payne, *Necrocorinthia*, p. 5, note 3; Coldstream, *op. cit.*, pp. 104, 346, 347.
[72] Coldstream, *op. cit.*, p. 105.
[73] R. Young, *Corinth,* XIII, pp. 13-14; aryballos, 40-1, pp. 33, 48; pomegranate vase, 21-2, pp. 28, 47-48.
[74] A. Stillwell, *Corinth,* XV, i, pp. 7-11.

conversion of the site to a pottery factory dates from *ca.* 700-650 B.C.[75] The area was admirably adapted for this purpose: clay beds on the sides of the ravines bordering the promontory, a water supply, stone for building, and paths leading up from the lower terrace and to the central village by the Temple Hill. The remains of this first period of activity are very scanty, some traces of walls under a later Terracotta Factory and over the graves of the Geometric cemetery, but sherds of Late Geometric and Early Protocorinthian were found in considerable quantity. They were interpreted as indicating the manufacture of pottery, rather than as habitational debris. A few were inscribed, our earliest examples of the Corinthian alphabet and a testimony to the literacy of some Corinthian workmen.[76]

A very puzzling feature of this early establishment is the remnant of a heavy wall of a defensive type.[77] Its substantial construction (2.40 m. in thickness, preserved for *ca.* 70 m.) of rubble with large stones and compartmented structure between two faces, as well as its position at the west edge of the promontory, seems to identify it as a fortification wall. The pottery found in the earth filling indicates construction before 650 B.C. and a partial rebuilding, at least, in the late seventh century. The wall apparently remained standing until the early fifth century. While it has been identified as part of an enceinte for the city of the early seventh century, there is considerable question that Corinth had such elaborate fortification until the fifth century when the Persian attack on Greece and the Peloponnesian War drove home the need for great enceinte walls. Other remains of such an early wall have not been found and it seems preferable, certainly more complimentary, to think that Corinth, like Sparta, relied on the valor of her citizens. In any case Acrocorinth may well have seemed sufficient refuge for the population scattered in small villages on the terraces. Perhaps we should consider that the wall was designed to protect only the village in which the Potters' Quarter was situated, although no other traces have been found on the promontory.

In small establishments of the type exemplified by the Potters' Quarter the pottery industry of Corinth grew throughout the seventh century. Innovation and invention, some from foreign influences, some of local origin, continued to maintain and to advance the craft. While Geometric traditions continued well into the seventh century, Orientalizing motifs and figured decoration had started *ca.* 725 B.C., and by 700 B.C. the black-figured technique with incised detail became regular, the latter perhaps, as Payne suggested,[78] through imitation of metalwork. From the east came new, exotic shapes: the ring vase, pomegranate vases and tall pyxis, and towards the close of this Protocorinthian phase, from *ca.* 650 B.C., an important new shape, the

[75] Stillwell, *op. cit.*, pp. 11-14.

[76] *A.J.A.*, XXXVII, 1933, pp. 605-610; L. H. Jeffrey, *The Local Scripts of Archaic Greece,* pp. 120-121.

[77] Stillwell, *op. cit.*, pp. 14-15; R. Carpenter, *Corinth*, III, ii, pp. 82-83; R. Scranton, *Greek Walls*, pp. 56-57, 85-88, 132-133.

[78] Payne, *Necrocorinthia*, p. 7.

alabastron.[79] Its adoption probably represents an addition to the list of Corinthian exports, olive oil, for the shape is proper for holding oil rather than for costly scent, as that of the tiny aryballoi. Perhaps we should infer that need of grain in Corinth was now being supplied in part from Sicily and that Corinthian landowners were able to specialize their agriculture more to olive oil. Wine production, to judge from the lack of amphoras, was minimal and not for export.

Of the indigenous Corinthian shapes, the kotyle, oinochoe and skyphos underwent refinement. These vessels, essentially for ordinary household use, formed a very large part of the export ware—for themselves rather than for contents, as in the case of the aryballoi and alabastra. For example, the pottery found at Megara Hyblaea, to mention only one foreign market,[80] indicates the popularity abroad of the good household pottery and the scent: there are many pouring vessels, oinochoai, with a few olpai (just becoming popular ca. 650 B.C.), thousands of cups, mainly small skyphoi, many pyxides and aryballoi.

At home in Corinth, however, the specialized vases, holding scent and high-grade oil, do not seem to have found a ready market, either for funerary dedication or in ordinary use. Perhaps the North Cemetery is not typical, but the lack of Protocorinthian pottery in its graves is surprising. As noticed above, no Early Protocorinthian at all was found. The graves of the seventh century were very scantily and poorly furnished,[81] for only eight of sixty-five contained any offerings and among them were few of the specialized export types: seven aryballoi, one alabastron, no pyxides, and one pomegranate vase. As in the previous century most of the pottery was of ordinary types and decoration and some of it handmade. Yet, the excavation of Protocorinthian houses near the Sacred Spring reveals that by the mid-seventh century ordinary households in Corinth were well stocked with household pottery.[82] Even so, to judge by the published pottery from the central excavation,[83] specialized and fine pottery was not in general use. While no sanctuary of this early period in the central region has yet been excavated, the material from the shrine of Demeter and Kore on the slope of Acrocorinth points in the same direction. It, too, is of local rather than export type.[84] Perhaps we should conclude that in the early seventh century the ordinary Corinthian was able to provide well for his household needs, make

[79] Payne, op. cit., pp. 269-270.

[80] Vallet and Villard, Mégara Hyblaea, 2; the excavators have made careful statistical records of the pottery discovered (pp. 9-10). Working from these and using their chronology I calculate that between 750 and 710 B.C., 10 hydriai, 86 kraters, 66 oinochoai, 431 cups, 4 plates, 7 pyxides and 24 aryballoi of Corinthian origin were found at Megara Hyblaea. Between 710 and 625 B.C. there are no hydriai, 47 kraters (a falling off of these shapes), but 318 oinochoai, 15 olpai, 6275 cups, 11 plates, 242 pyxides, 650 aryballoi, 772 conical oinochoai (also for scent). The significance lies, of course, not so much in the absolute numbers as in the ratios between types and periods.

[81] R. Young, Corinth, XIII, pp. 50-52.

[82] I am indebted to Mr. C. K. Williams for this information.

[83] Weinberg, Corinth, VII, i, pp. 51-54.

[84] Stroud, Hesperia, XXXVII, 1968, p. 300.

humble dedications in the new sanctuaries which were being established, but as yet did not have the means to purchase many small luxuries. Yet this same period must have seen a marked increase in the diversification of labor and craftwork.

About 700 B.C., as noticed above, the early archaic temple on Temple Hill was constructed.[85] About the same time a great temple was built for Poseidon in his sanctuary on the Isthmus.[86] The building of these large temples, of course, was the work of an organized community whose leaders could command resources of material and labor. The work itself would provide employment and raise the level of living for Corinthian workmen. Some, no doubt, worked on the new buildings in their off-season of agriculture, but others would have begun to specialize in the new activities, not only construction itself, but the building crafts of stone-cutting and carpentry and the making of architectural terracottas.[87] We may assume that the metal-working crafts received the same stimulation—bronze-working to make the new hoplite armor, to provide more costly dedications for the great temples, even bronze for architectural uses.[88] Shipbuilding, too, would have been stimulated. In addition to Thucydides' often-quoted remark about the shipbuilder, Ameinokles (I, 13), it is obvious that already in the eighth century Corinth had the capital and skill to build ships for colonization and its extending trade. The farmers and workers had their new sanctuaries, too, for the shrine of Demeter is characterized by its excavator as popular, the recipient of small and inexpensive votive offerings.[89] In short, urbanization began to work rapidly in Corinth in the first half of the seventh century, and a local market of some size was coming into existence. We can see the results after the middle of the century in the Potters' Quarter and, finally, as the process worked out, in the graves of the North Cemetery.

In the Potters' Quarter, between 650 and 600 B.C., an interesting building, the South Long Building, as it is called, was constructed.[90] Apparently the structure was used for the sale of the Quarter's products. It was long and narrow, compartmented into small rooms and faced on a roadway running between itself and the "fortification" wall. Thus, it provided a row of shops and booths where pottery could be sold, presumably both to traders for export and to local residents for use. The construction of such a building indicates the growth of the local market to which we have pointed. To judge from the large quantity of broken pottery dumped on the roadway, by no means all wasters from the kilns, either production was too great for the market or

[85] See note 6 above.

[86] O. Broneer, *Isthmia*, I, Princeton, 1971, pp. 1, 3, 55.

[87] A considerable number of very heavy, large roof tiles from the temples at Corinth (*Hesperia*, XXIV, 1955, pp. 156-157) and at Isthmia (*Isthmia*, I, pp. 40, 45-53, 55) have been found. Fragments of the same type have been discovered also at Perachora.

[88] For example, bronze was used to seal the joints of the floor in the first storage chamber of the Sacred Spring (Williams, *Hesperia*, XL, 1971, p. 3).

[89] Stroud, *Hesperia*, XXXVII, 1968, p. 300.

[90] Stillwell, *Corinth*, XV, i, pp. 15, 18.

the shopkeepers and buyers were excessively heavy-handed. Such sale at the works may be construed also as indicating that the growth of an agora for specialized marketing purposes was tardy.

There are other hints to the same effect. Corinth was still a group of scattered villages, essentially rural in character, so produce would have been individually raised or consumers could go directly and easily to the producers. If craft establishments were being built where most suitable for their activity rather than in some existing center, each, like the Potters' Quarter, could most conveniently sell its products on the spot. Probably there was some peddling of wares, but that would have been transitional to the establishment of retail shops in a more fully built up community. Then, too, the development of an agora for political purposes would hardly have been of concern to either an aristocracy or a tyranny. Neither would have desired frequent assemblies or need a variety of offices and special buildings for its political activity and administration.[91] On the whole the growth of industrial Corinth seems to have been much like that of residential Corinth—piecemeal, scattered, and using convenient natural facilities. The Potters' Quarter was one mile from the central settlement, another potters' establishment of the sixth century has been found at Anaploga,[92] a Tile Works of the same period was built to the northeast where the modern road winds up from the coastal plain; a fulling establishment has been identified at Anaploga.[93] Even in the central settlement itself there was evidently no aversion to craft workshops. Some were set up in houses, as the smelting operation in the newly discovered Protocorinthian houses near the Sacred Spring indicates.[94] Slag from smelting operations has been found in the classical levels to the east of the Sacred Spring, and a dyeworks was established in the early sixth century along the stream to the north of Peirene.[95] Apparently as Corinthian crafts developed, the new craftsmen, situated in advantageous locations, simply undertook new or complementary avocations. Herodotos' comment on the tolerance displayed by Corinthians to craftsmen seems to have a foundation in the physical appearance of the community. The urban monumentalization of the heart of the growing " city " was long delayed.[96]

---

[91] For what it is worth in this connection, Periander is said to have prohibited loitering in the agora (Nikolaos Dam., frag. 58, 1) and not to have allowed all those wishing to live in the town to do so (Diogenes Laertius, I, 98; Herakleides Pont., V, 2). Perhaps too much significance should not be given these notices, for they fit into the pattern of sumptuary legislation ascribed traditionally to tyrants and into the moralizing vein of thought characteristic of sixth-century Greece. However, in the case of Corinth Periander's prohibition on residence in the town may be a reference to an attempt to enforce the freezing of the *kleroi* (see note 68 above). Perhaps, too, the notice may be an attempt to account for the sprawling, village-like, appearance of Corinth, despite the luster of its tyrants.

[92] *B.C.H.*, LXXXVII, 1963, p. 726.

[93] *Ibid.*

[94] See note 16 above.

[95] See note 21 above.

[96] A reflection of this vigorous craft activity appears in the clay tablets from Penteskouphia.

The enlargement of the local market is reflected also in the furnishings of the graves in the North Cemetery from *ca.* 600 B.C., where the presence of certain specialized types of pottery indicates that a funerary market was being established.[97] In contrast to the scantiness of offerings in the graves of the seventh century, offerings of pottery became normal, averaging 3.6 vases per grave. The pottery itself, although seldom exceptional in quality, was evidently deliberately selected and grouped for burials. For example, in about fifty per cent of the graves trefoil oinochoai of globular shape, not found among export pottery or in the central settlement, were buried with the dead, evidently made for that purpose. Pyxides and miniature vases were used specifically for childrens' graves, while for some adults imported kylikes were deemed appropriate. A grave excavated at Examilia in the Corinthia[98] reveals another aspect of this funerary market; in it twenty-six vases were found, all, except for one cup, from a single shop, bought for the funeral. But, to judge from the North Cemetery graves, traditional burial practices remained strong in Corinth. Ordinary skyphoi of the type used in households remained a standard offering and, along with some aryballoi and alabastra, a few burials still contained handmade pottery as in previous centuries. Certain new shapes, kothons, large column-kraters and round-mouthed olpai, developed mainly for export, were lacking.

The appearance of the Corinthian Style, marked by new shapes, new types of decoration, and a mode of manufacture which, in an antique sense, might be called "mass production," reveals another step in urbanization. Weinberg, in his publication of the Corinthian pottery from the central excavation,[99] notes that production was substantially greater than previously and catalogues 125 pieces of Early Corinthian, 625-600 B.C., in contrast to the 90 of the preceding century. Among the pottery were some fine pieces with figured decoration, but it is interesting that aryballoi and alabastra were still few in number and the new kothons rare. In the sanctuary of Demeter a very considerable amount of pottery was dedicated in the late seventh and sixth centuries. Again, there were some fine pieces, but much of it consists of small and miniature vases,[100] of types which were turned out in great quantity at the Potters' Quarter and the other works in Corinth. Some, of course, were exported, but Corinthians bought thousands of these cheap vases for dedication in graves and sanctuaries and for the household. The inventiveness of the Corinthian potter was still applied for the export market, as well as his industry for the "mass production."

Potters are represented digging clay, stoking kilns, and shipping pottery. It is of some interest in this connection that scarcely a representation of the traditional round of agricultural work appears in the whole repertoire of Corinthian vase painting (Payne, *Necrocorinthia*, pp. 116-117).

[97] H. Palmer, *Corinth*, XIII, pp. 78-81.

[98] P. Lawrence, *Hesperia*, XXXIII, 1964, pp. 93 ff.

[99] Weinberg, *Corinth*, VII, i, pp. 55, 72-73.

[100] Stroud, *Hesperia*, XXXVII, 1968, p. 320.

The production of pottery in the Early and, to some degree, in the Middle Corinthian phases, from *ca.* 625 to 575 B.C., was characterized by its quantity, by the adoption of new shapes and by a new method of decoration. It was still a vigorous expanding craft. The alabastron, which had appeared *ca.* 650 B.C., remained popular to the end of the century, but then it gradually gave way to a new type of large aryballos, globular in shape. This aryballos is regarded as an eastern form, indicative of renewed direct influence from the Near East. From that quarter, too, came a new repertoire of decoration, probably through the importation of textiles. From them Corinthian potters selected congenial designs: an Assyrian-type lion, solid rosettes, palm trees and floral complexes, as well as figured motifs of marching warriors, banqueting scenes and various eastern monstrosities.[101]

But however healthy sale was on the now large local market in Corinth the renewed effort to hold the export markets was short-lived. The record of Megara Hyblaea is again revealing. Between 625 and 575 B.C., while Corinthian import was still large, the market was held by old products in new shapes, the scent and fine-grade olive oil in aryballoi, alabastra and kothons, and by innovations: amphoras, round-mouthed olpai instead of oinochoai, convex-sided pyxides instead of concave-sided. But the cups fell off markedly in popularity. This ominous note is confirmed by a consideration of the imports for the period from 575 to 550 B.C. A new shape had been developed in Corinth, which met with some reception, the column-krater, but all the rest is trivial. The market for drinking and pouring vessels, the oil and the scent had virtually disappeared.[102] The overseas trade had fallen to Athenian wares.

A variety of causes are advanced for this sudden collapse of much of the Corinthian pottery export. In the colonial regions local production had grown from the early days of the new settlements to respectable proportions and could supply ordinary and some fine pottery. The Corinthian potters could not maintain the momentum of the Early Corinthian period and for the products of the following generation archaeologists begin to use the terms " shoddy," " stereotyped," " hasty," and " mass production." There was, of course, no technical change in production but a careless manner of decoration was practiced, and there was a tendency to concentrate on a few shapes with the result that a larger number of more distasteful products were turned out. Some potters did make an effort, as previously, to innovate, but oddities like mastoi, amphoriskoi, bottles and flasks belong to the category of bric à brac and mantle ornaments rather than to functional pottery. The Athenian potters were working to improve the latter by refining their own shapes and developing new

[101] Payne, *Necrocorinthia,* pp. 53, 67, 118, 147.

[102] See note 80 above. A similar calculation for the period from 625 to 575 B.C. shows: 101 amphoras (an innovation), 21 dinoi (an innovation), 832 pitchers of various types, mainly olpai, 652 cups (about one-tenth of the import for the preceding period), 18 plates, 231 pyxides, 674 aryballoi, 910 alabastra (a new shape), 162 kothons (a new shape). For the period from 575 to 550 B.C.: no amphoras, 56 kraters (a new shape), 21 pitchers, 240 cups, no plates, 16 pyxides, 3 aryballoi, no alabastra, 28 kothons; the market had collapsed.

motifs and styles of decoration. After 550 B.C. Corinthian production was characterized by mechanical reproduction of old types, by the making of miniature vases, and
by the substitution of easy linear and floral decoration for more elaborate figured
scenes. The production was for a few markets in the Corinthian colonial area in the
Ionian Sea and for Corinth itself.

But in Corinth the local market was invaded after 575 B.C. by Athenian pottery,
both by fine ware, as might be expected, but also by ordinary household ware. The
excavation of four household wells in the central region tells the story. One was
filled with household debris of the period 600-540 B.C.; about fifty per cent of the
pottery was Athenian.[103] A second well, filled in the second quarter of the sixth
century, provoked the comment " a surprisingly large " amount of Attic.[104] A third
well seems to have been filled with the remains of a burned-out potter's shop; again,
among the Corinthian pottery was a surprisingly large amount of Attic.[105] The
fourth well, filled *ca.* 500-480 B.C., also contained much Attic pottery.[106] While the
local market for pottery was declining to a considerable degree, fortunately Corinthian crafts had long been diversified, so that the decline of one industry could be
compensated for by others. Evidently Corinthians could afford the new Attic imports.

CONCLUSION

At the outset of this study we proposed to discuss the urbanization of Corinth
under the aspects of its physical growth, its political organization and foreign policy,
and, finally, its economic growth, using pottery production as an index. It remains
to draw the threads together.

While excavational evidence is still scanty, it seems clear that Corinth, the
" city," was a sprawling community of scattered villages throughout the Geometric
and much of the Archaic Periods. The largest and most important village was in the
region of Temple Hill, but that was only one of a number situated on the terraces
where water supply and paths made settlement desirable. As craft industries developed, their establishments followed the same pattern; for potteries, in particular, a
conjunction of the material needs of clay, water and communication was necessary. In
their case it is likely that families in possession of such advantageous locations capitalized on the situation to develop the craft. Other families seem to have set up
smelting operations and shops in their residences. Between the clusters of houses
and workshops were open fields, tilled by the villagers and gradually filled in, presumably by attraction to the central settlement. Presumably, too, the wide extent of the
area covered by these scattered villages was a factor in the slowness shown in the
construction of an enceinte wall, which could have given form and a definite boundary

[103] E. Brann, *Hesperia,* XXV, 1956, pp. 350-374.
[104] O. Broneer, *Hesperia,* XX, 1951, p. 294.
[105] O. Broneer, *Hesperia,* XVI, 1947, pp. 237-238.
[106] M. Campbell, *Hesperia,* VII, 1938, pp. 557-611.

to the city. Perhaps the wall's great circumference, when ultimately built, resulted in part from the still sprawling nature of the city. In its growth as a complex of villages Corinth was following the pattern of other city states in the Peloponnesus, where creation of an urban center was very slow, as the examples of Sparta, Elis and Arcadia indicate.

Despite the obvious advantages of Acrocorinth as a refuge acropolis, its distance and the difficulty of ascent from the scattered villages precluded its early and steady development as the main religious center of the growing community, unlike the Acropolis at Athens. Instead, Temple Hill served that function and provided a visible center for urban growth. It is perhaps significant in this connection that most of the architectural terracottas of the archaic period were found in the region of the hill, by no means all to be connected with the successive phases or roof repairs of the temple itself.[107] On Temple Hill the primary stage in monumentalization was the construction of the large temple at the start of the seventh century. Other evidence of archaic construction in the area indicates the founding and embellishment of sanctuaries, provision for water supply, extension of residential areas and the establishment of some craft shops but hardly the organization of an agora. As discussed above, neither the political needs of archaic Corinth nor its pattern of growth would tend to stimulate the formal organization of space for that purpose.

Throughout their early history as a community the Corinthians seem to have been a unified political and social group. But it is important to differentiate the nature of the political cohesion between that of the Bacchiad kingship and that of the Bacchiad aristocracy. In the time of the kingship presumably the unity was furnished by ties of an Homeric nature—acknowledgment, sometimes grudging, sometimes enthusiastic, but always essentially personal, of the single leadership of an hereditary king seated at Corinth. But under the aristocracy effective ties of an institutional nature which could operate the state continuously as a political unity began to work. The basis of government, despite its family character, was considerably broadened. Offices of state were defined, selective, and limited in tenure, while officials, if not elected by, were presumably recognized by an assembly of the people. It is noteworthy in this connection that the "tyrant" Kypselos obtained a popular mandate by election to the kingship, *basileia*. His office was in name a revival of kingship and held in his family (itself a Bacchiad cadet branch) for three generations, although Greek historical tradition labeled him a tyrant. We have suggested that this new unity of the aristocracy was expressed also, at the community level, by a political synoecism. Membership in the state was transformed from the former ethnic basis of the Dorian tribes into a new territorial basis of eight units. This was presumably to take into account population shifts in an enlarged Corinthia, not to enable greater political participation of the citizens *per se*.

---

[107] I owe this observation to my wife, Mary Campbell Roebuck, who is studying the architectural terracottas from Corinth.

In foreign affairs the Bacchiads were concerned for the welfare of the state as a whole and able to utilize its resources for that purpose. Some of their actions, the organization of the aristocracy, the take-over of land north of the Isthmus, lie at the beginning of recorded history. But the traditions of the colonization of Syracuse and of Corcyra indicate that these were planned acts of state. The Bacchiads, too, were able to control internal dissension and to defend Corinth from Pheidon of Argos. Bacchiad purposes in foreign policy must remain conjectural, but there seems to have been concern not only about overpopulation and the means to remedy it, but also for Corinthian power abroad. The take-over of Perachora and the colonization of Corcyra reflect concern for sea traffic in the Gulf of Corinth and on the route to the west. Presumably this was no more at the outset than the transference of the concept of Corinthian control of its land to control of its " sea." But from this developed the fiscal concern of collecting tolls at the points where the sea traffic touched and ultimately the commercial, and fiscal, idea of putting a *diolkos* across the Isthmus. Involved with these considerations, of course, was that of keeping the sea clear of pirates. As Thucydides observed (I, 13, 2), " The Corinthians are said to have been the first to handle maritime matters in a manner closest to the present." In short we should credit the Bacchiad aristocracy with the political synoecism of Corinth, that is, with the creation of an effective state, in the latter half of the eighth century B.C.

This creation of a political community in the Corinthia provided the basis for the economic organization and urbanization of the community. Not only was the agrarian sector strengthened by the addition of territory and relief of overpopulation, but the crafts responded. Pottery production showed the first stimulation by developing special types primarily for export, to be shipped along the regular sea route through the Gulf of Corinth and to the west. Early in the seventh century Corinth was ready to diversify and enlarge its craft production as the stimulus provided by the construction of great new temples was felt. Sanctuary markets were added to the household and export markets. By the end of the seventh century a funerary market in pottery was added to the enlarged local and export markets. It is tempting to equate this rise in material prosperity and the appearance of new groups of workers among the population with the repudiation of the Bacchiad control *ca.* 650 or 620 B.C.; further, to associate the downfall of the tyranny with the economic pinch of decline in pottery export *ca.* 575 or 550 B.C. Be that as it may, Corinth did not become a city state in a phoenix-like birth nor can the community be characterized simply as " rural " or " commercial." The process was long-drawn-out from the time some Corinthians began to navigate the Gulf regularly in the early eighth century until the people elected Kypselos to a new type of kingship and then repudiated it in the sixth century.

CARL ROEBUCK

NORTHWESTERN UNIVERSITY

THE SETTLEMENTS OF PHILIP II
WITH THE GREEK STATES
IN 338 B.C.

THE purpose of this article is to examine one phase in the extension of the Macedonian hegemony over Greece—the settlements made by Philip II with individual Greek states as a sequel to the war of 340–338 B.C. and as a preliminary step to the establishment of the League of Corinth. "Settlements" is a somewhat inexact term; for, while Philip made formal treaties with his enemies upon their surrender,[1] he gave certain adjustments in favor of his allies a different legal basis, making use of the Amphictyonic Council[2] and the new League of Corinth.[3] Our knowledge of these settlements is very scanty, for none survives in documentary form. Only in the case of Athens has it been possible to reconstruct the full procedure of negotiation and treaty-making.[4] Generally speaking, it may be said that the separate settlements molded the individual units of Greece with which Philip was preparing to deal collectively through the League of Corinth; but what part did they play in the establishment of the League? For instance, Hampl has suggested[5] that the treaties of settlement were

---

[1] The most complete statement about the treaties made by Philip with members of the hostile Athenian coalition is that of Aelian (*Var. hist.* vi. 1): after Chaeronea, the Greeks, in terror of Philip, ἑαυτοὺς κατὰ πόλεις ἐνεχείρισαν αὐτῷ φέροντες. καὶ τοῦτό γε ἔδρασαν Θηβαῖοι καὶ Μεγαρεῖς καὶ Κορίνθιοι καὶ Ἀχαιοὶ καὶ Ἠλεῖοι καὶ Εὐβοεῖς καὶ οἱ ἐν τῇ Ἀκτῇ πάντες. οὐ μὴν ἐφύλαξε τὰς πρὸς αὐτοὺς ὁμολογίας ὁ Φίλιππος, ἀλλ' ἐδουλώσατο πάντας, ἔκδικα καὶ παράνομα δρῶν. As well as expressing a view very hostile to Philip, the statement contains one mistake, some inaccuracies, and some possible omissions. Elis was not a member of the Athenian coalition but had an alliance with Philip, although it had not sent aid to him at Chaeronea (see below, n. 18). Thus it should scarcely be included in this list. The Greeks are said to have surrendered κατὰ πόλεις, and three cities are mentioned: Thebes, Megara, and Corinth; then two league organizations: the Achaeans and the Euboeans; and, finally, a geographical expression: all those on Akte. The most obvious omission would seem to be Athens (others are the members of the Athenian confederacy; the cities of the Boeotian League; Leucas; Corcyra; Acarnania; Ambracia; Cephallenia [see below, n. 16]). These might be included in the general reference to the Greeks, but the writer's γε seems to indicate a definite list copied from his source. It is possibly implied that, in the case of the omitted states, Philip himself took the initiative in opening negotiations, as he did with Athens. Certainly, this view should not be pressed. In any case the phrase κατὰ πόλεις apparently indicates that the separate units of the Athenian coalition made separate settlements, i.e., that Philip did not make a general settlement with the coalition as a whole and that he did make settlements with its individual units, whether they were city-states, like Megara, or federal-league organizations, like the Achaeans.

[2] In the case of Phocis and Locris (see pp. 77 f).

[3] In the adjustment made between Sparta, Argos, Messene, and Arcadia (see pp. 88 f.).

[4] A. Schaefer, *Demosthenes und seine Zeit* (2d ed.; Leipzig, 1887), III, 20–29.

[5] F. Hampl, *Die griechischen Staatsverträge des 4. Jahrhunderts v. Christi Geburt* (Leipzig, 1938), p. 52. Hampl considered that the League was based on a *koine eirene* only and made no provision for the relationships of a *symmachia*. Accordingly, he has suggested that certain evidence (Arrian *Anabasis* ii. 1. 4; Diod. xvii. 63. 1) of alliances between Philip and individual Greek states refers to the alliances made by Philip at various times before the congress of Corinth, in particular, to the separate treaties made just after Chaeronea.

also alliances binding the separate states to Philip; if, however, the League itself was a symmachy,[6] which seems correct, that procedure would have been unnecessary. Some evidence, however, has been found for it in the Athenian settlement. Then, as is well known, the League treaties guaranteed the constitutions which the member-states had at the time of their entrance into the League. Philip is usually credited with an attempt to arrange governments friendly to himself in the Greek states. Was this provided for by the separate treaties, as Schwahn has implied?[7] Finally, many boundary revisions were made after Chaeronea. It has been suggested by Treves in specific connection with those in the case of Sparta: "The Hellenic League had obviously both the task of demarcating and the authority to guarantee the new boundaries. To that end, Aristotle, as is well known, . . . , drew, at Philip's request, the δικαιώματα of the Greek states. The symmachy thereby legalized the *status quo*."[8] If we may ex-

tend this to the territorial revisions in general, it implies that ownership of territory would have been stated in principle in the separate settlements but that a point-by-point demarcation and ratification would have been made by the League on the expert advice of Aristotle's treatise. These are some of the questions of procedure and practice which arise from a consideration of the problem of the settlements; but there are also matters of more general interest.

Philip designed the League of Corinth to conduct the affairs of Greece in a peaceable, legal fashion under his hegemony and that of his successors.[9] At the second session of the League in 337 B.C., he was elected commander-in-chief to lead this united Greece against Persia.[10] If such an organization was to function efficiently, Philip had to remove at the outset, as best he could, the causes of strife between various states and to insure the support of his plans by their citizens and governments. For that, more than the documents calling the League into existence would have been necessary. The groundwork had been laid by a decade of propaganda,[11] designed to win the good will of the Greeks, so that in every state, with the exception

---

[6] For the establishment and organization of the League see, in particular, the articles of U. Wilcken, "Beiträge zur Geschichte des korinthischen Bundes," *Sitzungsber. München*, 1917, pp. 1–40; "Alexander der Grosse und die korinthische Bund," *Sitzungsber. Berlin*, 1922, pp. 97–118; "Über eine Inschrift aus dem Asklepieion von Epidauros," *Sitzungsber. Berlin*, 1922, pp. 122–47; "Zu der epidaurischen Bundesstele vom J. 302 v. Chr.," *ibid.*, 1927, pp. 277–301; "Philip II von Makedonien und die panhellenische Idee," *ibid.*, 1929, pp. 297 ff.; J. A. O. Larsen, "Representative Government in the Panhellenic Leagues," *CP*, XX (1925), 313–29, XXI (1926), 52–71. For more recent treatments see W. Schwahn, "Zu *IG*, II, 160 (Philipps Landfrieden)," *Rh. Mus.*, LXXVIII (1929), 188–98; *Heeresmatrikel und Landfriede Philipps von Makedonien*, Klio, Beiheft XXI (N.F. VIII [1930]), 1–63; F. Schehl, "Zum korinthischen Bund vom Jahre 338/37 v. Chr.," *Jahreshefte*, XXVII (1932), 115–45; A. Momigliano, "La κοινὴ εἰρήνη dal 386 al 338 a.C.," *Riv. fil.*, LXII (1934), 487–514; Hampl, *op. cit.*, pp. 34–56; these are primarily concerned with the question whether the League is to be defined as a *koine eirene* or a *symmachia*. As Larsen, however, has pointed out, the organization is referred to as a *symmachia* in an inscription (review of Hampl, *CP*, XXXIV [1939], 378).

[7] *Heeresmatrikel und Landfriede*, pp. 36–38.

[8] P. Treves, "The Problem of a History of Messenia," *JHS*, LXIV (1944), 102–6 at 105. I had already attempted to reconstruct the adjustment made between Sparta, Argos, Messene, and Arcadia (*A His-*

tory of Messenia from 369 to 146 B.C. [Dissertation, Chicago, 1941], pp. 53–57); but, as Dr. Treves kindly pointed out in a letter, the problem needed a fuller consideration of the evidence. Since that time his criticisms have been published in the note mentioned above. The significance of the *dikaiomata* in Philip's settlements is discussed by H. Nissen ("Die Staatsschriften des Aristoteles," *Rh. Mus.*, XLVII [1892], 168–71) and mentioned incidentally in a discussion of Philip's personality by A. Momigliano (*Filippo il Macedone* [Florence, 1934], pp. 134–35); see also below, appendix.

[9] J. A. O. Larsen, "Federation for Peace in Ancient Greece," *CP*, XXXIX (1944), 160–61.

[10] Wilcken, *Sitzungsber. München*, 1917, pp. 25–28, and *Sitzungsber. Berlin*, 1929, pp. 309–10; but see Hampl, *op. cit.*, p. 46, n. 1.

[11] For a discussion of Philip's propaganda see, in particular, E. Bickermann and J. Sykutris, "Speusipps Brief an König Philipp," *Ber. sächs. Akad. d. Wiss.*, Phil.-hist. Kl., LXXX (1928), 20 ff.; Wilcken, *Sitzungsber. Berlin*, 1929, pp. 310 ff.

of Sparta,[12] there was a substantial group of Macedonian partisans, some by conviction, others by self-interest. The treaties which brought the League into existence set forth the principles of the organization and provided for its functioning;[13] but there was in them no mention of the penalties, rewards, and adjustments which Philip had to make in accordance with his general plans for Greece and which were necessitated by his own actions and those of the Greek states before Chaeronea. These would have found their proper place in the separate settlements, which should thus have offered Philip a means of removing the trouble-spots which were deemed harmful to the new league. Thus an examination of the separate settlements should also have its place in a general estimate of Philip's quality as a statesman. How did he use the opportunity?

In making the settlements, Philip had to take into account the results of the diplomatic and military activity of the years before Chaeronea—the alignments, alliances, and shifts of alliance, which gave various states claim to his good will or offered cause for punitive action. Not all the Greek states had taken part in the war of 340–338 B.C.; some had participated actively on Philip's side; and some were members of the Athenian coalition opposed to him, while others had remained inactive,

prudently waiting on events. Philip's own allies, who co-operated in the campaign of 339/8 B.C., were Thessaly, Epirus, and Aetolia.[14] To them, in the course of the campaign, were added northern Phocis and the Epicnemidian Locrians.[15] The opposing states were Athens and the remnants of the Second Confederacy; the Boeotian League, headed by Thebes; the Euboean League; the Achaean League; Corinth; the towns on Akte; Megara; Leucas; Corcyra; Acarnania; Ambracia; Cephallenia; Amphissa; southern Phocis.[16]

[12] Paus. vii. 10. 3; Sparta's resistance to Philip's demands and its abstention from the League are, perhaps, a better indication.

[13] Wilcken, *Sitzungsber. Berlin*, 1929, pp. 299 ff. The main evidence for the content of these treaties is the speech of Pseudo-Demosthenes (xvii), written *ca.* 330 B.C. by an anti-Macedonian; the fragmentary inscription (Ditt. *Syll.*[3], No. 260), which has been emended in accordance with the views of the various scholars dealing with the League (Wilcken, *Sitzungsber. Berlin*, 1929, pp. 316–18; Schwahn, *Rh. Mus.*, LXXVIII [1929], 188; Schehl, *op. cit.*, pp. 141 ff.); the document from Epidaurus containing the treaty of the League of Demetrius and Antigonus founded in 302 B.C. (*IG*, IV², 1, 68). The sources are discussed by H. O. Raue, *Untersuchungen zur Geschichte des korinthischen Bundes* (Dissertation, Marburg, 1937), pp. 3–8.

[14] Philip had strengthened his control of Thessaly in 344 B.C. by taking the position of *archon* and had weakened the unity of the state in 342 B.C. by the creation of the tetrarchies. Thessaly had benefited, however, by the restoration of its traditional prestige at Delphi and by its strong representation in the college of *naopoioi* there (see n. 38). In 343 B.C. Aetolia had been won over by Philip, who had established his brother-in-law, Alexander, as king in Epirus, allowing the latter an extension of territory in Chaonia (Pickard-Cambridge, *CAH*, VI, 248–49).

[15] Philip apparently found it useful to establish good relations with the Epicnemidian Locrians and northern Phocis for the better conduct of the campaign of 339/8 B.C. (G. Glotz, "Philippe et la surprise d'Elatée," *BCH*, XXXIII [1909], 530–41). The Opuntian Locrians presumably would be already pro-Macedonian, as they had benefited by the settlement of 346 B.C. (*ibid.*, p. 531).

[16] The sources contain several lists of members of the anti-Macedonian coalition, won over by Demosthenes in 343/2 or in 340 B.C., when the "Hellenic League" was formed. Demosthenes himself in the speech *On the Crown* (xviii. 237) claimed the Euboeans, Achaeans, Corinthians, Thebans, Megarians, Leucadians, and Corcyreans (Plutarch seems to have copied this list in his *Vita Demosthenis* 17). In the *Vitae decem oratorum* (851b) a list is given which omits the Leucadians and Corcyreans but adds the Locrians, Byzantines, and Messenians. The list is part of a quoted decree, honoring Demosthenes and giving a general account of his services to the state; but the inclusion of Messene is either a mistake or indicates that the reference must be taken as a reminiscence of the Messenian-Athenian alliance of 342 B.C. (*IG*, II², No. 225; Roebuck, *op. cit.*, pp. 51–52). There is no further evidence concerning the Locrians, but it may be assumed that Amphissa is meant, so that its presence on the Athenian side is reasonable (Oldfather, P.-W., XIII, 1211); the same probability would hold good for Byzantium (on the authenticity of the decree see Ladek, "Über die Echtheit zweier auf Demosthenes und Demochares bezüglichen Urkunden in Pseudo-Plutarchs Βίοι τῶν δέκα ῥητόρων," *Wiener Studien*, XIII [1891], 99 ff.). The other lists, found in *Vitae decem oratorum* (845a) and in Pseudo-Lucian (*Dem. enc.* 38) are of a general nature, citing only some of those states mentioned in the list in the speech *On the Crown*. The passages in Aeschines (iii. 94–98) record-

Athens and Thebes were the most powerful members of this coalition, but the
others had sent contributions of men and
money or had indicated their adherence.
Of the "neutral" states, Argos, Arcadia,
and Messene seem to have had alliances
with both Athens and Philip[17] but had a
claim on Philip's patronage by their pro-
Macedonian activity in 344/3 B.C. and a
convenient excuse for not sending aid to
Chaeronea in the blocking of the Isthmus
by Corinth and Megara. Elis did not take
part at Chaeronea but had an alliance
with Philip and showed its sincerity, at
least after the event, by joining him in the
invasion of Laconia in the autumn of 338
B.C.[18] Sparta itself, since Philip had
checked its encroachments on its neighbors in 344 B.C., had withdrawn almost
entirely from Greek affairs. With these
political alignments in mind, let us turn
to the examination of the settlements.[19]

WESTERN GREECE

In western Greece, Philip evidently
considered that Ambracia was the key
point for insuring his control over the region. It offered access to the Ionian Sea
from Macedonia and formed a wedge of
territory between Epirus, Aetolia, and
Acarnania, from which an eye might be
kept on them. Accordingly, in 343/2 B.C.

Philip had developed a claim through the
convenient, if legendary, activity of his
Heraclid ancestors and had made prepara-
tions to occupy the country.[20] At that
time, however, Athens had succeeded in
preventing Philip's invasion by sending a
force to Ambracia and gaining the support
of Acarnania and the large islands in the
Ionian Sea.[21] After Chaeronea, Philip was
in a position to make good his claim. A
garrison was placed in Ambracia,[22] while,
in Acarnania, Philip's partisans apparently came into control so that the pro-
Athenian leaders were forced to take refuge in Athens.[23] If Philip had already laid
claim to Ambracia as part of his hereditary possessions, he might have administered the district through the garrison
commander or, more probably, have de-

[19] I shall discuss only the settlements made with the
states of the Greek mainland. The conventional chronology for the year 338/7 B.C. is followed. For convenience it may be summarized: autumn, winter, and
spring, 339/8—the adjustments with Phocis and Locris; late August, 338—the battle of Chaeronea; September–October, 338—the settlement of western and
central Greece and the negotiations with Athens; end
of October, 338—the treaty with Athens; November–
December, 338—the Peloponnesian settlements; winter, 337—the first meeting of the League of Corinth;
spring, 337—the second meeting of the League of Corinth (see Wilcken, *Sitzungsber. München*, 1917, pp. 23–
24, *Sitzungsber. Berlin*, 1929, p. 299; Glotz, *op. cit.*, pp.
530–41; P. Cloché, "Les Naopes de Delphes et la
politique hellénique de 356 à 327 av. J.-C.," *BCH*, XL
[1916], 131–32; Beloch, *Gr. Gesch.*, III, 2 [2d ed.;
Berlin–Leipzig, 1923], 298–99.

[20] Bickermann and Sykutris, *op. cit.*, pp. 22, 29 ff.;
there is some controversy about the date of Philip's attempt on Ambracia (Dem. vii. 32, ix. 27, x. 10; Glotz-
Cohen, *op. cit.*, III, 322, 324).

[21] Dem. ix. 34, xviii. 244; for discussion and further
evidence see F. R. Wüst, *Philipp II von Makedonien
und Griechenland* (Leipzig, 1938), p. 94, n. 1. Although
Acarnania is said to have been responsible for a contribution of 2,000 hoplites to the forces of the "Hellenic League" of 340 B.C. (Aesch. iii. 97–98), its name is
not included in the lists of Athenian allies, so that it is
reasonable to assume that the state did not officially
oin the coalition but sent only volunteers (Wüst, *op.
cit.*, p. 119, n. 2).

[22] Diod. xvii. 3 (335 B.C.): after dislodging the garrison placed there by Philip, the Ambraciotes established a democracy.

[23] Diod. xvii. 3; Ditt., *Syll.*[3], No. 259; two of them,
Phormion and Karphinas, were granted the right to
exercise their hereditary citizenship, and others were
allowed to reside in Athens.

ing the purported contributions of the members of the
"Hellenic League" add the Acarnanians and all the
Peloponnesians; but Acarnania seems to have been
divided in loyalty (see below, n. 21), and Demosthenes
specifically excepted Arcadia, Argos, and Messene
(xviii. 64), while Elis (see n. 18) and Sparta are known
to have been inactive at Chaeronea; the towns on
Akte surrendered to Philip after Chaeronea (Aelian
op. cit. vi. 1; Lycurgus *Leoc.* 42), so that they presumably belonged to the Athenian coalition. Since Athens
and Thebes occupied southern Phocis before Chaeronea, the inhabitants would perforce have had to aid
them (Glotz, *op. cit.*, pp. 539–40). Ambracia and Cephallenia may be added, from our general knowledge of
the situation in western Greece (Glotz-Cohen, *Histoire
grecque* [Paris, 1936], III, 324, 332).

[17] Roebuck, *op. cit.*, pp. 51–52.

[18] Dem. ix. 27, xviii. 295; Paus. v. 4. 9; Glotz-
Cohen, *op. cit.*, III, 322–23, 331–32.

pended on an oligarchy of his own adherents. We have no evidence of what happened in the islands of Corcyra, Leucas, and Cephallenia; but there, too, Philip's partisans probably would assume control and send their political opponents into exile.

In the case of Philip's allies, Epirus had already been enlarged in 342 B.C. by an extension of territory in Chaonia. The Aetolians, however, in return for their cooperation, had apparently asked for Naupactus,[24] which was in the possession of the Achaean League.[25] Philip, after he had occupied Delphi in the spring of 338 B.C., took the city, despite the resistance of the Achaean garrison, and proceeded to award it to Aetolia.[26] Its loss would form one of the terms of the later settlement with the Achaean League,[27] but the account of Strabo mentions an adjudication by Philip which probably decided between the Aetolian claims and those advanced by the western Locrians, who would estimate the moment favorable, at least for stating their position.[28] Thus, in western Greece, Philip completed the plans entered upon in 343 B.C. to insure his hold on the district, but he did so without unduly increasing the power of any one of his allies there.

CENTRAL GREECE

Philip had, in 346 B.C., secured a voice for himself in the affairs of Greece in general and of central Greece in particular by

championing the Delphic oracle in the Sacred War and, at its conclusion, by taking for Macedonia the two seats of Phocis on the Amphictyonic Council. Thebes, however, by its control of the Boeotian League, had been in a position to exercise a preponderating influence in central Greece and had looked with increasing hostility and suspicion on Philip's encroachment. Although he had sought to work with Thebes, such an arrangement proved impossible. Thus, if central Greece was to be quiescent, the power of Thebes would have to be destroyed.[29] This meant a reduction of its influence and an increase in that of the other cities to make a more equable balance. While this and the establishment of pro-Macedonian governments would go far to insure the Macedonian hegemony, Philip, as in western Greece, took the extra precaution of installing a Macedonian garrison and further strengthening the influence of Delphi and of the Amphictyonic Council, of which he had demonstrated his control in the incident of Amphissa.

Philip's policy seems to have been inaugurated in the autumn and winter of 339/8 B.C.; for, during that time, Phocis, of which he had occupied the northern part, was granted concessions which went far to restore it as a potential makeweight to Thebes. In 346 B.C. the Amphictyonic Council had thoroughly crippled Phocis: its towns were destroyed and the inhabitants organized into villages, a heavy indemnity of sixty talents per annum imposed, and the Phocian League, if it survived at all, reduced to little more than an agency for the collection of the indemnity.[30] The Phocians had made payments in half-yearly instalments of thirty talents from the autumn of 343 until the

[24] Dem. ix. 34.

[25] Ibid.; Theopompus, Frag. 235 (Jacoby, Frag. gr. Hist.).

[26] Strabo ix. 4. 7 (427); Theopompus, Frag. 235; Glotz-Cohen, op. cit., III, 359.

[27] See below, pp. 83 f.

[28] Strabo ix. 4. 7 (427); Oldfather, op. cit., p. 1214. Strabo's expression, Φιλίππου προσκρίναντος, would seem to indicate that Philip had to make a decision on conflicting claims. Since Naupactus had been captured from the enemy and since each of the claimants was allied to Philip, it is unlikely that he would refer the matter to the League of Corinth, as he did later in the case of Sparta (see appendix).

[29] J. Kaerst, Geschichte des Hellenismus (3d ed.; Leipzig, 1927), I, 263–64; Wüst, op. cit., p. 169.

[30] Diod. xvi. 60; Busolt-Swoboda, Griechische Staatskunde (Munich, 1926), pp. 1448–49.

spring of 338 B.C.; but after that date the sum was reduced to ten talents paid annually, as the payment of that amount in the spring of 337 B.C. indicates.[31] About the same time, the rebuilding of the towns and their fortifications—an indication of sovereignty—was commenced,[32] and it seems likely that the League organization was restored to its former position.[33] In Phocis, as elsewhere, Philip's partisans would have taken advantage of the situation and the popular appeal of the concessions to consolidate their control of the government.[34] As the penalties had originally been imposed by the Amphictyonic Council, its decisions would have been necessary to modify them, so that it may be supposed that Philip would have had the concessions made by the Council in the autumn of 339 B.C.

The Council had also weakened Epicnemidian Locris in 346 B.C. by bestowing the important fortress of Nicaea upon the Thessalians, by whom it was garrisoned until Philip decided that it was safer in Macedonian hands (probably in 342 B.C.). In the summer of 339 B.C., however, Nicaea had been captured by the Thebans.[35] Accordingly, Philip proposed, when soliciting the alliance from Thebes in 338 B.C., that it be restored to its rightful owners, the Epicnemidian Locrians, whose cooperation he had apparently engaged by the promise of its return. Although, since the Thebans refused the alliance, this could not have been carried out until after Thebes was defeated, there is no reason to suppose that it was not done, as Nicaea had lost its strategic importance after Philip occupied Elateia. Philip, as general for the Amphictyonic League, would have been able to make the offer; but the final reversion would depend on the decision of the Council,[36] taken possibly in the autumn of 339 B.C. It is perhaps significant in this connection that the delegate from east Locris (although an Opuntian) to the Delphic board of naopoioi, was absent in the autumn of 339 B.C. but returned to the meeting held in the autumn of 338 B.C.[37]

Philip had made his influence felt in the Delphian organization not so much

---

[31] Ditt. Syll.³, No. 230; Glotz, op. cit., pp. 537–38; E. Bourguet, Fouilles de Delphes, Vol. III, Part V, "Les Comptes du IVᵉ siècle," p. 63.

[32] Paus. x. 3. 3, 33. 8, 36. 3. Pausanias ascribes the rebuilding of the Phocian towns to the aid of the Athenians and Thebans before the battle of Chaeronea and implies that the Phocians themselves took part in the battle on the Athenian side. The statement, however, can be true only for the fortifications of the towns in the area occupied by the Athenians and Thebans—north and east of Mount Parnassus. Philip presumably allowed reconstruction in his area of occupation and permitted it to continue throughout Phocis after the battle (Schaefer, op. cit., III², 39; Glotz, op. cit., pp. 538–41; Beloch, op. cit., III, 1, 573, n. 4; Momigliano, Filippo, p. 157, n. 1).

[33] The inscription (Ditt. Syll.³, No. 231) dated 342/1 B.C. mentions one Phocian archon from Medeon and four Phocian witnesses without mention of their towns; but the later inscription of the same type (Syll.³, No. 232), dated to the spring of 338 B.C., lists four archons, a secretary, and five witnesses from various towns, which probably indicates an organization acting for Phocis as a whole—at the very least, that the individual towns were reorganized (Glotz, op. cit., pp. 535–37).

[34] Mnason of Elateia is known as a pro-Macedonian, although his activity may have fallen in the period of Alexander rather than in that of Philip (Schaefer, op. cit., III², 39; H. Berve, Das Alexanderreich auf prosopographischer Grundlage [Munich, 1926], II, No. 539).

[35] Glotz, op. cit., pp. 528–30.

[36] See the fragment from Philochorus: ἀξιοῦντος Νίκαιαν Λοκροῖς παραδιδόναι παρὰ τὸ δόγμα τὸ τῶν Ἀμφικτυόνων (M. P. Foucart, "Étude sur Didymos d'après un papyrus de Berlin," Académie des Inscriptions et Belles-Lettres, XXXVIII, Part I [1909], 204–9). The decree of the Amphictyons which is referred to would be the decision of 346 B.C., depriving Locris of Nicaea (for discussion see Glotz, op. cit., pp. 531–32; Wüst, op. cit., p. 160).

[37] The lists of delegates to the board of naopoioi in Delphi have been studied by Cloché (op. cit., pp. 78–142; "Les Naopes de Delphes et la création du collège des tamiai," BCH, XLIV [1920], 312–27), who points out their connection with political events but warns against a rigid parallelism. The lists of the meeting in the autumn of 339 B.C., at which only 19 delegates were present (Cloché, BCH, XL [1916], 117 ff.; BCH, XLIV [1920], 312–27; Bourguet, op. cit., p. 169, No. 47, ll. 66–78), and of the meeting of autumn, 338 B.C., to which 31 delegates came (Cloché, BCH, XL [1916], 123–24; Bourguet, op. cit., p. 175, No. 48, ll. 8–22), are particularly interesting for our purposes.

through the Macedonian representation on the Amphictyonic Council as by using the Thessalians, with their traditional prestige, as his agents both in the Council and on the board of *naopoioi*. This method had worked successfully and, perhaps, had done something to smooth over irritation in an organization in which the feeling for tradition was very strong.[38] The Thessalian *hieromnemones*, however, who had served Philip's interests since 346 B.C., were identified with the Council's severe penalties against Phocis and had been very active in supporting a Thessalian hegemony in Council affairs. As Philip's policy with respect to both Phocis and Locris ran counter to the policy of 346 B.C., he apparently found it wiser to make a change which would facilitate his plans. Thus two new Thessalian *hieromnemones*, Daochos and Thrasydaios, appeared in the spring of 338 B.C. As well as making them the authors of the change in political policy, Philip took certain steps through them to increase the efficiency and prestige of the oracle and to give it a more international aspect. The reduction of the Phocian indemnity would mean a considerable loss to the treasury. Thus, to insure a better financial administration, a new treasury board, the *tamiai*, was established in the autumn of 339 B.C. to supervise the work of the *naopoioi* and to serve as a link between them and the Council. This measure at first caused some dissatisfaction among the *naopoioi*, particularly

among the members from those states which already had a political grievance against Philip. The irritation, however, was only temporary, and the *naopoioi* were playing their due part again in 338 B.C. and in the succeeding years.[39] In the spring of 338 B.C. a new Amphictyonic coinage appeared, designed to establish a uniform currency in the Amphictyonic district.[40] Philip himself probably presided at the Pythian Games held shortly after the battle of Chaeronea; and in the following years the activity of *tamiai* and *naopoioi* secured new buildings and furnishings to replace the depredations made by the Phocians.[41]

The restoration of Phocis and the increase of the influence of the Amphictyonic Council would, in itself, contribute much to the weakening of the power of Thebes and the Boeotian League in central Greece. Philip, however, took further steps to depose Thebes from its leadership in the League, to weaken the city's power, and to bind the loyalty of both Thebes and the League to himself. The procedure of the settlement is not entirely clear, but it seems probable that a distinction was made between Thebes and the other towns of the League. Possibly a settlement was made first with Thebes, as the circumstances after the battle would dictate, and then, when a government favorable to Philip had been installed, a general settle-

[38] Membership on the Council was very firmly fixed by tradition. Megalopolis and Messene, apparently hoping for Philip's support, had tried, *ca.* 344 B.C., to secure Council seats but seem to have failed. Even Sparta's withdrawal in 346 B.C. seems to have been misrepresented by Pausanias (Wüst, *op. cit.*, p. 18, n. 5; G. Daux, *Delphes au II*ᵉ *et au I*ᵉʳ *siècle* [Paris, 1936], pp. 329–30). The lists of *naopoioi* mentioned in n. 37 show a steady attendance of the Thessalian delegation, which was larger than that from any other state (Cloché, *BCH*, XL [1916], 80 ff.; XLIV [1920], 314–15). A Thessalian, Cottyphos, had also held the presidency of the Amphictyonic Council from 346 to 339 B.C.

[39] It is interesting to note that Delphi itself had no representative at the meeting of the *naopoioi* in 339 B.C., which Cloché attributed to pique at the creation of the board of *tamiai*, for, in its case, there would be no political motive (*BCH*, XLIV [1920], 322–23). Before the board of *tamiai* had been created, a commission of the Delphian *prytaneis* had administered the funds. On the significance of the changes at Delphi see Glotz, *op. cit.*, pp. 541–46; Bourguet, *op. cit.*, p. 14; for Daochos and Thrasydaios, *ibid.*, p. 170.

[40] Busolt-Swoboda, *op. cit.*, p. 1302; Wüst, *op. cit.*, p. 161, n. 3.

[41] Diod. xvi. 60; Dem. v. 22, ix. 32; Busolt-Swoboda, *op. cit.*, p. 1296. For the restoration of the objects pillaged by the Phocians see Bourguet, *op. cit.*, p. 177, commentary on ll. 23–24.

ment with the League.[42] In the case of
Thebes, Philip is said to have taken ransom for the prisoners and the dead and to
have allowed the political exiles to return.
From them he appointed a council of
three hundred, which would insure a government favorable to himself. Once appointed, this council proceeded to conduct
a purge of anti-Macedonians, which resulted in executions, banishments, and
confiscations.[43] Further to safeguard
Macedonian interests in the region, a
garrison was placed in the city.[44]

The League itself evidently remained in
existence, and Thebes retained its membership;[45] but the dominating influence of
the city was broken by the restoration of
Orchomenus, Plataea, and Thespiae,[46] all
formerly destroyed by Thebes. The Theban representation was changed on the

board of *naopoioi* in Delphi; for, in the
meeting of 338 B.C., held after Chaeronea,
Thespiae and Tanagra sent delegates.[47]
Boeotian territory remained intact, except for the loss of Oropus to Athens[48] and
the reversion of Nicaea to the Locrians.
Thus in central Greece a new balance of
power among small, weak states was established; Philip's diplomatic hold on the
region was further increased through the
Amphictyonic Council, and his military
control strengthened by the garrison
placed in Thebes, the nodal point of the
district.

ATHENS AND EUBOEA

A speedy settlement with Athens was
of the highest importance to Philip, for
the anti-Macedonian sentiment there was
stronger than in the other states and the
defeat of the city's land forces was only
half the battle. Its fleet was still the
strongest on the Aegean, and, with the
well-fortified base of Piraeus, Athens, if
besieged, could have afforded Philip considerable trouble had resistance been prolonged. Then, too, the trade carried on by

[42] Aelian (*op. cit.* vi. 1) states that Thebes surrendered to Philip, and Justin (ix. 4. 6–10) lists terms such as would be given to the city itself. The evidence indicating that the League was allowed to survive and that other towns were restored hints that a settlement was made with the League as representative of Boeotian interests as a whole. In any case some settlement in treaty form was made (Diod. xvi. 87. 3).

[43] Justin ix. 4. 6–10. Schaefer (*op. cit.*, III², p. 20, n. 1) has followed the view that a distinction should be made between the actions of Philip and those of the restored government. Justin plainly states that Philip had some Thebans put to death and others banished and that he made confiscations, but he goes on to describe the trials conducted by the restored government; thus he appears to be rather loosely attributing the results to Philip. Philip did, however, arrange that Demades should receive lands in Boeotia (Suidas *s.v.* "Demades"). The purge is presumably exaggerated, since enough anti-Macedonians were found to rise in strength against Alexander in 335 B.C.

[44] Diod. xvi. 87. 3; Paus. ix. 1. 8, 6. 5. Wüst (*op. cit.*, p. 169) connects this measure with the organization of the Corinthian League. There is no evidence to support the view, and it seems likely that Philip would avoid making such an overt gesture of military control in connection with the League, when it could have been arranged in the immediate aftermath of Chaeronea so that it would seem a natural military precaution. According to a principle of the League treaties, no city was to receive a foreign garrison (Ps.-Dem. xvii. 8). Thus, although the garrisoning of Ambracia, Thebes, Corinth, and Chalkis was against the spirit of the League arrangements, it was probably a *fait accompli* by the time of the constituent assembly, so that the Greeks would scarcely raise the point there (for bibliography see Glotz-Cohen, *op. cit.*, III, 371, n. 125).

[45] Arrian *op. cit.* i. 7. 11; the passage mentions Theban *Boeotarchs*. Evidently, the anti-Macedonian faction remained sufficiently strong and Thebes sufficiently powerful in the League to assure itself of considerable voice in affairs. Hyperides (i. 18) indicates that the League was in existence in 324 B.C. For discussion of the significance of the passage in Hyperides see A. Aymard, "Un Ordre d'Alexandre," *REA*, XXXIX (1937), 5–28; on the Boeotian League in the fourth century see Busolt-Swoboda, *op. cit.*, p. 1431, n. 4; Beloch, *op. cit.*, IV, 2, 426.

[46] For Plataea and Orchomenus see Paus. ix. 1. 8, 37. 8, iv. 27. 10; Diod. xvii. 13. 5. Alexander, too, had a share in their restoration (Arrian *op. cit.* i. 9. 10; Plutarch *Alexander* 34; *Aristides* 11). Schaefer adds Thespiae, since the Thespians dedicated a statue to Philip (Dio Chrys. xxxvii. 42 [466]).

[47] Cloché, *BCH*, XL (1916), 125. A Theban delegate had attended in 339 B.C. (Bourguet, *op. cit.*, p. 169, No. 47, l. 72), but none was present in 338 B.C. (*ibid.*, pp. 175–76, No. 48, ll. 8–22).

[48] Paus. i. 34. 1; Schol. to Dem. xviii. 99; Demades Ὑπὲρ τῆς δωδεκ. 10; Diod. xviii. 56. 7. Hyperides (*Euxenippos*) describes the territory of Oropus being divided among the Athenian tribes. The fragment referring to Oropus, which is ascribed to Aristotle's *dikaiomata* (*Opera Aristotelis*, ed. Acad. Boruss., Vol. V [Berlin, 1870], Frag. 570) is associated with this revision made by Philip (Nissen, *op. cit.*, p. 169).

the city was of importance not only to itself but to the whole of Greece, so that, to avoid economic disturbance also, Philip would have wished to come to terms. Thus he was influenced by very potent practical considerations, as well as disposed by his Philhellenic sentiment to offer more generous conditions than those given to Thebes.[49] The conduct of the negotiations, in which the orator, Demades, played such a large part, is well known and needs no repetition, save to note that Philip himself took the initiative, first, in sending Demades to Athens and then in setting his terms before the delegation of Demades, Aeschines, and Phocion, although they had apparently been empowered to discuss only the release of prisoners.[50] Philip's considerate behavior in returning the prisoners without ransom and in sending back the bones of the dead helped to influence the Athenians to accept the terms which Demades proposed to the assembly.[51]

The terms of the treaty have to be pieced together from various sources; but it is clear that, as in the case of Thebes, they were designed to destroy the real power of the state, although allowing it more outward signs of independence. The strength of Athens had, of course, lain in its naval supremacy and control of key points in the Aegean and in the Thracian Chersonese. Accordingly, the confederacy was dissolved,[52] but the city itself retained full independence[53] and the control of certain islands settled by Athenian cleruchs —Lemnos, Samos, Skyros, Imbros, and

Delos.[54] In addition, it received Oropus from Boeotia. Since full independence was retained, no Macedonian forces entered Athenian territory,[55] and Athens was able, as we have noticed, to offer hospitality and citizenship to refugees from its former allies. In addition, there was no purge of anti-Macedonians—Demosthenes, in fact, pronounced the funeral oration over the Athenian dead.[56] The treaty also stipulated that the Athenians be allowed to enter Philip's proposed league.[57] That is possibly to be construed as a pointed invitation rather than an open choice. In most discussions of the treaty it is stated that the freedom of the seas was guaranteed for each party, but that seems very doubtful.[58] It is likely, however, that

[49] Kaerst, op. cit., I, 264–65; Wüst, op. cit., pp. 169–70.

[50] See the excellent account of Schaefer, op. cit., III², 20–29.

[51] Pol. v. 10. 1–5; Justin ix. 4. 4; Diod. xvi. 87, xxxii. 4; Plut. Phocion 16; Demades Ὑπὲρ τῆς δωδεκ. 10; Demosth. Ep. iii. 11–12.

[52] Paus. i. 25. 3; Diod. xxxii. 4; Beloch, op. cit., III, 1, 572, n. 3 (for the Chersonese).

[53] Paus. vii. 10. 5.

[54] Lemnos (Arist. Ath. pol. 61. 6, 62. 2), Samos (ibid. 62. 2; Plut. Alex. 28; Diog. Laert. x. 1. 1; Athenaeus iii. 99d; Diod. xviii. 56. 6), Skyros (Arist. Ath. pol. 62. 2), Imbros (ibid.), Delos (IG, II², 1652).

[55] Aristides xiii (182), xix (258).

[56] Glotz-Cohen, op. cit., III, 365–68; Wüst, op. cit., pp. 170–71. Momigliano (Filippo, p. 162) has interpreted the continuance of anti-Macedonian activity in Athens and the military reorganization as indicative of a merely provisional adherence to the Macedonian hegemony.

[57] Plut. Phocion 16. The account is a condensed and somewhat ambiguous version of Athens' treaty-making with Philip. Phocion advised accepting the separate peace offered by Philip but objected to Athens' sharing in the koine eirene and the synedrion of the League before Philip's military demands from the Greeks became known. The passage allows two interpretations: first, that there were (a) a separate peace, (b) a distinct and later proposal to enter the League, (c) military demands, made known after the League was formed; second, that the proposal to enter the League was only a clause in the separate treaty with Philip; in any case, no military demands were connected with the separate treaty. The second interpretation seems preferable, as the phrase τὴν ἄλλην πολιτείαν seems to link (a) and (b). Schaefer has interpreted it thus (op. cit., III², 29, n. 3). If this is correct, it seems a plausible suggestion that such a stipulation was a part of all the separate treaties, although there is no evidence for the others. Syll.³, No. 260 refers, of course, to the treaty made upon Athens' entry into the League of Corinth (see n. 13).

[58] This term is usually read into the treaty (Schaefer, op. cit., III², 29, n. 1; Glotz-Cohen, op. cit., III, 364), and a reference made to Ps.-Dem. xvii. 19. That passage, however, refers to the regulation of the League of Corinth. There appears to be no reason to ascribe such a term to the separate treaty except that the Rhodians, on receipt of the false news of Athens'

Macedonian vessels were prohibited the use of the Peiraeus, just as their land forces remained off Athenian territory.[59] This separate treaty, too, is usually interpreted as establishing an alliance between Athens and Philip; but none of its terms seems to indicate any intention of joint action, and it is probable that Philip would not have forced the situation, since the League of Corinth was, in any case, to arrange mutual alliances.[60] Thus Athens, on the whole, received very generous treatment and indicated her co-operation with Philip both by entering the League on its formation and by returning to participation in affairs at Delphi in the autumn of 338 B.C.[61]

Closely related to the settlement of Athens was that of Euboea. Since the island was a key point for communication by sea between northern and central Greece, its control had been a bone of contention in the struggle between Athens and Philip. Athens, in 341 B.C., had succeeded with the aid of certain Chalcidians —Callias and Taurosthenes, in particular —in winning over Chalcis and making it the nucleus for the formation of a Euboean League.[62] After the battle, the Euboeans, presumably the League organization, surrendered to Philip,[63] so that the pro-Athenian leaders were forced into exile to Athens, where they were made citizens.[64] There is no evidence for the terms of the settlement, but it is likely that the League organization remained intact, with Philip's own partisans in charge.[65] Chalcis, of course, with its advantageous situation on the Euripus, was later known as one of the fetters of Greece, and it is probable that, like Ambracia, Thebes, and Corinth, it was garrisoned by Philip, although its full development lay rather in the period of Alexander.[66] The reversals of government would result in the usual crop of banishments and confiscations, but there is no evidence for any particularly punitive measures. As Athens had done, Euboea returned to its participation in Delphic affairs in the autumn of 338 B.C.[67]

destruction, had seized some Athenian cargo (Lycurg. *Leoc.* 14–15, 18; Schaefer, *op. cit.*, III², 29, n. 1). Its release would be a matter of negotiation between the two states, and the occasion would scarcely arise again, since the Athenian fleet was left intact. Such a term, to be effective, would have had to be binding on all states, as provided for in the League regulation.

[59] So Schaefer (*op. cit.*, III², 27, n. 6) with reference to Ps.-Dem. xvii. 26, 28. The reference is to a League regulation (see sec. 28 at the end); but such a provision would be an obvious complement to the barring of troops from Athenian territory and would also concern only the two parties to the agreement.

[60] Diodorus (xvi. 87. 3) calls the settlement φιλίαν τε καὶ συμμαχίαν; but his language, as frequently, need not be taken as technically accurate. Polybius (v. 10. 5) states that Philip made the Athenians συναγωνιστάς, instead of enemies—only a general expression or possibly to be referred to the later treaty of the League. Glotz-Cohen (*op. cit.*, III, 364) construed the treaty as an alliance, apparently on the grounds of the term guaranteeing freedom of the seas; but, as argued above, its authenticity is doubtful. Hampl's view that all the treaties were alliances was based on the conception that the League was a *koine eirene* only, which seems incorrect (see above, nn. 5 and 6). Wüst (*op. cit.*, p. 168) considered that an alliance was made, but Schwahn (*Heeresmatrikel und Landfriede*, p. 36, n. 3) that there was no alliance.

[61] No Athenian delegates had attended the meeting of the *naopoioi* in autumn (339 B.C.), but they and nine contractors were present again for the meeting of 338 B.C., about two months after Chaeronea (Cloché, *BCH*, XL [1916], 120–21, 125; XLIV [1920], 317–18; Bourguet, *op. cit.*, pp. 175–76, No. 48, ll. 13–14; p. 177, n. 1).

[62] *IG*, XII, 9, p. 153; Aesch. iii. 89, 91–92, 94 ff.; Glotz-Cohen, *op. cit.*, III, 329–31.

[63] Aelian *op. cit.* vi. 1; see above, n. 1; Schol. to Aristides *Panath.* 178. 12.

[64] Hyperides i. 20; Aesch. iii. 85–87.

[65] The League was in existence, possibly as a result of a refounding, in 298–294 B.C., when Demetrius held Euboea (*IG*, XII, 9, No. 207; the regulations of this document seem to presuppose a league organization). The view that the League was dissolved by Philip (Schaefer, *op. cit.*, III², 38; Wüst, *op. cit.*, p. 174) is not supported by any evidence and seems very unlikely, since Philip's general policy was to support federal organizations.

[66] Strabo x. 1. 8 (447); Pol. xxxviii. 3. 3; Arrian *op. cit.* ii. 2. 4.

[67] Cloché, *BCH*, XL (1916), 117, 123–24; Bourguet, *op. cit.*, p. 175, No. 48, l. 12.

MEGARA AND THE STATES OF THE NORTHERN PELOPONNESUS

Megara, Corinth, the Achaean League, and the towns on Akte had been members of the Athenian coalition. None, however, had been a particularly formidable adversary against which Philip needed to take severe action. Yet Corinth had considerable strategic value as the gate-keeper of the Peloponnesus.[68] Thus in the settlements it is singled out to house a Macedonian garrison, as Ambracia and Thebes had been. Although the terms of the settlements are almost completely lost, Hyperides' speech against Athenogenes throws a flash of light on the events in Troezen immediately after the battle of Chaeronea. They are probably typical of the sudden reversals of government which occurred in many of the anti-Macedonian states. Athens, in the flush of excitement following the battle, called on its near-by allies for aid, among which were Troezen and Epidaurus.[69] Although the Troezenians passed a decree voting aid, they would scarcely have had time to send their troops across the gulf. In the meantime, a Macedonian partisan, Athenogenes by name, who had come from Athens in the course of the war (with malice aforethought?), called upon Mnasias of Argos for aid and brought about a change of government. Like the other refugees, the exiled Troezenians fled to Athens and were made citizens.[70] Philip must have made his settlement with the new pro-Macedonian government,[71] which was apparently sufficient guaranty of the

city's loyalty to keep it independent of Argos, for it continued to send its own delegates to the meetings of the naopoioi in Delphi.[72]

In Megara there was probably a change of government similar to that in Troezen, followed by the surrender of the state to Philip.[73] None of the terms of settlement are known; but Megara, which had not sent delegates to the meeting of the naopoioi in 339 B.C., did so again in the autumn of 338 B.C.[74]

Corinth, like Athens, at first made ready for a siege[75] but on Philip's approach, or possibly after an internal revolution, gave up the idea of resistance and surrendered.[76] Philip garrisoned Acrocorinth[77] and, when the time was ready, called the first meeting of the delegates to the new league in Corinth. No other penalties are known to have been imposed, although, if Corcyra and Ambracia were regarded as Corinthian colonies, they would presumably be freed from any jurisdiction which the city had exercised over them.[78]

The Achaean League surrendered[79] and seems to have been generously treated. Its extra-territorial possession, Naupac-

[72] Troezen sent a delegate in autumn, 339 B.C. (Cloché, BCH, XL [1916], 117; Bourguet, op. cit., p. 169, No. 47, l. 76), but not to the meeting held in the autumn of 338 B.C. Probably, then, the revolution in Troezen is to be dated in September–October, 338 B.C. A Troezenian delegate was present again in 335 B.C. (BCH, XL [1916], 128).

[73] Aelian op. cit. vi. 1.

[74] Cloché, BCH, XL (1916), 117, 123–24; Bourguet, op. cit., p. 176, No. 48, l. 21.

[75] Lucian On the Writing of History 3.

[76] Aelian op. cit. vi. 1. Corinth, with strong economic interests at Delphi, sent its delegates to the meetings of the naopoioi in both 339 and 338 B.C. (Bourguet, op. cit., p. 169, No. 47, ll. 74–75; p. 175, No. 48, ll. 17–18).

[77] Plut. Aratus 23; Pol. xxxviii. 3. 3.

[78] Wüst, op. cit., p. 94, n. 1. Demosthenes' reference (ix. 34) to Ambracia as "Corinthian" is probably to be interpreted as indicating its traditional affiliation only.

[79] Aelian op. cit. vi. 1; above, n. 1.

[68] Plut. Apophthegmata Laconica 221 F; when a Spartan saw the camp of Philip near Corinth, he reproached the Corinthians for being bad gate-keepers of the Peloponnesus.

[69] Lycurg. Leoc. 42.

[70] Hyperides Athenogenes 29–35.

[71] Aelian op. cit. vi. 1. Philip made his settlements in the Peloponnesus after his arrival there (Arrian op. cit. vii. 9. 5), probably in November, 338 B.C. (above, n. 19).

tus, was lost to Aetolia,[80] but the League itself was not dissolved.[81] Further, its government seems to have been more stable than those of many other of the Greek states, as there is an indication that no revolutions took place.[82]

Elis, although it had sent no aid to Philip at Chaeronea, had been allied to him since 343 B.C. as the result of an oligarchical revolution in the state.[83] The policy of the oligarchs had been maintained with difficulty against democratic opposition,[84] so that, when Philip entered the Peloponnesus, the Eleans, apparently to allay suspicions as well as to satisfy a desire for revenge, joined him in the invasion of Laconia.[85] There is no indication that Elis received any direct reward for this aid, but the sanctuary at Olympia was later enhanced by the erection of the Philippeion,[86] and the Eleans themselves set up an equestrian statue to Philip.[87]

[80] This would probably be one of the terms of settlement which would thus legally confirm its reversion to Aetolia (see above, p. 77).

[81] Polybius (ii. 40. 5, 41. 9) remarks that the League was dissolved by the early Macedonian leaders, but it was in existence in 324 B.C. (Hyperides i. 18).

[82] In Pellene a tyrant, Chairon, came into power with the support, or the acquiescence, of Alexander (Ps.-Dem. xvii. 10; Athen. xi. 509b; Paus. vii. 27. 7). It was charged by the writer of Ps.-Dem. xvii that this was a breach of the regulation of the Corinthian League which guaranteed the governments existing at the time of its foundation. It is probable, then, that there was no disturbance before Pellene's entrance into the Corinthian League, or that would have provided additional material to the pamphleteer. Also, Pellene was the only Achaean state not to co-operate with Agis in 331 B.C., which may be explained by the presence of this tyrant and the continuance of anti-Macedonian governments in the other cities of the Achaean League (Aesch. iii. 165; Ernst Meyer, P.-W., XIX, 362–63).

[83] Paus. v. 4. 9; above, n. 18; for discussion and further evidence see Beloch, op. cit., III, 1, 541.

[84] Plut. De ira cohib. 457 f.; Apophth. reg. 179a; Glotz-Cohen, op. cit., III, 332.

[85] Paus. v. 4. 9. According to Aelian (op. cit. vi. 1) the Eleans surrendered to Philip after Chaeronea. This is a mistake, possibly originating in a reminiscence of the hostility noticed in the preceding note.

[86] Paus. v. 20. 10.

[87] Ibid. vi. 11. 1.

SPARTA, ARGOS, ARCADIA, AND MESSENE

It remains to discuss the adjustment made by Philip in the relations between Sparta and his allies, Argos, Arcadia, and Messene. This problem was of a different nature from that of the other settlements. Naupactus could have been given to Aetolia, Nicaea restored to Locris, and Oropus given to Athens without difficulty, since they had all been in enemy possession and Philip, as victor, had them at his disposal. Sparta, however, was not a member of the Athenian coalition and had not taken any action hostile to Macedonia. Yet the relations of Sparta and its neighbors constituted the "Peloponnesian problem" of the fourth century, so that some settlement was necessary in the interests of a quiet Greece.

The ownership of the border districts of Thyrea and Cynuria had been a point of contention between Argos and Sparta for generations, with both sides developing, in the course of time, a claim by appeal to the traditional division of the Peloponnesus by the Heraclidae.[88] Sparta, however, had usually been able to make good its claim by force of arms. Sparta had also had a long dispute with Megalopolis over the Belbinatis and with Tegea over the Skiritis and Karyae.[89] After the establishment of Messene as an independent power in 369 B.C., its Laconian frontier became a subject of dispute, for Sparta retained territory to the west of Taygetus—the Ager Denthaliatis, the coastal territory in southeastern Messenia, and some of the perioecic towns farther to the west along the coast of the gulf.[90] This dispute would merge into the same general issue as a result of Epaminondas' policy in supporting Argos, Arcadia, and Messene

[88] Ibid. ii. 20. 1, 38. 5, vii. 11. 1–2; Isoc. Panath. 91.

[89] Paus. viii. 35. 4; Livy xxxviii. 34. 8; Pol. ix. 28. 7; Theopompus, Frag. 238 (Jacoby, op. cit.); Beloch, op. cit., III, 1, 575, n. 1.

[90] Roebuck, op. cit., pp. 38–39, 56–57.

as a bloc against Sparta. Thus Messene, too, developed a claim based on its version of the traditional division of the Peloponnesus by the Heraclidae.[91] This contention would, of course, fit neatly into Philip's propaganda and plans, for he claimed to be a Heraclid and had adopted Epaminondas' solution of the Peloponnesian problem. Not only was the issue one of traditional prestige and even of economic advantage in the possession of additional territory, but the passes by which Sparta had access to the fertile plains of its neighbors and thence to the outside world lay through these border areas. Sparta had never recognized the establishment of Messene[92] and had shown little disposition to acquiesce in its own diminished power, for southern Arcadia had been invaded in 352 B.C.[93] and further aggressive action had been planned in 344 B.C.[94] The armed intervention of Thebes

had saved Megalopolis in 352, and the strong diplomatic *démarche* of Philip in 344; but, before Chaeronea, no change had been made in the control of the border territory. Although Philip had no grievance to find in Spartan action after 344 B.C.,[95] what guaranty was there that they would remain quiescent? It remained to complete the work already begun.

After Philip had received the surrender of Megara, Corinth, the towns on Akte, and Achaea, he proceeded to Argos, the traditional homeland of his ancestor Heracles. The Argive political leader, Mnasias, had already shown his zeal by assisting the pro-Macedonian party in Troezen, and Philip was warmly welcomed in Argos.[96] Thence he proceeded to Arcadia, where he may have taken steps to mend the rift in the Arcadian League,[97] as well as to sponsor the terri-

[91] *Ibid.*, p. 44; see Isoc. *Archidamus* 17 ff. for the Spartan claims. Treves (*op. cit.*, pp. 103–4) has cogently argued that a national Messenian tradition must have been developed in the century preceding the refounding of the city and received renewed impetus, reflected by Alcidamas' *Messeniakos logos* and Isocrates' *Archidamus*, upon the refounding. Certainly, there are traces of it in the sources before 369 B.C. For example, to the passages noticed by Treves might be added some of the fragments of Hellanicus, which show a tendency to connect Attic and Messenian history (L. Pearson, *Early Ionian Historians* [Oxford, 1939], p. 213) and the evidence of a treaty(?) between Athens and the Messenians in the middle of the fifth century B.C. (*IG*, I², 37; Merritt, *Hesperia*, XIII [1944], 224–29). How much of this tradition was truly Messenian, however, and how much Athenian fabrication, inspired by political opportunism to take advantage of the sporadic outbreaks of a serf population, would be a very difficult problem to resolve. In any case it seems probable that only when there was some actual hope of establishing Messenian ownership to land within their natural boundary, Taygetus, with the help of Thebes or Macedonia, would the Messenians make full use of the opportunity to utilize and embellish their national traditions. This legendary material would provide the sources on which Aristotle based his *dikaiomata* (see appendix); for, as Nissen pointed out (*op. cit.*, pp. 168–70), mythological tradition had as much validity as legal decisions to the Greek mind of that period.

[92] Roebuck, *op. cit.*, pp. 44–47.

[93] Diod. xvi. 39; Glotz-Cohen, *op. cit.*, III, 256–57.

[94] Roebuck, *op. cit.*, pp. 49–50.

[95] The Spartans had remained aloof from the diplomatic entanglements and intrigues of the years immediately preceding the war. They had, however, continued to take a part in Delphic affairs, except for the meeting of the *naopoioi* in autumn, 339 B.C. Cloché has explained this abstention as caused by resentment at the creation of the board of *tamiai* (*BCH*, XL [1916], 122–23; XLIV [1920], 318–19). The Spartans also sent four delegates to the meeting held in the autumn of 338 B.C., some two months after Chaeronea, which, then, took place before the invasion of Sparta by Philip and, presumably, before his intentions were known (Cloché, *BCH*, XL [1916], 127–28; Bourguet, *op. cit.*, p. 176, No. 48, ll. 20–22).

[96] Plut. *Erot.* 760a–b. Argos sent delegates to the meetings of the *naopoioi* in both 339 and 338 B.C. (Cloché, *BCH*, XL [1916], 121–25; Bourguet, *op. cit.*, p. 169, No. 47, ll. 72–74; pp. 175–76, No. 48, ll. 17, 19).

[97] On the reconstitution of the League see Beloch, *op. cit.*, III, 1, 574; 2, 173–77. Beloch's attribution to Philip of the reorganization of the Arcadian League rests mainly on the dating of the inscription (Ditt. *Syll.*³, No. 183) to the period after Chaeronea. It is an honorary decree for an Athenian, Phylarchus, voted by the Council and the *myrioi* of the Arcadians. The decree contains a list of 50 *damiourgoi* from 10 member-states, including Megalopolis, Mantinea, the Maenalians, and the Cynourians. The two last-mentioned became members of the city-organization of Megalopolis in 369 and 361 B.C. (Paus. viii. 27. 3–4; Hiller von Gaertringen, *Ath. Mitt.*, XXXVI [1911], 355–58). The decree omits, however, most of the towns of northern Arcadia, including Stymphalus, one of whose citizens served as general for the Arcadian League in 366 B.C. (Xen. *Hell.* vii. 3. 1). Thus the decree would seem to

torial claims of Megalopolis and Tegea. From Arcadia he invaded Laconia in the late autumn of 338 B.C. and laid it waste.[98]

There is a certain amount of fragmentary information in the sources concerning the invasion and the subsequent territorial adjustments; but it represents two conflicting traditions, derived from the claims of the two parties to the dispute. Thus it has led to different interpretations in the modern treatments. There are three main literary sources: passages in Polybius, particularly the debate of Chlaineas, the Aetolian, and Lyciscus, the Acarnanian, before the Spartan assembly in 210 B.C.;[99] a poem of Isyllos, the Epidaurian

poet,[100] who wrote paeans celebrating the "miracles" of Asclepius in the early third century B.C.; some of the *Apophthegmata Laconica* of Plutarch.[101] It has been stated that Polybius' evidence is valuable for the "conflicting political ideologies prevailing in the age of Philip V . . . but almost valueless as evidence for *our* reconstruction of the history of the age of Demosthenes." That is true of the manner and spirit in which the passages are written and of the judgments expressed on Philip in them; but is the factual material, some of it attested from other sources, false and to be ignored?[102] Isyllos' poem and the *Apophthegmata* might seem in themselves to be worthy of little credence; but Isyllos lived only two generations after Philip's invasion of Laconia, and, since his poem was set up in the sanctuary of Epidaurus, it should represent a popular tradition of so recent an event. The *Apophthegmata*, for their part, apparently depict successive steps in the negotiations between Philip and the Spartans.

It seems clear from Polybius that Argos, Arcadia, and Messene invited Philip to support their claims to the disputed territories at the opportune moment after the battle of Chaeronea, probably when he had arrived at the Isthmus or at Argos.[103] As pointed out above, Philip would

---

represent the condition of the League at a period before the Maenalians and Cynourians were completely absorbed by Megalopolis, before Stymphalus joined the League, and when Mantinea and Megalopolis were not at odds—that is, before 366 B.C. The period is difficult to fix, however, because of the internal dissensions which rent the League in its formative stage and which, presumably, are not all mentioned in the sources. Beloch's view that such a period is best found at the time of the settlements after Chaeronea involves rejecting Pausanias' evidence as mistaken and placing the final absorption of the Maenalians and Cynourians into Megalopolis at some unknown date after 338 B.C. Cary, on the other hand, has argued that the document belongs to the year 369, 368, or 367 B.C., before northern Arcadia was drawn into the League (*JHS*, XLII [1922], 188–90). Yet, if Stymphalus provided a general in 366 B.C., it seems likely that the city was a League member of tried loyalty and several years' standing, so that the period 369–367 B.C. seems very brief in which to fit the decree. Cary's view is probably to be preferred as doing no violence to the existing evidence, although that of Beloch has usually been followed and rests on historically sound considerations (Hiller von Gaertringen, *Klio*, XXI [1927], 10, who has withdrawn his former dating of the decree in 361 B.C.; Momigliano, *Filippo*, p. 162; Wüst, *op. cit.*, p. 173; none of these scholars refers to the argument of Cary). Whatever Philip's action with respect to the League may have been, he was regarded by the Megalopolitans as a great benefactor of their state (Pol. xviii. 14; a stoa bordering on the agora was erected in Philip's honor, Paus. viii. 30. 6, 31. 9). It is possible, of course, that such an honor was only in gratitude for the territorial adjustments made in favor of Megalopolis.

[98] See below, n. 107.

[99] Pol. xviii. 14; ix. 28–31, 32–39. "The speeches of Chlaeneas and Lyciscus of Acarnania are to be regarded as essentially based on a genuine record" (F. W. Walbank, *Philip V of Macedon* [Oxford, 1940], p. 87, n. 1).

[100] *IG*, IV, 950; Wilamowitz, "Isyllos von Epidauros," *Philologische Untersuchungen*, Vol. IX (1886), poem E. It is usually accepted that the Philip mentioned is Philip II, not Philip V, and that Isyllos' *floruit* is to be placed *ca.* 280 B.C. (R. Herzog, *Die Wunderheilungen von Epidaurus*, *Philologus*, Supplementband XXII, Heft 3 [1931], 41 ff.).

[101] They are collected by Schaefer, *op. cit.*, III², 44–46. References to the *Apophthegmata* are to the edition of the *Moralia* by W. Nachstädt, W. Sieveking, and J. Titchener (Leipzig, 1935).

[102] See appendix.

[103] Roebuck, *op. cit.*, p. 54, n. 19; as indicated above (n. 95), the Spartans attended the meeting of the *naopoioi* in 338 B.C., which would have taken place in October. Philip, then, would have had no dealings with them up to this point, and he apparently made no attempt to deal with Peloponnesian affairs until his arrival there (Arrian *op. cit.* vii. 9. 5). Thus the negotiations with Sparta would not have started until he was at Corinth or on his way to Arcadia.

desire a settlement in their favor to complete the policy embarked upon in 344 B.C. Accordingly, he would make his wishes known to the Spartans, hoping that he could intimidate them into acquiescence. Some of the *Apophthegmata* mention an exchange of letters between Philip and the Spartans, in which he made certain requests which were refused.[104] The nature of the requests is not specified, but it is reasonable to suppose that they

were the territorial adjustments, since another apophthegm quotes an observation to the effect that Philip would make Greece inaccessible to the Lacedaemonians.[105] If the nature of the replies has been correctly stated by Plutarch, they were scarcely likely to appease Philip. Others of the *Apophthegmata* indicate that the requests of Philip were debated and refused, a vote taken for war by the Spartan assembly, and discussions held on the proper military policy, the decision being in favor of fighting in Laconia.[106] Thus, if the *Apophthegmata* may be taken as really indicating the course of events, they show that Philip made an attempt to come to a settlement with the Spartans by negotiation, which was refused. There was, then, nothing wilful in the invasion save in the nature of the demands themselves, which, it seems, were the demands for cession of the border areas. Philip, as we know, did invade Laconia and lay it waste;[107] but he does not seem to have made a serious effort to destroy the state and its institutions. It was sufficient for the moment to weaken the Spartans and give his allies an opportunity to occupy the disputed territory.[108]

Isyllos, however, presents us with another tradition. Philip is said to have invaded Laconia with the purpose of destroying the royal house and the Lycurgan institutions. He failed in this, so that the Spartans, who had invoked the aid of

[104] Archidamus, No. 1 (*Apophth. Lac.* 218 E): Philip wrote a rather stern letter to Archidamus, to which the latter replied impertinently (since Archidamus is reported to have died in Italy on the day on which the battle of Chaeronea was fought, the attribution to him of certain of the *Apophthegmata* is incorrect [see Schaefer, *op. cit.*, III², 44, n. 5]). *Incert.*, No. 28 (*Apophth. Lac.* 233 E): Philip wrote, upon arriving in Laconia, "Whether they wish him to come as friend or foe"; they replied, "Neither." This is couched in the normal language of a request for passage through the territory of another state (cf. Agesilaus, Nos. 42–43 [*Apophth. Lac.* 211 C–D]). *Incert.*, No. 53 (*Apophth. Lac.* 235 A): Philip made a request by letter, to which they replied, "No." Agis, No. 16 (*Apophth. Lac.* 216 A–B): Agis went alone as an envoy to Philip. The anecdote retailed by Stobaeus would fit here (*Flor.* vii. 59): Philip came to Laconia, encamped, and threatened stern measures unless the Spartans carried out his orders; one of the Spartans, hearing the threats, said that he was very glad that nothing prevented warriors from dying (this same story is told by Cicero *Tusc. disp.* v. 14. 42; Frontinus *Strategemata* iv. 5. 12; Valerius Maximus vi. 4. E 4). Another apophthegm may refer to a moment when Philip's requests had been presented but not officially answered—Damindas (*Apophth. Lac.* 219 E): it was observed that the Lacedaemonians would suffer terribly unless they came to terms with Philip (εἰ μὴ τὰς πρὸς αὐτὸν διαλλαγὰς ποιήσονται).

Schaefer has arranged these and some of the other *Apophthegmata* in a different order to fit his reconstruction of events (*op. cit.*, III², 44–46). Archidamus, No. 4, and Agis, No. 14, are placed before the battle of Chaeronea; but, as has been noticed, the attendance of the Spartans at the meeting of the *naopoioi* in 338 B.C. seems to indicate that no contention had taken place publicly between them and Philip until after that date. Then, Archidamus, No. 1, and *Incert.*, No. 28, are placed after Chaeronea, but the nature of the demands is not explained by Schaefer. He considers that Philip invaded Laconia and forced the Laconians to ask for peace (there is no evidence of this) but that the terms offered were so harsh that the Spartans preferred death (hence Damindas, *Incert.*, No. 53, and the anecdote of Stobaeus). It is suggested that the terms were that Sparta should enter the League and serve against Persia; but so obdurate was the Spartan attitude that Philip yielded to it and, instead, deprived the Spartans of their border territories by a judicial decision binding on both parties to the dispute.

[105] Agis, No. 14 (*Apophth. Lac.* 216 A).

[106] Archidamus, No. 4 (*Apophth. Lac.* 218 F): in the war against Philip, some advised that battle should be joined far from their homeland, but Archidamus replied that winning was sufficient (the same story is told of Phocion, Plut. *Phocion* 16). Eudamidas, No. 4 (*Apophth. Lac.* 220 E): the citizens chose war against the Macedonians.

[107] Paus. iii. 24. 6, v. 4. 9, vii. 10. 3; Pol. ix. 28. 6–7, 33. 8–12; *Incert.*, No. 53 A (*Apophth. Lac.* 235 A–B); Orosius (iii. 14) linked Thebes and Sparta as suffering the penalties of executions, banishments, and confiscations at the hands of Philip. There is no other evidence of this, so that it is apparently only a perverted condensation.

[108] See appendix.

Asclepius, saw the god's hand in the matter and instituted a festival of Asclepius Soter.[109] The account must represent some Spartan popular tradition, such as Isyllos, a follower of the archaic Doric tradition, would be predisposed to fasten upon. It is another question, however, how truly it represents Philip's intentions. Wilamowitz, following the view that Philip's aim was to establish friendly governments in the Greek states, considered that Sparta was the only stumbling block to such a scheme. Philip tried to carry out his aim but failed because the bitter Spartan resistance would have made it too costly. In reprisal, the land was laid waste, and the Spartans were deprived of their border territory.[110] The requests and the negotiations of the *Apophthegmata* would, then, refer to a demand by Philip that the Spartans depose their king and reform their political institutions. It seems a better explanation, however, that the devastation of their land and the loss of territory would, in the Spartan mind, be confounded with a blow at the very existence of their state. Isocrates' *Archidamus* reveals how the Spartans had identified the loss of Messene in 369 B.C. with the feeling that their traditional prestige and way of life were lost;[111] the adjustment of Philip was but a corollary to the policy of Epaminondas. Further, an attack on the hoary traditions of Sparta would make a much better literary theme[112] than would a boundary adjustment. Therefore, no

precise significance need be attached to Isyllos' words. If the question is considered in the light of Philip's other settlements, there seems no reason to believe that he envisaged the destruction of the Spartan institutions.[113] He would, of course, desire friendly governments; but only in the case of Thebes is there evidence that Philip interfered personally to insure that result. Elsewhere the reversals seem to have taken place by the spontaneous action of his partisans. Thus the restored exiles and his own followers held magistracies and conducted internal purges. Similarly, where political and territorial changes had been deemed necessary, Philip had sought to give them as valid a legal sanction as possible. The Amphictyonic Council had been used to restore Phocis and grant Nicaea to Locris; the territorial transfers of Naupactus to Aetolia and of Oropus to Athens were made from enemy states which he had defeated.

Sparta, however, was not one of the enemy states opposed to Philip at Chaeronea; nor were Argos, Arcadia, and Messene among the allies who had aided him there. Since the procedure used in the other cases would not apply, a new one was devised. The changes which Philip had made *de facto* were made *de iure* by an arbitration process of the League after it was established, and the title of Philip's

[109] *IG*, IV, 950. 57–79; Wilamowitz, *op. cit.*, pp. 24 , 31–35.

[110] Wilamowitz, *op. cit.*, pp. 31–35.

[111] Roebuck, *op. cit.*, p. 44. Some notion of the Spartan reaction to the loss of their territory in 338/7 B.C. may be seen in *Apophth. Lac.* 192 B: when Antiochus, serving as ephor, heard that Philip had given the land to the Messenians, he asked whether he had also given them the military power to hold it. In the *Archidamus* see, in particular, secs. 8, 12, 16, 21, 25, 48, 89, 98, and 110.

[112] Isyllos thought of states in such terms—see his poem A.

[113] Beloch (*op. cit.*, III, 1, 574, n. 3) interprets Isyllos in a general sense only, arguing that Philip's policy was to preserve existing governments as a principle in founding the League of Corinth. That was true after the League had been founded and has some justification in the cases of Athens and the Achaean League. In many states, however, there is evidence of a change in the personnel of the government to Philip's own partisans and, since it is well known that they were wealthy oligarchs, presumably in most cases a change from democracy to oligarchy. Beloch (*ibid.*, pp. 574–75) also suggests that Sparta was not destroyed in order that its neighbors should be kept dependent on Macedonia. That, too, would be only partially true, for, in the Peloponnesus, as in central Greece, the result of Philip's changes was to establish a balance of power among small, weak states.

allies to the territories was confirmed. Philip's wishes would be known to the arbitrators and hardly disregarded. It is scarcely an objection that Sparta was not a member of the League. If the Spartans refused to sign a treaty relinquishing the territory, the only course left was to take it from them by force and then to give the transaction a legal basis through the League of Corinth.[114] After the revolt of Agis, too, when Sparta was not a member of the League, the settlement was turned over to the *synedrion* by Antipater. This reconstruction of the settlement also accounts for the divergent tradition in our sources. The anti-Macedonian tradition, put forward by Sparta when the issue was raised on later occasions, as before Tiberius, represented it as a personal, violent act of Philip, which it was *de facto*.[115] The pro-Macedonian tradition represented it as a legal settlement of the respective claims of the contestants, made by the League, which it was *de iure*.[116] Tiberius, incidentally, decided the claim in favor of Messene.

If our reconstruction of this adjustment is correct, Philip then attempted to give it as valid a legal sanction as he was able, while still putting his policy, conceived in 344 B.C., into effect. The result was similar to that achieved in central Greece—a balance of power among small, weak states, with the potentially dangerous one held in check by the obligations of the others to Philip.

CONCLUSIONS

What answers may be made, from this examination of the settlements and the circumstances surrounding them, to the questions raised in the introduction? In the first place, it is to be noted that Philip

made formal treaties of settlement with the members of the anti-Macedonian coalition. It is stated only in the case of Athens that an alliance was also made; but, as has been noticed, the known terms of the treaty do not seem to indicate this. Philip apparently planned to insure alliances with both former friends and enemies by the organization of the League of Corinth as a symmachy, which would place all the Greek states on a similar footing. Then there is no hint in the treaty terms, so far as they are known, that changes of government, either in personnel or in form, were arranged by them. It is likely that, when such changes occurred, they would, as in the case of Troezen, be spontaneous acts of Philip's partisans on receipt of the news of his victory. In some states, as in Athens and the Achaean League, there seems to have been no change. The treaties were made, then, in some cases with previously anti-Macedonian governments, which, as in the case of Achaea, later led to trouble. There seems to be no reason to connect territorial changes with action by the League, save in the important and exceptional case of Sparta. The separate treaties or, as in the case of Nicaea, the Amphictyonic Council would have arranged the revisions.

The more general problem of whether Philip used the settlements to correct some of the political ills of Greece must be taken into account with his policy before Chaeronea and with the purpose of the new league. It is apparent that the settlements put the crowning touch on a policy which had been formulated well in advance of the opportunity to make them. Philip had endeavored to seize Ambracia in 342 B.C. and had supported the anti-Spartan bloc in the Peloponnesus in 344 B.C. Evidence appears, however, of a reasoned solution for the key problems of the various areas of Greece. The former

[114] See appendix.

[115] Pol. ix. 28. 7; Tac. *Ann.* iv. 43. 1.

[116] Pol. ix. 33. 11–12; Tac. *op. cit.* iv. 43. 3.

systems of political control were destroyed —those of Thebes in central Greece, of Athens in the Aegean, of Sparta in the Peloponnesus. To replace them Philip initiated a subtle balance by building up the power of the weaker states, but none unduly. In central Greece, Phocis was restored and the influence of the Amphictyonic Council increased; in the Aegean, some of the islands were freed, some left under Athenian control; in the Peloponnesus, Argos, Arcadia, and Messene were strengthened. Thus better balances of power were set up which were not entirely sterile. They did not prevent the revolt of Thebes in 335 B.C. or the war of Agis of Sparta in 331 B.C., but they may have done something to prevent them from spreading. To create this balance, certain changes had been necessary; but Philip had been adept in finding traditional precedents for them and had sought to give them as much validity as possible by the use of treaty forms, decrees of the Amphictyonic Council, and the arbitration of the new league.[117] Philip may be more justly criticized for displaying his military control in the garrisons of Ambracia, Thebes, Corinth, and probably Chalcis. These had, however, all been enemy states, and such a precaution should not appear unreasonable for the initial stages of a new order.[118] Certainly, the Greeks could not complain that it was an innovation.

Philip planned that all the sovereign political organizations of Greece were to be members of the League of Corinth. The settlements show a disposition to favor federal organizations. Of the hostile states, the Achaean, Boeotian, and Euboean leagues were apparently allowed to survive. Among his allies, Philip had mended the rift in the Arcadian League, restored the Phocian League, and added Naupactus to Aetolia and Nicaea to Locris. While this may in part be ascribed to the practical convenience of dealing with relatively few large units rather than a host of separate cities,[119] Philip must also have hoped for a solution of political difficulties in general by federations, as, of course, his own scheme of a panhellenic league and the measures taken to form artificial combinations of states for the purpose of representation in it would indicate.

These various political remedies were not, it may be supposed, entirely altruistic. They were designed to organize Greece in Philip's interest as a quiet and co-operative ally, which would enable him to turn his attention to the projected war against Persia. But his conquest was not essentially military, and he attempted to deal with the psychological problems which arose. Care was taken to avoid personal antagonism, for only in Thebes did Philip interfere personally as a military victor in the political organization of the city. Elsewhere his partisans made the changes. Naturally, Philip allowed such reversals of government, but he may have hoped that the bitterness following upon them would be directed primarily upon their fellow-citizens by the sufferers. The League, of course, attempted to insure that no counterrevolution would take place. It was not a healthy state of affairs, but Philip tried not to leave time for antagonism and resentment to grow. As

---

[117] Wüst (*op. cit.*, p. 174) has emphasized the view that Philip's territorial changes were designed to restore the "Old Order" in Greece as it was before Thebes, Athens, and Sparta had enlarged their territory at the expense of their neighbors. Emphasis on the "Old Order" was, of course, a part of his propaganda but scarcely a serious political aim. It was designed to facilitate the imposition of the Macedonian hegemony.

[118] See above, n. 44.

[119] This is not to suggest that the separate settlements arranged the political units which were to be represented in the League. Various combinations based on military strength were made for that purpose (for a recent study see Raue, *op. cit.*, pp. 43–66).

soon as possible, he turned the attention of the Greeks to the formation of the League and to the war on Persia, rumors of which were set in motion very soon after Chaeronea.[120] Philip failed in this reorientation of Greek political thought, as the events after his death showed. The failure was not caused merely by lack of time for his policies to work themselves out but by the inability of Greek political thought to reconcile local "nationalism" with a true national unity.

APPENDIX

THE ARBITRATION OF THE CORINTHIAN LEAGUE FOR ARCADIA, ARGOS, MESSENE, AND SPARTA

Dr. Treves has observed (*op. cit.*, pp. 105–6) in the course of his criticism of the view of the Spartan settlement which I had previously sketched (*op. cit.*, pp. 53–57): "At the utmost, all that one can surmise is that the territories which Sparta was compelled to surrender in the autumn of 338 B.C. were then merely 'occupied' by hostile troops, and that the annexation took place, legally and formally, only after the work of the League began." This is, I think, substantially correct, except for the term "annexation" and the view of the League's activity which it implies, stated elsewhere as a "task of demarcation and guarantee" and a legalization of the status quo. His criticism is based primarily on the objection to accepting Polybius' tradition, favorable to Philip, as evidence for the period of Chaeronea. One should perhaps distinguish between Polybius' judgment (v. 10. 1; xviii. 14—his own views; ix. 33 —the view put in Lyciscus' mouth) and the factual content of the material. The judgment on Philip is favorable, but the factual basis should be either disproved or established independently. Treves considers that Pol. ix. 33. 11–12 means that "the Spartans agreed, though under compulsion, to become a party to the agreement and to submit their disputes with their neighbors to the arbitration of the

League." It is objected that this procedure can scarcely be correct, for Sparta did not adhere to the symmachy until forced to do so after its defeat at Megalopolis in 331 B.C., and that the Spartans were not therefore bound by its decisions; also, that Justin (ix. 5. 1–3) states that the representatives of the member-states of the League were summoned to the constituent meeting, only after the territorial claims had been settled by the king to their satisfaction. First of all, is there any evidence besides that of Polybius for a settlement through arbitration? An inscription (Ditt., *Syll.*³, No. 665. 19–20) refers to a settlement by judicial procedure ([κ]ρ[ί]σεις). The literary tradition, too, has preserved a somewhat confused record of a settlement by judicial process. Strabo mentions a Messenian-Lacedaemonian dispute in the time of Philip (viii. 4. 6), while Tacitus refers to it as decided *ex vero* by Philip (*op. cit.* iv. 43. 3). Pausanias records that Philip acted as arbitrator between the Argives and the Lacedaemonians (vii. 11. 2). In the case of the Arcadian-Lacedaemonian dispute, Livy has a reference to its settlement by an old decree of the "Achaeans" (xxxviii. 34. 8; is "Achaeans" written by mistake for "Hellenes," since the Achaeans are mentioned so frequently in this chapter?). Thus, this evidence taken as a whole would seem to amplify and confirm that of Polybius for an arbitrated settlement by the League. As we have noticed, Treves states that the League's activity was one of demarcation and legalization of the status quo (the state resulting from the forcible occupation of the territories); but Polybius' evidence is readmitted so far as to be interpreted that the demarcation and the guaranty are alluded to by κριτήριον (ix. 33. 12); so, too, the [κ]ρ[ί]σεις of the inscription. Polybius, however, uses κριτήριον as object of καθίσας; κριτήριον might, in itself, be used to mean a "judgment"; but, when used with καθίσας, it can scarcely mean anything else than "tribunal" (see Liddell-Scott-Jones, *Greek Lexicon*, κριτήριον, 2). Thus Polybius' phrase will mean "setting up a tribunal," not "making a decision." What, then, was the function of this tribunal—demarcation and ratification of a boundary already established or determination of the ownership of the terri-

---

[120] According to Wilcken, Philip began to circulate rumors of a Persian war shortly after the separate peace with Athens (*Sitzungsber. München*, 1917, p. 13).

tory? Treves has pointed out that Aristotle drew, at Philip's request, the *dikaiomata* of the Greek states to this end of demarcation and guaranty of boundary lines. A fragment (No. 276) from the Marcian *Vita* of Aristotle indicates the purpose of the *dikaiomata*: καὶ τὰ γεγραμμένα αὐτῷ δικαιώματα Ἑλληνίδων πόλεων ἐξ ὧν Φίλιππος τὰς φιλονεικίας τῶν Ἑλλήνων διέλυσεν, ὡς μεγαλυρρημον⟨ήσαντά π⟩οτε καὶ εἰπεῖν· ὥρισα γῆν Πέλοπος. Thus they are specifically connected with the Peloponnesian adjustments. One of the surviving fragments, however (No. 571, *Opera Aristotelis*, ed. Acad. Boruss., V, 1572) refers to the expedition of Alexander of Epirus to aid the Tarentines, which was made *ca.* 333 B.C. (Hackforth, *CAH*, VI, 300–301). Schaefer has suggested (*op. cit.*, III², 55, n. 1) that the *dikaiomata* were not published (according to Diog. Laert. v. 26, in one book) until the time of Alexander and were designed to counteract the rising tide of discontent against the settlements made by Philip. Nissen (*op. cit.*, pp. 168–71) resolved the difficulty by assuming that the *dikaiomata* were compiled for Philip's use but not published until later, and then in an expanded form to include "Rectifications" for the western Greek states. There is, then, some difficulty in accepting the statement in the *Vita* literally. In any case it throws no light on the action of the League but tells us only that Philip's adjustments, or his opinions on them, were based on Aristotle's researches. The procedure by which Philip made them is not mentioned. Should we not, then, accept the evidence of Polybius literally—that a tribunal was set up under the auspices of the League to act in this case and, as the evidence for *judicial* action indicates, that it decided *ownership* in favor of Philip's allies? If the League was founded to preserve the peace of Greece and organized as a symmachy, its guaranty of the decision would be automatic. Further, the scope of its activity would extend to nonmembers, should the latter menace that peace; for, after the war of Agis in 331 B.C., Antipater referred the settlement to the *synedrion* of the League (Diod.

xvii. 73. 5; Q. Curtius vi. 1. 19). Sparta may have gone so far as not to send a representative to defend its case before the tribunal; but would that prevent a decision's being taken? That Sparta would not consider itself bound by the decision goes without saying. It had never recognized the establishment of Messene and had withdrawn from the peace conference of 362 B.C. on that account (Roebuck, *op. cit.*, p. 46). So far as the objection raised on the evidence of Justin is concerned, I think Treves has suggested the correct solution: the territories were occupied before the first meeting of the League, so that the question was settled *de facto*. Justin would scarcely notice the arbitration which confirmed it *de iure*, in such a condensed account as he gives. This distinction between the ratification of an occupation and a determination of ownership by the League might seem to be trivial. So far as the practical result was concerned, it made no difference; but the procedure was important. It was in accordance with Philip's usual gilding of the bitter pill, as, for example, in his use of the Amphictyonic Council both in 346 and in 338 B.C.; and it would establish a precedent for what, in the course of time, might prove to be an equitable method of procedure in territorial disputes. The League did make use of such procedure by arbitration in the subsequent case between Cimolus and Melos, which was referred to Argos (Ditt., *Syll.*³, No. 261; Larsen, *CP*, XXI [1926], 55). The case of Sparta was of more importance and thus needed a larger tribunal picked from the League members; possibly the *synedrion* acted as a committee for the purpose. Other territorial adjustments were, of course, made after Chaeronea, but, as we have noticed, they were a part of the separate treaties made with enemy states or handled through the Amphictyonic Council. Accordingly, there seems to be no reason to suppose that territorial adjustments were a regular part of the League's work at the time of its foundation.

DALHOUSIE UNIVERSITY
HALIFAX, CANADA

COMMENT
From The Second International Conference
On Economic History

Recent work in early Greek economic history, as M. Will has indicated in his admirably clear and thorough report, has been concerned mainly with colonization and the agrarian crisis in Attica at the time of Solon. Studies of colonization in South Italy and Sicily have removed the presumed evidence for pre-colonization trade and have emphasized the essentially agrarian motivation of the Greek settlement. On the other hand, Greek expansion in the eastern Mediterranean was more complex. Relations with Anatolia, the Levant, Egypt and the Pontus are to be assessed also in terms of cultural influences and of trade. The Ionian Greek cities were relatively late in initiating overseas trade and the founding of colonies. For the Greek expansion as a whole, however, motivation is sought in the agrarian difficulties of early Greece. It is suggested that a rapid growth of population followed upon the attainment of stability in the Aegean in the eleventh century B.C. Internal colonization, the exploitation of marginal land, accomodated this increase to some degree. Yet, in the eighth century, the relatively large population, lack of fertile land and the continuous fractionalization of land holdings caused distress which turned the Greeks to the remedy of emigration. Relief was obtained in part by the exodus of colonists, in part by the growth of trade, particularly by the importation of grain into the Aegean. In Athens, Solon's skilfull reorganization brought an economic ordering to that *polis*.

This unilinear explanation of the Greek expansion, which finds support in the literary evidence of agrarian difficulties in Athens in the time of Solon and in Boeotia in the time of Hesiod, appears somewhat suspect, for neither Attica nor Boeotia were active in the early phases of colonization. It tends to obscure the role of trade as a stimulant to colonization, both at the outset of the movement and throughout its course. I should like to raise the question, whether Greek expansion was not the product of prosperity rather than of poverty. The Greeks evidently had the ships and the energy, as well as the manpower, to conduct a rapid and large-scale expansion in the late eighth and seventh centuries. From the last quarter of the seventh century a complex system of trade was developed by which grain was imported into the Aegean. It would be desirable also to trace the growth of local industry in Greek communities and to discuss the effects of both foreign and local trade on the structure of society in the early *polis*. Such discussion, however, leads into the complex problems of urbanization in Greece and the economic organization of the city state. Perhaps it is sufficient in this connection merely to refer to the revolutionary activity of the sixth century in which the city state acquired its typical form. I should like, however, to make a few observations about urbanization in Ionia. This is premature, pending the fuller publication of archaeological work on the early sites, but the current impression of Ionian mediocrity in the seventh century needs revision. Ionian tardiness in colonization and trade may indicate that its urbanization was more, not less advanced than that of European Greece. Ionia's main effort, in the late seventh century, seems consciously mercantile in motivation.

Trade as a Stimulant to Colonization.

I should make it clear at the outset that I agree with the view that Greek overseas colonization was not stimulated by a search for commercial outlets for the surplus production of Greek industry. Yet, the need for basic metals, tin, copper and iron, and the desire to acquire exotic luxuries may well have stimulated the first overseas trading ventures in which the goods acquired were paid for by an agricultural surplus.

In the Homeric economy, which is surely that of Greece in the ninth and early eighth centuries, metals were in short supply and their sources obscure, but not entirely local [1]. Only the heroes possessed fine bronze arms and armor. Iron was rare. Gold and silver objects were prized heirlooms or gifts of friendship. While heroes boasted mainly of their wealth in animals and land, they were very sensitive to the flashing beauty of arms, of jewellery, ivory carvings and fine textiles. These were scarce and highly prized. Such possessions were not, of course, regularly acquired by trade, but, in the case of the textiles, by manufacture in the household, in the case of the others, by war, piracy, ransom or as gifts.

By the beginning of the seventh century, however, some cities, such as Corinth, began to field their soldiers in the full panoply of hoplite armor and weapons [2]. Throughout the century there was a rapid transition to the new arms and method of fighting. The ability to make war effectively was enlarged and mercenary soldiering became a profession. In this same period sanctuaries were enriched by lavish dedications of bronze: great cauldrons, tripods, vessels of new and elaborate shapes. Evidently the supply of iron, of bronze or of its components, tin and copper, had increased substantially. Further, objects of gold, as well as oriental luxuries, appeared in relatively great quantity in Aegean Greece [3]. These phenomena coincide with the earliest ventures of Greek colonization, to the Levant and to South Italy. The Levant, of course, was the source of the oriental luxuries, but also of metals, the copper, iron and silver of Cyprus and of North Syria. Italy, too, was a center of metal-work in the Early Iron Age. While small local deposits of ore in the Aegean were presumably mined as they were discovered, it is difficult to account for the new and extensive uses of metal by the Greeks as exclusively from local sources. The literary tradition, while scanty, gives little hint that metals were procured locally, but legends of early Greek metal-working point to the Levant [4], with which a continuous, if tenuous, connection had been maintained throughout the Dark Age.

An extensive system of local trade by sea must have existed in the Aegean to provide the seaworthy ships and the knowledge of building and navigating them which facilitated the expansion. There are several indications of this. Ships and naval scenes became decorative motifs in Late Geometric vase painting, even on the pots from such rural areas as Boeotia and Attica [5]. The motives may be the product

1. D.H. F. GRAY, "Metal-Working in Homer", *JHS* 74 (1954) pp. 1-15; C. ROEBUCK, *Ionian Trade and Colonization* (New York, 1959) pp. 38-41, 97-98, 102.

2. H. L. LORIMER, "The Hoplite Phalanx with Special Reference to the Poems of Archilochus and Tyrtaeus", *BSA* 42 (1947) pp. 76-138.

3. ROEBUCK, *op. cit.* pp. 84-88.

4. ROEBUCK, *op. cit.* p. 102, n. 93.

5. G. S. KIRK, "Ships on Geometric Vases", *BSA* 44 (1949) pp. 93-153.

of new artistic ability and stylistic taste, but the ships must have existed to serve as models. In the late eighth century technical advances were made in ship-building, as Thucydides' notice of Ameinocles, the Corinthian, attests [1]. The poet, Hesiod, reluctant as he himself was to go to sea, reveals that local trading was a normal activity and that the peasant usually possessed a boat. In the *Works and Days* [2] instructions are given to hang up the rudder and store the boat for the winter (45, 624-29). There is an auspicious day to begin the building of a boat (808-809), just as to begin the various agricultural activities. The farmer risked a part of his small surplus in trade, either by venturing in his own craft or by consigning the goods to a semi-professional trader who made up a larger cargo for an extensive voyage (630-34; 641 ff.). Farming, of course, was the basic source of livelihood, but it provided the surplus for local trade by sea and the risk of trade brought profit. Such local voyaging provided the skill and experience for longer ventures where needed metals and luxuries might be obtained. How else, too, can we explain the very extensive dissemination of the Athenian Protogeometric and Geometric pottery styles than by local Aegean sea-trade, although the pottery itself was not an article of trade?

Pre-colonization Trade and Early Settlements.

Pre-colonization trade from the Aegean to Italy has been denied in recent studies of the ceramic evidence [3]. I do not question the reclass-

---

1. R. Carpenter argues that Ameinocles invented the pentekonter ("The Greek Penetration of the Black Sea", *AJA* 52 [1948] pp. 1-10), but Kirk has pointed out some difficulties to the acceptance of this view (*op. cit.* pp. 141-142). In any case, the pentekonter seems to have come into use in the early seventh century.

2. The evidence of the *Works and Days* for agrarian distress in Greece seems somewhat over-labored. Evidently marginal land around Ascra was still available in the time of Hesiod's father, who came from Aeolis to settle there. In addition to the produce of a man's own farm, the timber (428), acorns and honey (232-33) of the hills were available. Presumably pasturage for sheep and cattle (591) was offered by the wooded hill slopes. The substantial free-holding farmer, of which group Hesiod was typical, could achieve by hard work a store of grain to feed his household for a year and a surplus to trade. The household was not inconsiderable: husband, wife, children, a slave or two and, when needed, a hired man. Even Hesiod, not the first or last farmer to deplore man's condition of labor, was prepared to enjoy the good things of life in the early summer when veal and lamb were added to the diet (582-96).

3. G. VALLET, *Rhégion* et *Zanclé* (Paris, 1958) pp. 204-05. Vallet, however, admits that the process of Chalcidian colonization indicates commercial considerations and thinks that Ischia, the earliest foundation (*ca.* 770 B. C.) was established to procure Italian metal (pp. 56-58), perhaps by exchange of Greek textiles, wine and oil. R. M. Cook has argued that Ischia was essentially an agrarian foundation (*Historia* 11 [1962] pp. 113-114).

ification of the pottery, but point to certain considerations which seem to indicate a period of trade before settlement. The absence of imported Greek pottery, dated before the colonial foundations, is hardly decisive, as a consideration of the trade of Aegina indicates. Perishables, such as textiles and hides, may have been the Greek articles of exchange. Also, it has been pointed out[1] that the area of Mycenean trade in southern Italy anticipates, to a remarkable degree, the area of historical Greek colonization and that trade was continued in the sub-Mycenean period from the Ionian islands. A continuity of artistic influence, if not actual importation, has been observed in Apulia. Siting of the early Chalcidian colonies of the historical period, particularly that at Pithekoussai on the island of Ischia in the Bay of Naples, seems more suitable for trading posts than for agrarian settlement. The security offered by Ischia would have been advantageous both to an agrarian settlement and to a trading post, but it scarcely seems necessary to sail from Chalkis to the Bay of Naples to find a safe and reasonably fertile island for a small colony of farmers, who would not have known the route. The view that easier acquisition of Italian metal was the aim of settlement seems reasonable. Certainly, however, we should agree that the large scale settlement of Sicily and of southern Italy which followed the Chalcidian ventures was mainly agrarian in motivation. We should also recognize, with Vallet, that Italy speedily became a large and important commercial market for Greek products[2]. The Greek colonies, too, became a sort of staging ground for further exploration and trade in the western Mediterranean.

Rhodians, perhaps from their Sicilian colonies, or, perhaps using these as ports of call, sailed to southern France and to Spain[3]. The pottery found at St. Blaise and Cap Couronne predates the colonial foundation at Massalia, ca. 600 B.C., by a generation. There are also indications of preliminary trade in Spain before the Phocaean settlement at Emporion, contemporary with that at Massalia. Herodotus told of Colaeus' voyage to Tartessus and bronze helmets and vases have been found at scattered points in southern and eastern Spain. Motives of trade seem predominant in the secondary areas of colonization, southern France and Spain. Rhodians and, later, Phocaeans were interested in the carrying trade between the west and the Aegean. It was only after the Persian occupation of Ionia that Phocaeans sought

---

1. See the observations of S. A. Immerwahr in the review of Taylour, *Mycenean Pottery in Italy and Adjacent Areas* (*AJA* 63 [1959] p. 298).

2. VALLET, *op. cit.* pp. 57-58.

3. Rhodian activity in southern France: F. VILLARD, *La céramique Grecque de Marseille* (Paris, 1960) pp. 73, 110; in Spain: ROEBUCK, *op. cit.* pp. 95-96, 137.

another permanent settlement in the west, on Corsica. Two generations earlier they might have established it in safety.

In the Greek expansion from the Aegean to the southeastern
Mediterranean the motive of trade is unmistakeable. There was never
a complete break in contacts between the Aegean and the Levant
after the Mycenean Period, whether the connection was maintained
by Cypriotes and Phoenicians or by Greeks from the Aegean Islands [1].
These latter forays were probably semi-piratical, but from the ninth
century the Greek islanders were sailing with some regularity to the
Syrian coast. There the trading post of Al Mina was founded before
750 B.C. [2]. Al Mina, of course, has been recognized as the point of
origin for the North Syrian goods which influenced Greek artistic
motifs and techniques of production. It is also important to recognize
that Greece could pay for such luxuries and that the metal of Cyprus
and North Syria were available to Aegean traders. In the Levant
there could not be a follow-up of agrarian colonization as there had
been in South Italy and Sicily. Instead, a process of trade was developed with the southeastern Mediterranean which culminated in the
foundation of Naukratis in Egypt by 600 B.C. [3]. There wheat, linen
and papyrus could be procured as well as the objects of luxury. The
small number of settlers in the few Greek trading posts did little to
relieve the over-population in the Aegean; perhaps more was accomplished by the employment of Greeks in Egyptian and Assyrian mercenary service. Significant relief, however, was afforded by the importation of wheat from Egypt. As I have argued elsewhere [4], serious
colonization of the Pontus began in the same period as the development of Naukratis. The movement into the Pontus was mounted from
the staging ground of the Propontus, where agrarian settlement had
begun by 700 B.C. The Pontic settlements are characterized by
Herodotus as *emporia*, trading posts, and their purpose was the
procurement of preserved fish and, in the sixth century, grain.

From this very brief review of the function of trade in colonization,

1. E. GJERSTAD, *Swedish Cyprus Expedition* IV 2 p. 315; V. DESBOROUGH, *Proto-
geometric Pottery* pp. 180-85, 303-04; Ch. CLAIRMONT, *Berytus* 11 (1955) pp. 98-100;
G. M. A. HANFMANN, "Eastern Greek Wares at Tarsus", *The Aegean and the Near
East* (New York, 1956) pp. 167, 173-75.

2. Al Mina: ROEBUCK, *op. cit.* pp. 62-64, 102, 104; Al Mina apparently was not
the only early Greek foundation in the area, for the date of the Greek settlement
at Tell Sukas has been pushed back as the result of recent Danish excavation.

3. ROEBUCK, *op. cit.* p. 62; *idem*, "The Grain Trade Between Greece and Egypt",
Classical Philology 45 (1950) pp. 236-47.

4. ROEBUCK, *Ionian Trade and Colonization*, pp. 110-30; A. J. Graham (*JHS* 81
[1961] pp. 198-99) and, most recently, P. ALEXANDRESCU ("Autour de la Date de
Fondation d'Histria", *Studii Clasici, Bucarest*, 4 [1962], pp. 46 ff.) favor rather earlier
dates for the founding of some colonies.

I suggest that the initial stimulus to Greek expansion from the Aegean was to acquire metals and luxury goods. The directions of the expansion, both west and east, were perhaps indicated by some continuity of Mycenean trade, actual or in tradition. The means to trade, ships and an agricultural surplus, however small, had been developed by the Greeks in the tenth and ninth centuries. Until a professional class of traders developed, the leaders in such trade must have been the landowners, nobles or substantial farmers, who had the capital to build the ships and stock them with produce. These initial commercial ventures were followed by a wave of migration to Sicily and to Italy, Thrace and the Propontus to found agrarian settlements. Perhaps some landowners found it profitable to export their «crofters", then to convert the land to the production of olive oil and wine as export of the latter products became profitable. By the last quarter of the seventh century a new and strong commercial motive was apparent, which led to the establishment of trading posts in France and Spain, Egypt and the Pontus and to the volume trade of the sixth century. This trade exported olive oil, wine, pottery and silver in quantity and procured grain, metals and exotic luxuries. It brought the professional trader into existence, developed a complex system of coinage and exchange and was far-reaching in its effects on the economic organization of the *polis*. A comparison of the wealth and power of Greek states in the latter part of the sixth century as contrasted to their position in the eighth indicates the effect of trade on the economy of Greece. In the latter part of the sixth century the motivation of Greek colonization seems to change once again. Political refugees were willing to move to a better life in the colonial areas and tried to select their sites with an eye to the exploitation of trade[1]. It is only a step to the consciously political motivation of Athenian colonization in the fifth century.

Urbanization in Ionia.

The Ionian Greeks, to judge by the present evidence, did lag considerably behind Corinth, Chalkis, Rhodes and the Cyclades in initiating overseas trade and colonization. Their response to the orientalizing influences from North Syria, which were so influential in the

---

1. In Thrace, for example, Peisistratus of Athens not only used Thracian silver to finance his return to Athens, but established a lasting Athenian interest in the region. Tean refugees refounded Abdera after the Persian conquest of Ionia (Herodotus 1. 167) and, at the time of the Ionian revolt, Histiaeus and Aristagoras planned to establish a new Ionia in Thrace. In the west, Phocaean refugees tried to found a colony on Corsica and Samians, after the battle of Lade in 494 B. C., took over Zancle (Herodotus 6. 22-23; VALLET, *op. cit.* pp. 337-38).

development of Greek art, was late and indirect [1]. Does it necessarily follow, however, that we should use these criteria to class Ionia as mediocre in the seventh century? Ionia was the borderland between Greece and Anatolia. Not only the products of its crafts, but the ethnic origin and economic organization of its craftsmen and farmers may have been different than in the European Greek *polis*[2]. We should hardly judge early Ionian art, just being revealed by the excavation of such sites as Old Smyrna, by the standards of, say, Corinthian or even Rhodian orientalizing art. The art was at first provincial and derivative, but in other areas, such as the architectural urbanization of its cities, Ionia seems to have been ahead of European Greece[3]. To judge by the example of Old Smyrna, even the small rural cities of Ionia were populous and relatively prosperous in the eighth century and in the seventh well advanced in urbanization.

By the eighth century the population of Old Smyrna had increased greatly and habitation within the walls of the town was dense[4]. The physical layout of the town was unplanned and it was built up with close-packed, small, curvilinear houses, although the fortification wall was massive and well constructed. From *ca.* 750 B.C. the people were sufficiently prosperous to import some luxuries, olive oil from Athens,

1. For an evaluation of the growth and character of Ionian art see E. AKURGAL, "The Early Period and Golden Age of Ionia", *AJA* 66 (1962) pp. 369-79.

2. ROEBUCK, *Ionian Trade and Colonization* pp. 32-35; *idem*, "Tribal Organization in Ionia", *TAPA* 92 (1961) pp. 495-507.

3. E. AKURGAL, *AJA* 66 (1962) pp. 372, 374. Akurgal (p. 372) claims primacy for the Greeks in western Asia Minor in developing (750-650 B.C.), "probably under the inspiration of the Hittite small states of Anatolia and Syria, the first organized cities of the Hellenic world in the proper sense of a Greek *polis*." This inspiration seems very dubious when the isolation of western Asia Minor from the Neo-Hittite states is considered. Also, the essential institutions and values of the *polis* are the product of evolution in their own historical context rather than transferred from oriental models. Perhaps we should distinguish urbanization in a general socio-economic sense from the characteristic Greek *polis*. In both Ionia and European Greece the basic transformation from village to city seems to have been accomplished in the seventh century. In Ionia this urbanization may have been facilitated by initial colonial foundation and continuous military pressure; that is, the formation of compactly built and politically organized communities was natural and desirable. More complete social and political integration of the inhabitants was only achieved in the sixth century at the time of the tyrannies (ROEBUCK, *TAPA* 92 [1961] pp. 495-507). In European Greece such integration was contemporary if the Solonian, rather than the Cleisthenean, organization of Athens be taken as the basic ordering of the state. The subject, of course, needs discussion and extensive treatment in its various aspects. In this connection I am concerned only to protest agaitns the too facile categorization of Ionia as mediocre in the seventh century.

4. This reconstruction is drawn from J. M. COOK, *BSA* 53-54 (1958-59) pp. 13-22; see also AKURGAL, *AJA* 66 (1962) pp. 370-74.

wine from Chios and Lesbos, drinking cups from Corinth. Presumably they paid by exchanging their surplus agricultural products and, perhaps, distributing some gold from Lydia. About 700 B.C. an earthquake seems to have levelled the town and provided the opportunity to rebuild. Reconstruction was started, not only with energy, but with imagination and deliberate planning, for the structures were laid out uniformly on a north-south axis. An area was reserved for a sanctuary, although construction of a large temple was not begun until late in the century. There was provision for a public water supply. The private houses were large, with several rooms, and were solidly built of stone. The techniques of building and the skill of the masonry work are of as high quality as any known in contemporary Greece. Throughout the seventh century Smyrna continued to import luxuries, but now on a wider scale from Rhodes and the Levant as well as from the Aegean. Two facts are striking: the deliberately planned layout indicates that a community had formed whose government was able to exercise control over property within the town and to plan for the future; second, the high material standard of living was wide-spread and not confined to a small upper class, for the size and plan of the houses are uniform. This material well-being was apparently based on agricultural exploitation of the coastal plain of Smyrna and of the adjacent hillsides. Probably the land was worked in large part by native Anatolian labor in a serf-like status. Old Smyrna took almost no part in overseas colonization nor in the carrying trade developed by the maritime cities of Ionia. The town gives the impression of a solidly prosperous, countrified place, able to afford a large temple when that became fashionable, excellent fortifications and the luxuries brought by the carrying trade. The excavator suggests that the Greek population was about 1000 households, three or four times smaller than Erythrae and Colophon, also Ionian rural cities.

Unfortunately the evidence doses not allow a similar reconstruction of the architectural urbanization of any European or Ionian maritime city state. There are indications, however, that the European Greek sites were not more advanced than those of Ionia. In Corinth [1] the first monumental building about which we have knowledge, the predecessor of the present so-called Temple of Apollo, was built *ca.* 650 B. C. The construction was of mudbrick and timber on a roughly dressed stone foundation. In Samos the Hekatompedon of Hera had already been given such monumental form and, only a quarter century later, Old Smyrna was employing more advanced techniques in

---

[1]. Corinth: M. C. ROEBUCK, *Hesperia* 24 (1955) pp. 153-58; Samos: E. BUSCHOR, *AM* 55 (1930) pp. 20 ff.; BUSCHOR and SCHLEIF, *AM* 58 (1933) pp. 146 ff.

stone for its first large temple. In Athens [1] the excavation of house wells indicates that in the early sixth century, the period of Solon, the center of the Agora was cleared of its last private houses to become a purely public area. If architectural urbanization is a gauge in the growth of the *polis*, we should be chary in characterizing Ionia as mediocre.

In conclusion, I would like to suggest a further consideration. Perhaps we should recognize the possibility that the maritime cities of both Ionia and of European Greece, those advantageously situated for sea trade, ventured into trade and colonization for profit, rather than because of local agrarian discomfort. Their expansion was a demonstration of prosperity and strength. Some rural cities, like Old Smyrna, never needed to make such ventures, but could enjoy the benefits of the carrying trade of their maritime neighbors. Others, with smaller local resources, engaged in agrarian colonization. Another rural city, Athens, was active in the local Aegean trade of the tenth and ninth centuries. In the eighth and seventh centuries its Eupatrid landholders continued to export their olive oil and were able to buy foreign goods and to enjoy the magnificent ceremonial pottery from their local workshops. They followed the line of specialized agriculture and attempted to appropriate the holdings and produce of the small-scale farmers rather than themselves to engage in the growing carrying trade beyond the Aegean. In Athens, however, growth of a local market for the mass consumption of the products of its pottery industry a generation before Solon, indicates that the economy of the Aegean area was knitting together and no city could remain immune from its effects [2]. Solon's reform had to take into account the growth of a local urban market as well as agrarian distress.

1. E. BRANN, *Hesperia* 31 (1961) p. 306.
2. T. DUNBABIN, *BSA* 45 (1950) pp. 201 ff.; E. BRANN, *Hesperia* 31 (1961) pp. 314 ff.

TRADE-ROUTES AND COMMERCE OF THE ROMAN EMPIRE

By M. P. CHARLESWORTH, M.A.

FELLOW AND TUTOR OF ST JOHN'S COLLEGE
AND FORMERLY FELLOW OF JESUS COLLEGE, CAMBRIDGE;
SOMETIME PROCTER FELLOW OF PRINCETON
UNIVERSITY, U.S.A.

SECOND EDITION, REVISED

Exact Reprint of the Edition:

London, 1926.

ARES PUBLISHERS INC.

7020 NORTH WESTERN AVE.
CHICAGO, ILLINOIS 60645

ARES PUBLISHERS INC.

CHICAGO   MCMLXXVIII

TRADE AND POLITICS IN
ANCIENT GREECE

BY

JOHANNES HASEBROEK
PROFESSOR OF ANCIENT HISTORY IN THE
UNIVERSITY OF COLOGNE

TRANSLATED BY

L. M. FRASER AND D. C. MACGREGOR
FELLOW OF QUEEN'S COLLEGE   FELLOW OF BALLIOL COLLEGE

Exact Reprint of the Edition:
London 1933
ARES PUBLISHERS INC.
7020 NORTH WESTERN AVE.
CHICAGO, ILLINOIS 60645

ARES PUBLISHERS INC.
CHICAGO   MCMLXXVIII